Little Strangers

Little Strangers

Portrayals of
Adoption
and
Foster Care
in America,
1850–1929

Claudia Nelson

INDIANA
University Press
Bloomington & Indianapolis

Publication of this book is made possible in part with the assistance of a Challenge Grant from the National Endowment for the Humanities, a federal agency that supports research, education, and public programming in the humanities.

This book is a publication of

Indiana University Press
601 North Morton Street
Bloomington, IN 47404-3797 USA

http://iupress.indiana.edu

Telephone orders   800-842-6796
Fax orders   812-855-7931
Orders by e-mail   iuporder@indiana.edu

© 2003 by Claudia Nelson

The paper used in this publication meets the minimum requirements of American National Standard for Information Sciences—Permanence of Paper for Printed Library Materials, ANSI Z39.48 1984.

Manufactured in the United States of America

Library of Congress Cataloging-in-Publication Data

Nelson, Claudia.
Little strangers : portrayals of adoption and foster care in
America, 1850–1929 / Claudia Nelson.
        p.   cm.
Includes bibliographical references and index.
ISBN 0-253-34224-4 (cloth : alk. paper)
1. Adoption—United States—History. 2. Orphans—United
States—History. 3. Adoption in literature. I. Title.
HV875.55 .N449 2003
362.73'4'0973—dc21
2002014747

1 2 3 4 5 08 07 06 05 04 03

To my daughter Mary Isabel Nelson
(née Yi RuiFeng)
with love

Contents

Acknowledgments

Like adoptions, books are group efforts. I appreciate the generous help of family, friends, colleagues, and institutions. Martha Vicinus, Anthony Rotundo, and Mimi Tangum provided invaluable support in this study's initial incarnation as a proposal laid before the National Endowment for the Humanities; the NEH and Southwest Texas State University provided financial assistance for which I am deeply grateful. Anne Morey, David and Mary Nelson, Marilynn Olson, and the anonymous readers for Indiana University Press pored over my work in manuscript form and offered perceptive, constructive, and sometimes bracing comments. The book is richer for their suggestions. Versions of chapters of this book originally appeared as "Drying the Orphan's Tear: Changing Representations of the Dependent Child in America, 1870–1930" in *Children's Literature* 29 (2001) and as "Nontraditional Adoption in Progressive-Era Orphan Narratives" in *Mosaic, a journal for the interdisciplinary study of literature* 34, no. 2 (June 2001): 181–197; another chapter contains material from my article "'In these days of scientific charity': Orphanages and Social Engineering in *Dear Enemy,*" published in Roderick McGillis's collection *Children's Literature and the Fin de Siècle* (Greenwood Press, 2002). I thank Yale University Press, *Mosaic,* and Greenwood for permission to reprint that material here. And finally, my inspiration was provided by my daughter, who also spent much of her toddlerhood asking solicitously, "Are you going to work on your book about adoption now?" This book is for her, but also for Joseph, Marie, Elena and Robert, Sarah and Becca, Alice and Margaret, and Maia and Zoe—and for many others unknown to me.

Little Strangers

Introduction

Little Orphant Annie's come to our house to stay,
An' wash the cups an' saucers up, an' brush the crumbs away,
An' shoo the chickens off the porch, an' dust the hearth, an' sweep,
An' make the fire, an' bake the bread, an' earn her board-an'-keep. . . .

(Riley, ll. 1–4)

The 1885 poem "Little Orphant Annie," by Hoosier versifier James Whitcomb Riley, profiles a girl "bound out" to earn her own way in the world. In return for room and board, young Annie (based on a child who worked for the Rileys) serves as maid-of-all-work for a large family; at night, she tells ghost stories to her employer's offspring. After recounting what befalls disrespectful children who mock adults or refuse to say their prayers, she concludes with a message at once attractive to the powers that be and calculated to serve her own interests:

You better mind yer parents, an' yer teachers fond an' dear,
An' churish them 'at loves you, an' dry the orphan's tear,
An' he'p the pore an' needy ones 'at clusters all about,
Er the Gobble-uns'll git you
    Ef you
          Don't
             Watch
                Out! (ll. 41–48)

At once subservient and feisty, Riley's Annie uses oratory and imagination to convince her luckier peers of the existence of unseen powers who will avenge any unkindness offered her. Readers may notice, however, that these powers evidently see no reason to ameliorate her lot as slavey. Ultimately, Annie is probably on her own.

Originally published (as "The Elf Child") in the Indianapolis *Journal* and later in great demand at verse recitations public and private, Riley's poem may have lent its name to another popular text, Harold Gray's comic strip *Little Orphan Annie*, which began its run in 1924. But the cartoon Annie is no bound-out girl. Despite a rocky start in a Dickensian orphanage and endless subsequent tribulations, she is always reunited with Daddy Warbucks, and her role in his household is not to care for chickens but to be cherished and protected herself. While the *nouveau riche* Mrs. Warbucks wants Annie as a prop so that she can participate in the fashion for appearing charitable, the adoptive father feels an immediate and powerful love for his new daughter. Bruce Smith proposes, indeed, that Warbucks—a self-made man whose fortune, as his name implies, comes from defense contracts awarded to him during the First World War—is "a man with deeply hurt feelings who believed nobody liked him because he'd made money from the war"; thus "the orphan nobody wanted" becomes crucial to "the munitions maker nobody liked" because she is his connection to the world of feeling (13). And while his love attracts kidnappers and the jealousy of Mrs. Warbucks, it puts Annie at the family's center, not its margins.

The contrast between the situations of the two Annies suggests the dramatic changes that took place over many decades in the American understanding of the function of the displaced child. When Massachusetts enacted the nation's first comprehensive adoption law in 1851, the usual motive for taking an unrelated child into the family was the desire for cheap help; at that time, most formal or informal adoptions (as opposed to the temporary placements represented by binding out or apprenticeship) involved blood kin. It was comparatively unlikely that children separated from their families of origin by the death or incapacity of one or both parents would find new homes in which they would be deemed emotionally important. In a tradition that descended from the Elizabethan Poor Law of 1601, foster parents were supposed to provide food, clothing, and education in exchange for the child's services. Thus, child placement efforts focused primarily on adolescents or at least preteens, who were old enough to be of practical use; young children were often considered unplaceable and relegated to institutions. In contrast, by 1929—the first year that every state had an adoption law—most commentators held that the adopted child's main function, like Annie's for Daddy Warbucks, was to be loved by its new parents. The legal adoption of strangers' children had become a commonplace, as had the adoption of infants, even though the latter make a great deal of work and perform none.[1]

This book examines representations of adoption and foster care in writings produced between 1850 and 1929. It is a history not of displaced, adopted, and foster children but of the rhetorical uses to which such children were put. Because the focus here is not on real children and lived experience but on how an assortment of cultural critics, social-service workers, child-development experts, journalists, and writers of fiction used children real and imagined to advance a wide range of ideas, this study necessarily presents a distorted picture of reality. But the distortions involved are themselves suggestive, indicating as they do how commentators constructed images of displaced children to suit their own needs. Indeed, the very word "orphan" may be understood not only in terms of its dictionary meaning, but also as a rhetorical ploy designed to elicit a particular emotional response from its nineteenth-century audience, since in addition to children who had lost one or both parents to death, "orphans" frequently included abandoned children, illegitimate children, and the offspring of the destitute or depraved.[2] Identifying such youngsters as orphans rather than "foundlings," "bastards," or "paupers" was one way of detaching them from the suspicion of hereditary moral taint.

One factor that helps to explain this shift in understanding is that child placement over the final third of the nineteenth century had gained in importance because there were more displaced children in the United States than had ever before been the case. In the 1860s and '70s, Civil War casualties accounted for some of this rise; later, we may attribute it jointly to economic conditions that made it hard for the impoverished to keep their families together, to a rise in divorce and desertion, and to a new reluctance on society's part to leave homeless children to fend for themselves. The boom in immigration was also a significant factor: the 1.2 million newcomers who arrived from Ireland between 1847 and 1854 as a result of the potato famine would be followed from 1870 to 1900 by more than 11 million working-class European immigrants, many of them neither Anglo-Saxon nor Protestant, and by workers imported from East Asia. These influxes swelled the population of America's cities, inflaming religious prejudices and a xenophobia focused in part on displaced children, who, whatever their parentage, quickly came to figure in the public imagination as representatives of the ethnic "other." The assimilation of such "others" became a pressing social concern, one whose urgency for contemporaries can hardly be overstated.

At first, one response to the question of how these children might be made productive Americans was to found more public and private orphanages, whose inhabitants might be shielded from the contact with adult unfortunates that was a feature of life in almshouses.[3] But by the end of the century, while more and more children were passing through orphanages each year, observers were increasingly skeptical about the benefits of institutionalization. Critics complained that inmates of orphan asylums were being turned into automata. Regimented, repressed, and deprived of family life, they were said to grow up with neither enterprise nor character, threatening the communities in which they spent their lives. Immigrant or native-born, then, the products of such an upbringing might be viewed as embodiments of anti-American principles, devoid of the traits that would make the country strong. It is possible to discern in these charges anxiety about the increasingly regimented and repressed lives of ordinary adults in a newly industrialized society; displaced children, who might be raised en masse in what some social scientists presented as the human equivalent of factory farms, provided a convenient focus for arguments about the importance of individuality.

But the displaced child has often served as a symbol of America in a more positive sense. Noting that from *Tom Sawyer* to *The Wizard of Oz* to *Tarzan of the Apes*, "the American childhood story is almost always the story of an orphan," Jerry Griswold argues (with a nod to Leslie Fiedler) that our nation's classic childhood texts are "not marginal, but squarely within our central literary tradition," and that this centrality is inevitable because "the recurring story of maturation in American children's books embodies and speaks directly to our own particular cultural experience and to America's vision of itself: as a young country, always making itself anew, rebelling against authority, coming into its own, and establishing its own identity" (5, 241, 242). Nor need we limit our examination to the twelve canonical fictions that Griswold considers in *The Classic American Children's Story*; whether fiction or nonfiction, child-oriented or adult-oriented, the middle-brow texts of the period that the present study examines pullulate with adopted and foster children who demonstrate an astonishing ability to change society or to adapt triumphantly to its demands, whether by manipulating human nature, making money, warming hearts, or upholding truth, justice, and the American way. Superman's linking of foundlinghood and patriotism is no accident. The United States has long presented itself both as self-made orphan (it celebrates every year the anniversary of the severing of its relationship with the mother country) and as adoptive parent to countless immigrants. Because both foster parent and upwardly mobile child evoke the American dream, the rhetoric surrounding adoption and foster care often takes on nationalist overtones, suggesting that the displaced child is a distinctively American phenomenon. That this implication is false does not prevent such rhetoric from telling us much about the part that such displaced children have played in the reshaping of American childhood and the American family—indeed, the reshaping of America's understanding of itself.

For, as reformers and writers were well aware, child placement is the stuff of which engrossing narratives are made. Thus commentary on this subject exploits melodrama and archetype, from tales of abuses rivaling *Oliver Twist* to Cinderella stories of social rise, and milks the drama inherent in efforts to solve the problem of the displaced child. Moreover, late nineteenth- and early twentieth-century writings on the displaced child also reflect changing attitudes toward ethnic and religious minorities, child labor, social welfare, heredity and environment, personality and citizenship, gender, class, and the nature of childhood and the family. Along the way, they provide important insights into the complex relationship between nonfiction and fiction, for just as the latter incorporates truths about the real position of the young within American society, the former often constructs an image of the child that may have little to do with individual experience. In both forms, the dependent child typically becomes a metaphor that may be used either to critique or to support a variety of social institutions. It is the social criticism that gives such rhetoric its energy, but it is the figure of the child that gives it its appeal.

Attitudes toward dependent children evolved slowly, and in any generation we may find rhetoric more typical of earlier or later periods in American social history. To generalize, however, one might argue that until the mid-1880s, the dominant tendency in nonfiction texts was to see displaced children primarily in terms of the practical uses to which they might be put. Giving such children work on farms, in factories, or as domestic servants was said to benefit at once the employers; the children, who would be receiving board and keep and useful training; the taxpayers, who would not have to support these children in institutions; and the body politic, since children raised to habits of industry would make better citizens later on. Fiction, however, typically urged consideration for the child's feelings and lamented the emotional bleakness of the uncaring world. In contrast, the turn of the century was a transitional period, a time of social experimentation and recantation of earlier positions. Although adoptions motivated by emotion rather than utilitarianism were increasingly common and social measures aimed at protecting at-risk children were increasingly widespread, the drive toward reform spurred in nonfiction a counterbalancing conservatism and anxiety about the displaced child, while fiction suggested that this anxiety was misplaced. And, finally, the 1910s and '20s witnessed an intensification of an existing desire to idealize children in general and, sometimes, adoptable children in particular, so that more and more discussions of adoption and foster care were cast in terms of children's *and* adults' emotional needs—even while writers simultaneously sought to render them more convincing via appeals to science.

As the preceding paragraph has suggested, trends in one body of writing do not necessarily reflect trends in all. Just as it is useful to consider foster care, informal adoption, and legal adoption side by side, both because they illuminate one another by contrast and because the former sometimes shaded into the latter, we cannot afford to look at a particular kind of text in isolation. Organizing its findings chronologically, this book will sample the following: "orphan fiction" for children and adolescents, which in some cases addressed adults as well; stories and articles in women's magazines; legal writings; articles and conference presentations aimed primarily at social workers; and discussions of heredity and child psychology. In tone, literary quality, and evident purpose, these texts are diverse. This diversity is precisely the point, since it is essential to recognize that the displaced child is an omnipresent rhetorical trope in American writing of this period, an image informing not merely canonical literature but an assortment of ephemera that did at least as much as the major works to mold and reflect cultural perceptions. In this mixture of texts, we may discover how various kinds of writings for various kinds of audiences collide and collaborate to form patterns that may not be seen when we look at a genre in isolation. In discussing the terms upon which the debate about adoption and foster care was conducted, then, this book seeks in part to illuminate the extent to which imaginary, popular, and "real" representations of displaced children influence, overlap with, challenge, and contradict one another.

The remainder of this book expands on the ideas sketched so broadly and briefly in the foregoing overview. Chapter 1 explores two key events of the 1850s. The first of these is the publication of Susan Warner's monumental best seller *The Wide, Wide World* (1850), which did much to establish the orphan novel as a marketable commodity and to inspire subsequent fictions in the field. The second is the rhetoric following upon the 1853 founding of the New York Children's Aid Society, which dramatically expanded the practice of exporting destitute urban children to rural foster homes. While Warner's novel and the publications associated with the Society vary considerably in the degree of sympathy they extend toward the displaced child, both sets of writings call into question domestic and familial ideals that are sometimes seen as sacrosanct in mid-Victorian America.

Chapter 2 spans the period from 1860 to 1885 and discusses a rhetorical trope that recurs again and again during these years, namely the tendency to frame the problem of the displaced child in economic terms. The fiction of the time frequently uses orphans to highlight the instability of social class; as if to counterbalance the anxieties arising from this perception, nonfiction often presents various approaches toward displaced children as a matter of dollars and cents, readily calculated, prudently expended by the knowledgeable child-saver. As entries in a philanthropic ledger, displaced children—and the social problems that give rise to them—appear controllable.

My reasoning in concentrating on children's fiction in this and subsequent chapters rather than examining orphans in the works of, say, Henry James is not merely, to misquote Willie Sutton, that that's where the orphans are. Rather, I would contend that it is the nature of mass-market texts, whether for children or for adults, to respond to their culture's deep-rooted assumptions and anxieties; popularity often results from giving tongue to what one's contemporaries already think, and sometimes also from playing on their secret doubts about what they think they *ought* to think. Moreover, the audience for the children's texts presented in Chapter 2 and throughout this study appeared to the texts' authors to be separate from the specialized adult audiences for social-work conference presentations, sociological studies of the inheritability of criminal tendencies, state-by-state overviews of adoption law, and the like.[4] In juxtaposing texts written by distinct groups of authors and addressing distinct audiences, we may gain a better understanding of concepts that transcended genre. At the same time, another reason that I limit my survey of orphan fiction to tales for a young or multigenerational audience is precisely that orphan stories of this type form a coherent genre whose defining characteristics merit considerable study. The number of novels about displaced children intended for and read by an exclusively adult audience is much smaller, and these works, I would argue, do not constitute a genre, in that they do not adhere to a sufficiently extensive set of conventions.

Chapter 3 continues the examination of orphan fiction, following this body of literature as it begins to sketch a new and more sentimental function for the adoptee or foster child. In the years from 1886 to 1906, displaced children were increasingly imagined as long-lost heirs or members of the aristocracy of talent; although they clearly functioned as commodities within the literary marketplace, their proper "work" was presented as the spiritual and emotional uplift of adults. As Chapter 4 notes, this shift occurs against the backdrop of reforms associated with Progressivism, such as the efforts to curtail child labor and improve the living conditions of the poor, but other factors are relevant here as well: the rise of mass-market journalism, the anxiety about Taylorist production methods, and the backlash against the orphan-train movement, for instance. While displaced children in fiction and nonfiction alike became focal points for the expression of anxiety about the place of the individual in a mass society and about adult emotional incapacity (among other issues), their presence also evoked hostility, whether directed at the children themselves or at those who sought to take them in.

Chapter 5, which runs from 1907 to 1918, narrows the two previous chapters' focus on the Progressive Era to the more specific question of how women figured in the adoption rhetoric of the era. The decade, of course, witnessed an unusually active reshaping of feminine gender roles as suffrage agitation and increasing employment of women outside the home suggested a frontal assault on the boundaries between private and public. Discussions of adoption during this period often took the opportunity to participate in the debate over women's proper place, whether they offered women a convenient shortcut back to traditionalism (often a traditionalism that could be combined with a career) or became the excuse for attacks on conservative gender mores. Simultaneously, the eugenics movement and hereditarian theory retained vestiges of older views on women's influence over their children, so that while a good adoptive mother might not be able to salvage the wrong kind of child, a bad biological mother could prove all-powerful, overcoming her mate's genetic contribution to stamp her descendants forever with her mark.

Finally, Chapter 6 explores phenomena such as the standardization and bureaucratization of placement procedures, juvenile series books on adoption, and statistical studies of foster-care outcomes in light of 1920s concerns about the relationship of the individual personality and the corporate world, about the nature of normalcy and the conflict between science and sentiment, and about attaining "mastery" over one's self and one's environment. The decade constructed an image of adoptees and foster children as most remarkable when they could be deemed to have achieved full membership in the herd. If a major goal of the late-nineteenth-century orphan trains was to acculturate the children of immigrants to American customs and values, adoption in the 1920s retained this assimilationist stance but gave it a self-consciously modern flavor. Just as the adoption rhetoric of this era denigrated sentimentality while continuing to employ it, old ideas of retraining displaced children for productive citizenship were presented as new through their attachment to the latest catchwords and social preoccupations.

This study does not purport to be comprehensive. Rather, I seek to provide a series of core samples that in combination may suggest some of the varied and occasionally conflicting cultural uses to which representations of adoptees and foster children were put over eight decades of American life. Retrieving the lived experience of the young is always enormously difficult because overwhelmingly it is adults, not children, who tell children's stories, filtering them through layers of "memory and desire." It is with this co-opting, and with some of the social influences affecting it, that this book concerns itself.

1

The 1850s and Their Echoes

Two Case Studies

The America of 1850 inherited from colonial days a tradition of dealing with displaced children by putting them to work—or, alternatively, by encouraging them to leave town so that any money spent on them would come out of someone else's pocket. Both approaches remained standard at mid-century, but the question of what to do with orphaned, deserted, or destitute runaway children was becoming more complex. As the introduction to this study notes, such children were increasingly, and disturbingly, visible in the nation's cities, their numbers daily augmented by immigration, their presumed future that of the pauper or the criminal. Thus one common response to needy children was the desire to protect society from their depredations.

Simultaneously, however, the early and middle nineteenth century witnessed a flowering of interest in child development and a growing belief that nurturing the young was better calculated to produce worthy adults than punishing them. Child-rearing manuals had become a major American genre in the 1840s, when authors such as Catharine Beecher and Horace Bushnell suggested that children were not steeped in original sin, but rather were malleable creatures who might be led to virtue by informed and gentle parents. The insistence on "breaking the will" even of infants was going out of style, pushed aside by an emphasis on making good behavior pleasant. Hence commentators on needy children also sought to protect them from society—to extract them from the damaging milieu into which they had been born or thrust by loss and to transplant them into a morally nourishing soil.

Whether displaced children were deemed victims or threats, reformers believed that intervention was necessary. If the new theories of parenting stressed enlightened child rearing, they also warned that immoral or neglectful caregivers would produce bad children, beliefs that child-savers used to justify intervening in the domestic arrangements of the very poor. Orphanages, public and private, were one solution; rare in 1800, they had become common in the 1840s and '50s. But few children remained in them to adulthood, since superintendents perennially sought to make room for new admissions. By and large, orphanage inmates and noninstitutionalized children who had attracted the attention of child-savers experienced similar fates. Some could be given over into the custody of relatives. Others went to "working homes" that would provide both respectable employment and domestic security. And still others, although they were in the minority, found homes in which they were expected to be consumers rather than producers. Following the lead of Massachusetts in 1851, states began to enact general laws of adoption that facilitated the permanent transplanting of children into new families and bestowed upon legal adoptees rights (of inheritance, for instance) equal to those of legitimate biological children—sometimes over commentators' protests.[1] Together these ways of handling placement illustrate the coexistence of conflicting attitudes on the appropriate disposition and function of surplus children in mid-nineteenth-century American society, attitudes informed, in turn, by ideas about ethnicity, social class, religion, and the purification of the nation.

This chapter examines some of those ideas through the lens of two contrasting events: the 1850 publication of Susan Warner's seminal orphan novel *The Wide, Wide World* and the explosion of rhetoric surrounding the New York Children's Aid Society (founded in 1853), whose work, publicized by writers such as Horatio Alger and popular periodicals from *St. Nicholas* to *Harper's Monthly*, was to become synonymous in many people's minds with the relocation and consequent uplifting of street children. Neither of these events came out of the void. *The Wide, Wide World* followed in the footsteps of earlier orphan novels such as Catharine Maria Sedgwick's *A New-England Tale* (1822); like Warner's work, Sedgwick's takes as protagonist the daughter of an improvident father and a long-suffering mother, who falls to the care of a flinty aunt after having "been taught [true Christianity] even more by the example than the precepts of her mother" (Sedgwick 24), and who finally marries an idealized father-figure.[2] Similarly, in founding the New York Children's Aid Society, Charles Loring Brace borrowed from predecessors such as Robert Hartley and Unitarian minister George Merrill. Hartley's New York Association for Improving the Condition of the Poor (established in 1843) focused on ameliorating poverty by building character; to this end, middle-class volunteers sought to instill self-discipline and industry in the working class, a message that Brace directed more specifically to children and adolescents. And in 1850 Merrill, whose Boston Children's Mission had opened the previous year, began to ship "salvageable" children to foster and adoptive homes elsewhere in New England, and subsequently the Midwest as well. By the end of the decade, the Mission and the Society had each relocated approximately 1,300 youngsters—but the Mission, of course, had been first out of the blocks (Holloran 45). Although Brace is sometimes credited with having invented the device of the "orphan trains," he might better be considered its chief publicist.

But while they were not wholly new in conception, *The Wide, Wide World* and the New York Children's Aid Society are both landmarks in their respective fields because of the power and influence wielded by their representations of displaced children, representations that sometimes contradicted and sometimes reinforced one another. A best seller on two continents, Warner's debut book was the first American work to sell more than a million copies. *A New-England Tale* had been a critical and commercial success, but *The Wide, Wide World* was a sensation, inspiring countless imitations and helping to codify—and commodify—what would become a long-standing tradition of using the parentless child to critique respectability and domesticity. Sedgwick's account of the tribulations of her heroine is comparatively brief and matter-of-fact; Warner's obsessive detailing of her protagonist's grief, anger, shame, and moral struggles demands that we feel with the orphan, experiencing and responding to her exploitation and objectification and confronting our own resentments through hers.

Discussions of Brace's gargantuan placement efforts—particularly discussions authored by Brace himself—likewise have considerable rhetorical importance, albeit along somewhat different lines. Often as dramatically framed as Warner's narrative, they are redolent rather of a desire to protect society from presumed criminal elements than of a wish to heighten sympathy with the oppressed or to better children's lives for their own sake. Brace's publicizing of the Society's methods is frank about one of the organization's central strategies, its deliberate severing of the ties between impoverished urban children and birth families that often included two surviving parents. Catholic child-savers of the era complained bitterly about what they perceived, correctly, as religious bias on Brace's part; the New York Children's Aid Society was heavily invested in "rescuing" the children of Irish and central European immigrants from popery. But the bias was not Brace's alone, since his intended audience of socially concerned Protestants and prospective rural foster families clearly agreed that some families were made to be broken. Brace's newspaper and magazine articles, memoirs, and other writings perform a critique of domesticity that diverges in significant ways from Warner's, largely because his conception of the displaced child differs dramatically from hers. Both critiques, however, resonated with the middle-class American public.

At first glance, these two sets of writings might appear to have little in common beyond popular success. Yet they share an understanding of the displaced child as imbued with significance beyond the individual, even while the child's individuality becomes an object for examination in new detail. In tracing the intricacies of her protagonist's psyche and emotions,

Warner makes her imagined orphan representative of both the woes of the powerless and the noble aspirations of a moral nation. Similarly, discussions of the achievements of the New York Children's Aid Society stressed the possibility of effecting social change through the mechanism of the family, one child at a time. Both Warner and the Society were responding to the perception that inserting the young into new homes is a meaningful way of overcoming social problems. That adoption inevitably suggests a fresh start in life means that it lends itself to being read as an instrument for change on both the personal and the public levels. As a consequence, it tends to become also a stalking-horse for reformers' and commentators' pet obsessions—especially, in the cases explored in this chapter, the question of assimilation.

Displaced Children in Fiction: *The Wide, Wide World*

Variously claimed by critics as an early example of girls' fiction and as the archetypal work of sentimental writing for adults, Warner's text was to be a major influence on orphan novels for both audiences for the next sixty years. Typically, such narratives tell the story of an orphan girl who arrives in a new and distasteful situation and successfully adapts to her lot. But most later orphans and half-orphans, such as Kate Douglas Wiggin's Rebecca of Sunnybrook Farm (1903), Frances Hodgson Burnett's Sara Crewe (1887, expanded 1905), Eleanor H. Porter's Pollyanna (1913), and a Canadian example, L. M. Montgomery's Anne of Green Gables (1908), change their environments to suit themselves. Tellingly, Warner's Ellen Montgomery—who belongs to what Bernard Wishy calls the era of the "child redeemable" rather than the post-1860 era of the "child redeemer" (xi)—has relatively little influence on those about her. Although she converts her uncle by marriage to Christianity and softens the heart of the wild Nancy Vawse, she lacks the compelling personality of turn-of-the-century orphan heroines. Instead, she succeeds by learning to bear what is unpleasant, repressing her strong feelings and accepting a series of new settings in order to discover her spiritual home. In Ellen's case, assimilation is as threatening as it is ultimately desirable, since not all environments promise spiritual improvement.

We first encounter Ellen when she is ten years old and about to be wrested away from her dying mother, whose insensitive and newly bankrupt husband is forcing her to accompany him on a business trip to Europe; he claims that the voyage will restore her health but that there is not enough money to permit Ellen to come too. The pain of this parting reverberates throughout the narrative, which is studded both with false authority figures eager to stand between Ellen and her pious mother's spirit and with spiritual guides eager to bring Ellen to a true understanding of Christ. Heartbroken, Ellen is conducted to the countryside (apparently upstate New York) to live with her father's half-sister, Fortune Emerson, a sharp-

tongued domestic dictator fixated upon maintaining the strictest household economy and bringing her unwelcome charge to a due humility.

Their relationship never becomes affectionate, but after Ellen's parents
die—her mother of illness, her father in a shipwreck—she is invited to join
a more congenial and Christian household as a replacement for the dead
daughter of the house, Alice Humphreys, Ellen's erstwhile mentor, teacher,
and friend. This informal adoption is more than satisfactory to Ellen, who
has already identified this establishment as her ideal home. Nevertheless,
she must leave her new family at fourteen, when she belatedly receives
letters from both Montgomerys directing her to go to Edinburgh and live
with her mother's relatives, the Lindsays. Worldly and high-handed, the
Lindsays disapprove of Ellen's evangelical Christianity (effortfully acquired
after leaving her mother) and her American loyalties; they forbid her to
speak of her former adoptive brother and father. But the brother, John
Humphreys, the novel's ultimate authority figure in matters religious and
secular, comes to Edinburgh and impresses the Lindsays with his force of
character. A final chapter, unpublished during Warner's lifetime, clarifies
that Ellen returns to the Humphreys ménage, this time in the capacity of
John's wife.

Warner's dual themes here are religion and family, which, as Veronica
Stewart notes, she can reconcile only after a struggle (62). Both are represented as riddled with conflict: religion because Ellen believes that she cannot call herself a Christian until she can claim to love God better even than
her mother (from whom, of course, God appears to be separating her in a
particularly cruel way), and family because, as Warner makes clear, families are hierarchies within which the flawed, arbitrary, and short-sighted
may exercise complete dominion over their moral superiors. Under these
circumstances, it is essential to Ellen's spiritual quest that she be an orphan, not only because her "affection for her mother supplants her love of
Jesus" and thus inhibits her "rebirth through Christ" (Stewart 64), but also
because orphanhood gives her the mobility and the wide experience necessary to make an informed judgment about the nature of the ideal family,
and especially the ideal patriarch. While she has little or no choice about
whom she will live with at any given time, she is nonetheless free to withhold herself emotionally from her environment, assimilating or refusing to
assimilate as she deems best.

When Warner's novel appeared, American society subscribed to what is
often called the "cult of domesticity," an exaltation of middle-class family
life and especially the mother's role within it as the center of love, nurturing, and morality. Warner's comment that "love to her mother was the
strongest feeling [Ellen's] heart knew" (13) is typical of the era's idealization of maternity, as is the novel's portrait of Mrs. Montgomery as tender,
Christian, uncomplaining, and ever mindful of her daughter's welfare and
happiness.[3] Even so, Warner shows that this good mother has her flaws.
She lacks the near-omniscience that sentimental literature sometimes

attributes to virtuous maternity; not only has she erred in marrying Captain Montgomery (undomesticated, unchristian, and a poor provider)
against her family's wishes, she also posthumously instructs Ellen to leave
America for Edinburgh, inadvertently forcing her to trade heaven for Van-
ity Fair. As Stewart notes, her major sin is one of omission: "Just as Captain
Montgomery proves inept at navigating the public sphere of high finance,
Mrs. Montgomery fails to carry out her most crucial social function as wife
and mother," the conversion of husband and daughter to Christianity (63).
Her helplessness is endemic among the novel's female characters; even
such apparently strong figures as Fortune and Alice must confront their
limitations when they encounter men whose plans or views differ from
their own. But because Mrs. Montgomery, in particular, lacks the power of
shaping and containing masculine drives that the nineteenth century so
comfortably ascribed to women, Ellen must leave her in order to achieve
salvation.

In this need for separation, Ellen resembles the displaced children of a
lower order who were the clientele of the New York Children's Aid Society.
As Brace presented the latter group, they too traveled from city to country
in search of moral improvement, like Ellen learning rural skills and finding
themselves cut off from their families of origin. (One of Fortune's crimes is
to withhold letters and funds from Mrs. Montgomery and the Captain; to
advance what they saw as the children's best interests, Society personnel,
too, sometimes blocked birth parents' efforts to communicate with their
offspring [*Orphan Trains*].) But if Brace put the Society's placements in a
positive light, implying that from the child's standpoint change was always
for the better, Warner's narrator is ambivalent about the adults who surround the orphaned Ellen. Fortune, who lacks Mrs. Montgomery's aristocratic background and her Christian faith, denies Ellen schooling and religious guidance; her child-rearing philosophy is merely that children should
be docile and useful. Fortune's farm manager and eventual husband, Van
Brunt, is kindly but untutored, godless until Ellen converts him at the
novel's end, while wealthy acquaintances such as the Dunscombes, who
superintend Ellen on the first stage of her travels, are shallow and mean-
spirited. The Lindsays, class-conscious and anti-American, try to eradicate
her unsophisticated innocence and to water down her faith into mere conventional churchgoing. John Humphreys is a ruthless discipliner of both
horses and girls and inspires fear as well as love in Ellen, whom he trains
through affection but also through lectures and shaming. And even Alice
Humphreys, whose tutelage of Ellen most closely resembles Mrs. Montgomery's, replicates the mother's weaknesses as well as her strengths, not only
in her ill-health but also in her inability to separate from beloved relatives
even when it is God who mandates their absence (see Stewart 67).

Warner's point here, in other words, is not that the orphan must leave
its unhealthy environment in order to be cared for by more suitable people,
as Brace (like other child-savers) would argue. Rather, it is that orphan-

hood itself can be spiritually enlightening. Ellen's preceptors and experiences teach her that—especially for women, children, and the poor—life is uncertain, that human bonds are fragile because circumstance may snatch away the beloved, and that one's trust must be in God. On one level, her status as orphan is a metaphor for the solitude of the human soul striving toward the divine.[4] On another, it is a crucial part of her religious education, inasmuch as her travels bring her to household after household in which she must subordinate her wishes to others', an exercise that underscores God's demand for total surrender of the self. What Richard Brodhead calls the "discipline by intimacy" of the opening chapters, which show the closeness of the mother-child bond, gives way to a discipline by separation, in which, Brodhead argues, Ellen's desire to please her mother is transformed into obsession by the mother's absence (33–34).

Meanwhile, the replacement caregivers are impelled to exert their authority ever more strongly by their consciousness that they are not Ellen's "real" parents. Fortune resents any hint that she may be an inadequate foster mother, Alice follows her confession that she will be "a poor substitute for your mother" with a list of improvements needed in Ellen's conduct (238, 241), and Mr. Lindsay insists, "I will not have you call me 'uncle'—I am your father—you are my own little daughter and must do precisely what I tell you" (510). In other words, Ellen's subordination to others, which she must accept if she is to find God, is intensified by her status as displaced child because all these adults feel the need to demonstrate their position as Ellen's "sole guardian and owner" (381). As an orphan in a society without general adoption laws, Ellen is a possession whose "ownership" is uncertain until she finally becomes a wife.

While each parent-substitute requires Ellen's obedience and her acquiescence in the style of the new household, the demands vary with the social differences among her caregivers. As Brodhead observes, each household represents a "different social formatio[n] of the home's place and work," from Fortune's "old-style" home, which manufactures all that it consumes, to "the more genteel (and less productive) formation of a historically later phase, in the case of Alice and John Humphreys[, and] the altogether leisured, pleasure-oriented formation of a Europeanized gentry class, in the case of the aristocratic Lindsays" (31). Unlike Brace, Warner rejects the Romantic equation of rural simplicity with virtue and urban sophistication with vice, suggesting rather that true Christianity may be found, however infrequently, in any walk of life.

But if wealth and social class are irrelevant to religious feeling, they have a strong effect on an individual's understanding of the function of the displaced child. Although Fortune never had any desire for Ellen's presence in her home and seems to have acceded only out of duty to Captain Montgomery's plea that she take charge of his daughter, she fully intends to receive recompense for her hospitality in the form of Ellen's labor. Consequently, the girl is "forced" into "busy industry" (347): dishwashing at first, butter-making and spinning once she has gained more housewifely skill. When Fortune falls ill for a period of some weeks, Ellen has been sufficiently domesticated that her aunt can hand over to her all the household tasks.

Yet despite the narrator's disapproval of Fortune as narrow, unsympathetic, and impious, the demand that Ellen share in the quotidian work of the farmhouse is not criticized. Although Fortune does not mean to benefit Ellen, but to deprive her of time that would otherwise have gone in study, the child nonetheless profits from her chores: "the hours of spinning that wrought so many knots of yarn for her aunt, wrought better things yet for the little spinner: patience and gentleness grew with the practice of them; this wearisome work was one of the many seemingly untoward things which in reality bring out good. The time Ellen *did* secure to herself was held the more precious and used the more carefully" (419). The early-nineteenth-century habit of turning displaced children to practical account, then, is validated—but a shift has taken place, in that the narrative assesses the work assigned with an eye to the adult's gratification in terms of the benefits received by the child. In this sense Warner's novel resembles the Children's Aid Society rhetoric, which likewise takes a child-centered approach by stressing household chores' redemptive value for untrained children and downplaying the benefits for adults.

To be sure, most of Warner's adults are more interested in their own needs than in Ellen's, although their needs vary. In contrast to Fortune's utilitarian approach to surrogate parenthood, both the Humphreys and the Lindsay families see Ellen's function as primarily emotional. Shortly before her death, Alice explains that Ellen's job will be "to take my place, and take care of those I leave behind . . . to be to [my father] as far as you can, what I have been" (432). Ellen's household duties now consist primarily of tidying her new father's study, a task important for its symbolic value (it belongs to the daughter of the house) rather than for its practical aspects (the Humphreyses employ a devoted retainer who is fully capable of cleaning a room). Quickly Ellen becomes "the light of the house," as the retainer puts it (460), a role she certainly never had in Fortune's establishment. She cannot, it is true, expect to fill in completely for Alice, but "Deep as the gloom still over [Mr. Humphreys] was, Ellen never dreamed how much deeper it would have been, but for the little figure flitting round and filling up the vacancy" (461). And living in the house that holds Alice's brother, Ellen is now conveniently placed to receive the spiritual and intellectual instruction that John had begun to provide earlier. Here the situation reverses that in Fortune's home: while John is working for his own good in training up a wife for himself, as Joanne Dobson (231) and David Leverenz (188) have argued, he appears to Ellen to have in mind her happiness alone.

Adopting a child to replace a dead son or daughter was no new practice; indeed, it was among the most common of the *emotional* motivations for adoption at this time. Writing of the fledgling Chicago Orphan Asylum (opened in 1849), Clare McCausland notes that by 1851 it had admitted one hundred children, of whom seventy-six had been placed in homes. The remaining twenty-four were babies or young children—not good workers, in other words, and hence less desirable. But while many adults accepting older children expected to teach them "activities for a useful life," as McCausland's nineteenth-century source delicately puts it, others sought "to replace a 'lost loved one'" (17). This dichotomy lasted for some time. When, in 1873, Brace wrote a piece for *Harper's* describing the adults who accepted placements from the Children's Aid Society, he categorized the prospective parents very similarly:

> Farmers come in . . . looking for the "model boy" who shall do the light work of the farm and aid the wife in her endless household labor; child-less mothers seek for children that shall replace those that are lost; house-keepers look for girls to train up; mechanics seek for boys for their trades; and kind-hearted men, with comfortable homes and plenty of children, think it is their duty to do something for the orphans who have no fair chance in the great city. ("Laborers" 330)

A noteworthy characteristic of this list is the children's fungibility; Brace's description implies that whether prospective foster parents are looking for household help, "replace[ments]" for the dead, or objects of charity, any child of suitable gender and age is as good as any other. Warner, however, suggests that such is not the case with the Humphreys family, who want Ellen and Ellen alone because no one else combines great spiritual and domestic potential with an intense love for the lost Alice. (To put matters another way, we might say that they recognize that Ellen is an ideal pros-pect for assimilation into this particular household.) While the idea of adopting a substitute for a dead child was to fall out of favor by the end of the period discussed in this study, the Humphreyses' appreciation of Ellen as an individual looks distinctly "modern."

But the Humphreyses' ability to fathom the personality with which they are dealing contrasts with the third style of informal adoption illustrated in *The Wide, Wide World,* that practiced by the Lindsays. This family—Ellen's maternal grandmother and the grandmother's middle-aged son and daughter—sees the rearing of Ellen primarily as recreation. She becomes, indeed, a luxury item. This role for children accompanied the home's gradual transformation from a site of production into a site of consump-tion. Thus it is more common at the industrialized turn of the century, or in well-to-do urban settings, than it is at mid-century in rural locations; the Lindsays are the wave of the future because they can afford to be. In *Pricing the Priceless Child,* Viviana Zelizer traces "the construction of the economi-cally worthless child" (5). As the child ceased to contribute in meaningful *practical* ways to its family, its sentimental importance was magnified pro-portionately, a phenomenon apparent in miniature in *The Wide, Wide World.*

Zelizer dates sentimental constructions to childhood to the middle of the nineteenth century for the middle-class urban child, but notes that before the 1930s, when "Child labor laws and compulsory education . . . gradually destroyed the class lag," matters were different for the poor because industrialization widened employment opportunities for the working-class child, whose wages were often a mainstay of the family budget (6).

For Warner, however, the Lindsays' ultramodernity in viewing Ellen sentimentally is presented not as progressivism but as cause for concern. The narrator notes disapprovingly, "She was petted and fondled as a darling possession—a dear plaything—a thing to be cared for, taught, governed, disposed of, with the greatest affection and delight" (538). While Ellen is accustomed to being a possession, she prefers to be a possession with use value. But in the Lindsay household, the richest of the establishments with which Ellen becomes acquainted after leaving her mother, there are no duties at all, aside from attending the lessons that her relatives assume will correct the (nonexistent) flaws in Ellen's American education. Whereas Ellen's interaction with both Fortune and John is punctuated by humiliations of various kinds, then, her entrance into idleness and luxury is a protracted humiliation of a different sort.

Indeed, Ellen is reluctant to confess to her newfound aunt, Lady Keith, how she occupied her time at Fortune's house:

> "I had to sweep and dust," said Ellen colouring,—"and set tables,—and wash and wipe dishes,—and churn,—and spin,—and—"
> Ellen *heard* Lady Keith's look in her, "Could you have conceived it!"
> (507)

Now Ellen need no longer do her own mending, as she did at the Humphreys home, and there is no dusting of Mr. Lindsay's study. On the contrary, it is the Lindsays who perform personal tasks for her: "At eleven o'clock regularly every day she went to her grandmother's dressing room for a very elaborate bathing and dressing." Even though at fourteen she presumably can complete her toilette by herself, "Ellen was much too precious a plaything to be trusted to any other hands, even her own" (540). This existence, painted as effete, confining, and somewhat degenerate (one of Mr. Lindsay's orders is that the unwilling Ellen learn to drink wine), is also presented as an Old Country phenomenon. Correspondingly, the narrative makes much of Ellen's American patriotism; that she retains her admiration for national heroes such as George Washington is a sign that she will also retain her piety and her ability to work. We are not to desire her complete assimilation into her new family, because to exchange American ways for European ones is to regress morally.

While Ellen herself much prefers her life as Alice-replacement to either her subsequent role as favorite doll or her earlier existence at Aunt Fortune's beck and call, in fact none of the three contrasting approaches to informal adoption explored in Warner's novel permits the adoptee full scope for action, if action for women is defined in terms of the cult of domesticity. The domestic ideology that dominated sentimental literature asserted that feminine virtue should be all-powerful within the home, influencing men to higher things and placing women at the center of private life. Ellen's sole power over Fortune is that of irritating her, and since Van Brunt's conversion occurs after she has left the vicinity, and the narrator repeatedly suggests that the real domestic power in this family is his, she cannot be described as the center of the household. At the Humphreyses', Ellen's position as "light of the house" does not include being the source of morality. That job is John's; Ellen's task is to accept chastisement meekly when, as frequently happens, she falls short. And while we are clearly to read Ellen as the most moral inmate of the Lindsay ménage, her position as "dear plaything" bars her from exerting any influence for good.

We are left, then, with an understanding of the orphan's role in this 1850 text as varied but generally passive. Although Warner's novel contains many moments that foreshadow the emotionally powerful displaced child of the early twentieth century (even Fortune develops a grudging appreciation for some of Ellen's virtues), Ellen is not yet an example of such a figure. As is emphatically not the case with such later literary orphans as Pollyanna, her main task is to improve herself rather than the wider community, here usually depicted as either too good to need her ministrations or too unregenerate to succumb to them. In this, she again resembles Brace's vision of the displaced child as morally needy, although her class affiliations and the fact that she is twice taken in by blood relatives distinguish her from the clientele of the Children's Aid Society and other child-saving organizations. But if Ellen's family ties are not characteristic of later discussions of the displaced child, Warner's emphasis on Ellen's Americanism will be a constant theme throughout the period this study examines, in which displaced children are perennially considered in light of how American they are or may become.

"Orphans" on Trains: Framing the Efforts of the New York Children's Aid Society

Ellen, of course, is a first-generation American, only one step removed from the Old Country. But her "old country" is Britain, which Warner presents as more elegant, if less vigorous, than the United States; it is at her Scottish home rather than any of the American households she visits that she sometimes seems insufficiently ladylike. Her aristocratic roots identify her, literally, as radically different from the children who swarm through Brace's writings. They too are new Americans, but although the United States received many English and Scottish immigrants during and after the 1850s, Brace's profiled children are more likely to be Irish or perhaps German—as destitute as is Ellen at the beginning of her travels, but with no

wealthy relatives in the background. In order to communicate to his prospective supporters the urgency of the social problem with which he is
dealing, Brace dwells obsessively on the children's slangy speech, ragged
clothes, ignorance of Christianity, and unfamiliarity with the most basic
appurtenances of domesticity.

And the situation was urgent indeed. Immediately before the founding
of the New York Children's Aid Society, the flood of poor Irish immigrants
entering Boston and New York had swamped existing agencies for the care
of orphans and waifs. Orphanages quickly filled to capacity and beyond;
the population of street children rose alarmingly, as did the numbers of
children living with one or both parents but working in sweatshops or as
newsboys, crossing sweepers, and the like. Massachusetts responded to the
problem by passing its general adoption law (so that after 1851, it would
no longer be necessary to parlay connections and expertise into getting the
state legislature to authorize an adoption on an individual basis) and by
sending out more and more children to foster families; while these measures were not always adequate,[5] they at least represented an official commitment to adoption and foster care over institutionalization or neglect.
New York, in contrast, did not enact its adoption law until 1873.[6] If Massachusetts was long unusual in the strength of its commitment to placing
children in private homes, New York remained at the other extreme as
what Matthew Crenson has termed the "orphanage capital of the United
States" (50).

Brace was a man passionately committed to educating at-risk children.
In his view, both orphanages and factories crippled their inmates' chance
of learning the academic and emotional skills necessary to full citizenship.
Moreover, as the offspring of poor people who in many cases had only
recently entered the country, the children with whom he concerned himself were, he believed, already developmentally handicapped. Brace began
his career at a time of intense anti-immigrant feeling; the Irish influx horrified the native-born, who both doubted the new arrivals' ability to assimilate and insisted that assimilation take place immediately. Summing
up both Brace's thought and the climate of the times was an editorial in the
reformist *Massachusetts Teacher* in 1851, which saw the Irish influx as a tor-
rent of "muddy water" defiling the "pure" Commonwealth: "With the old
not much can be done; but with their children, the great remedy is education. The rising generation must be taught as our own children are taught.
We say must be because in many cases this can only be accomplished by
coercion" (qtd. Holloran 21).

While Brace did not write the *Massachusetts Teacher* editorial, the idea
that the destitute and/or immigrant child was a source of contamination,
but one that might be neutralized by retraining, was fundamental to his
presentation of his efforts throughout his career. An article that he contributed to the May 1882 issue of *St. Nicholas* compares the Society's clientele
to the feral "wolf-reared children" of Indian legend. These are children, he

notes, "who have been taught only in the schools of poverty, vice, and crime; whose ways are not our ways, and who have wolfish habits; whose brain makes them more cunning, more dangerous, than the animal, and who, if they grow up thus, will be more dangerous to this city than wolf or tiger to the villages of India" ("Children" 544). Nevertheless, "though wolves in human shape"—their biological parents—"have brought them up to crime and sin, they can be saved and made into reasonable human beings" (544). Such salvation depends, for the most part, on complete separation from their original families.

The metaphor of the wolf-reared child, like the Children's Aid Society's comparison of indigent adults to "social rats" motivated solely by "animal passions" (qtd. Ashby, *Children* 46), permits the erasure of certain assumptions central to the Victorian cult of domesticity. Warner's novel questions the inevitability of family as a site of virtue by highlighting the moral shortcomings of figures such as Captain Montgomery and Fortune Emerson. In "Wolf-Reared Children," Brace goes considerably farther: these parents are not merely insensitive and dictatorial but bestial, while the children lack the moral agency that Ellen displays. The young, it would seem, are almost infinitely plastic, so that in one kind of home environment they will be "reasonable human beings," in another unimaginably dangerous.

Brace's rhetorical move here is a logical, if melodramatic, response to two conflicting facts. First, as Brace was well aware, in the mid-nineteenth century America's cities were witnessing a boom in juvenile arrests; not surprisingly, the newly established reform schools in urban areas were disproportionately populated with immigrants, whose poverty and unsettled lives were conducive to delinquency and whose low status might have rendered them more liable to prosecution. Second, as we have seen Warner's novel illustrate, the surrounding society idealized domesticity and stressed the importance of family ties, even as it perceived and lamented a multitude of threats to the family's cohesiveness and power. To reconcile the concept of family as endangered moral nursery with the concept of the unassimilated child as moral danger, Brace found it expedient to define such children as anti-children, their families (if families they had) as anti-families: as he remarks, "[their] ways are not our ways." LeRoy Ashby has documented the Society's commitment to "'manufactur[ing]' orphans" both by downplaying children's existing family ties and by representing even concerned parents as depraved (*Children* 44–48). When the child's family, and even the child itself, were the objects of fear rather than of sentiment, the question of placement took on a new meaning.

Ellen Montgomery does not inspire fear in the adults who surround her, although she arouses dislike in Fortune (who regards her as rebellious and ungrateful), in the Dunscombes (who are offended by her sartorial failings and by what they consider her flaunted virtue), and even perhaps in her own father (whose readiness to divest himself of his daughter may reflect jealousy at her emotional importance to his wife or irritation at her indifference to himself). But Ellen is American born and has respectable relatives. Although her mother is sickly and her father somewhat irresponsible, Ellen possesses a known family history; she does not require assimilation into middle-class or national mores, and she has not asserted an untimely independence by earning her own living or evading adult supervision. A shopping expedition she makes on her mother's behalf to supply herself with clothes for her journey is evidently her first solo flight, and that a gentleman must intervene to save her from a scornful clerk underscores that she recognizes her need of adult help and guidance.

Ellen, in other words, is a lady, not a wolf. In contrast, indigent children were frightening because of their independence of socializing forces such as respectable mothers and schools; because of their visibility within the public sphere, as they loitered on street corners or supported themselves through peddling, petty crime, or prostitution; because of their bedraggled appearance, foreign speech patterns, or wildness, all of which suggested to observers that such children were the enemies of domestic stability. In Britain, the plethora of street children contributed to the founding of "ragged schools" and reformatories, the passage of acts covering compulsory education and limiting employment opportunities for the young, and the efforts of pioneering sociologists such as Henry Mayhew to identify and classify individual types. In the United States, it also contributed to the drafting of adoption statutes and to the implementation of large-scale relocation efforts such as the "orphan trains." Such projects accepted the 1840s dictum that environment was crucial; the potential social cancer represented by the ungovernable child could be eradicated by adoption or foster care, whatever that child's heredity or early life.

Thus although Brace, like Warner, consistently focuses on the individual child and its needs, the real point underlying the rhetoric may be the needs of society. In *Short Sermons to News Boys* (1866), Brace describes his motivations in founding the Children's Aid Society at a time when—he claimed— New York City contained more than ten thousand homeless youngsters, each of whom might be viewed as a potential "wolf."[7] Here again, the spotlight is on the needy individual, but the greater concern appears to be for society as a whole:

> Our great effort was to put these poor creatures—the vagrants, the houseless, the needy and criminal, and the uncared-for children of the great cities, where they could be most easily reached by Christian influences. . . . The hopeful field was evidently among the young. There, crime might possibly be checked in its very beginnings, and the seed of future good character and order and virtue be widely sown. (Qtd. Presser 481)

The point here is clear: to be "uncared-for" is to be allied with crime, disorder, and bad character, although, crucially, none of these failings is blamed on the child. Children whose natural caregivers have failed them through death or through poverty require missionary activity from the "Christian" middle classes, activity that Brace encouraged in a variety of forms.[8]

Between 1854 and 1929 the Society and its competitors recruited more than one hundred thousand children from the streets, and subsequently also from orphanages and other institutions, in order to reclaim them through emigration. Children deemed suitable for placing out were assembled into groups shepherded by a representative of the Society, who would accompany them onto a train, usually bound for the rural Midwest or South. At each stop, the group would disembark to be paraded before locals who, attracted by advertisements of the orphans' coming, had gathered with an eye to taking in a child. Those children who did not manage to attract a foster parent would reboard and try again in the next town.

As both historians and participants have documented, the possibilities for abuse and exploitation in this setup are obvious. For one thing, the Society could not vet the foster parents with any degree of care. At first, the children themselves were responsible for informing the agency of any difficulties with the placement; when agents were eventually employed to check on the children's progress, these agents were too few in number to visit more than a representative sampling of homes. Moreover, either party might dissolve the arrangement at will, leaving the child alone in an alien community. Nevertheless, the assumption was that the orphan train riders would be better off away from their original homes.

In recruiting foster parents, how the children were marketed was clearly important. The Society offered a blanket assurance, repeated in countless advertisements and other public statements, that its charges' criminality was incipient rather than actual, something to be ended by a change in environment before it had even begun. But we also have the packaging of the individual children. The orphan trains' stops appear to have been a cross between a horse fair and a musicale. Farmers would examine the children's muscles and teeth to assess physical condition, but often the children also recited poems or sang songs. One such song, reportedly composed by Brace himself, expresses the Society's party line about families of origin:

> No more complaining fills the street
> Of children who deserted roam,
> For here the houseless vagrants meet
> A benefactor and a home.
> And girls defenceless, wretched, poor
> Snatch'd from the haunts of vice and care
> From ill examples here secure,
> Instruction and protection share. (Qtd. Simpson 141)

That the orphan trains' stopovers presented the child both as object of charity, pathetic and redeemable, and as entertainment suggests a perception on Brace's part (a perception shared by Warner) that motives for taking a foster child were varied: even in the 1850s, not every host family was seeking a servant. Yet songs such as the one quoted above make explicit—

and for a small-town or rural audience rather than for wealthy and sophisticated urban philanthropists—that while foster families are, as Brace put
it, the child's "best asylum," birth families invert the domestic ideal. The
cult of domesticity classified the private sphere as the realm of morality,
where family members might be cleansed of the sins into which the public
sphere led them. But Brace consistently implied that family life among the
poor behaved like the public sphere in exposing the young to temptation
and moral contamination. To be sure, as Joel Schwartz observes, Brace was
unusual for his time in discussing family instability, including divorce and
remarriage, as a factor in delinquency (59). Yet even while he simultaneously acknowledged that the poor often love their children, he stressed
that for the poverty-stricken classes, parental love can damage a child. He
lamented that "in general, the mothers do not like to part with their children, even to get them in much better situations" (qtd. *Orphan Trains*),
summoning up a vision of a selfish mother standing in the way of her
offspring's advancement. As in Warner's novel, children must become orphans—whether actually or rhetorically—if they are to be saved; separation from the birth parent is morally essential.

Brace himself estimated that 47 percent of his orphan-train exports had
at least one living parent, "poor and degraded people, who were leaving
them to grow up neglected in the streets" (qtd. Carp 10). Ironically, he
sometimes presented such neglect as preferable to love. What the failure to
separate from one's child might lead to is illustrated by his account of an
interview with an Irish widow who earned her living by gathering swill—
a profession that conveys at once the mother's claim to respectability (she
is a member of the working poor and thus "deserving" by the standards of
many philanthropists) and the contamination of her environment. This
woman's daughter had first attended an industrial school and then been
placed out in the West. Missing her child, the mother forced her to return
to New York; the daughter, who had been doing well away from home,
turned to drink and to men, leaving her mother to mourn that "she, my
own darlint, strak me, and wanted to turn me out. . . . Ach, why did I tak
her out of her place!" (*Classes* 172). The double meaning of "place" here,
which conveys both "her situation as a domestic servant" and "the place
where she belongs," encapsulates much of the Society's philosophy.

As Brace wrote in 1872, his major reason for deciding in the 1850s to
transplant the children to farms, besides the farmer's perennial quest for
laborers, was that farm workers, as live-in help, must "share in [farmers']
social tone" (*Classes* 225). His project, in other words, was assimilationist.
Geared toward protecting the United States from what he termed the "dangerous classes" (those of low "social tone"), its primary focus was not on
establishing emotional bonds between dependent child and foster parent.[9]
Similarly, advertisements of the orphans' impending arrival did not focus
on the emotional rewards of opening one's home to such a child. Rather,
they sought to allay anxieties about the wildness of these "wolf-reared

children." Take one undated handbill that appears in Janet Graham and Edward Gray's 1995 documentary *The Orphan Trains:* "These children are well disciplined, coming from various orphanages in the East, both boys and girls, of different ages. They know nothing about street life. Families taking them must be well recommended. Adoption is not demanded. . . . [I]f not satisfactory [the children] will be removed after a reasonable trial."[10] This presentation of the situation inverts Warner's emphasis on custody quarrels and on the desire of Ellen's various guardians to insist upon their status and rights as parents; rather, the handbill stresses the potentially temporary and fragile nature of the bond to be created and presents the children as objects instead of subjects. While even in the early years of the Society's endeavors foster parents might develop intense attachments for their children, and vice versa,[11] the sentimental side of these arrangements did not loom large in the Society's writings.

Rather, and especially at the outset, what was highlighted were the practical advantages of taking in a child who will literally go to great lengths to get a home. Early advertisements seeking families to accept placements, as Marilyn Irvin Holt points out, touted the children as "sturdy workers" (138)—a focus that gradually disappeared over the last years of the nineteenth century, even though many families continued to evince interest in fostering dishwashers and chore boys. Similarly, an 1859 report on the Society's accomplishments remarked that children formerly "in the most extreme misery, we beheld sitting, clothed and clean, at hospitable tables, calling the employer 'father,' loved by the happy circle" (Brace, *Classes* 239). While this phraseology certainly emphasizes the children's emotional well-being as well as their newly civilized state, the point that the foster parent is most accurately described as an "employer" is taken for granted. The picture conjured up by Brace's words is less a vision of a devoted family than a vision of an idyllic job under the auspices of a benevolent boss.

Particularly in the early years of the Society's endeavors, of course, the riders of the orphan trains were generally not very young children. Typically they were between five and fourteen years of age; Brace's published articles represent them as old enough to make informed choices about their future. ("The Poor Boy's 'Astor House,'" which appeared in the April 1876 issue of *St. Nicholas,* observes that the Newsboys' Lodging House recruited emigrants via a placard addressed to the children themselves: "Boys wanting Homes in the Country must apply to the Superintendent" [361].) Parents motivated by emotion to adopt children have historically tended to prefer toddlers and, when feasible, infants; we need not be startled by Brace's assumption that one may best place an eleven-year-old (say) by emphasizing his usefulness, especially when legal adoption is unlikely. At the same time, we might remember two additional points. First, as we shall see, Progressive Era fiction often represented preadolescents as objects for sentimental adoption, an outlook that Brace—like Ellen Montgomery's Aunt Fortune—seems not to have shared. Second, it was Brace himself who decided that older children, especially boys, would form the bulk of his clientele, a determination that reflects not only a sense of the practical problems involved in shepherding across the country children too young to see to their own hygiene but also a sense that most foster parents would prefer children who could do chores.

Chores, indeed, were central to Brace's conception of his project of reform, just as the different attitudes toward work on the part of Ellen's various foster parents are important moral indicators in *The Wide, Wide World*. One of Brace's major reasons for opposing orphanages was that "the skills they taught had little practical use" (*Orphan Trains*), and the idea that the tenement child should learn to work was always paramount for him. Looking back on twenty years as a reformer, he wrote that "the principle throughout all the operations of the Children's Aid Society, is . . . to discourage pauperism, to cherish independence, to place the poorest of the city . . . on farms, where they support themselves and add to the wealth of the nation . . . to give education and work rather than alms" (*Classes* 397). Work, he added, was therapeutic: "There seems to me something, too, in labor in the soil, which is more medicinal to 'minds diseased' than work in shops. The nameless physical and mental maladies which take possession of these children of vice and poverty are more easily cured and driven off in outdoor than indoor labor" (400–401). Here again, the focus is not on the cult of domesticity but on the American work ethic. The question is not whether orphans should labor, but where.

Since many of Brace's orphan-train recruits might be defined as independent and self-supporting even in their lives as newsboys, factory hands, or bootblacks, his focus on the work ethic and "the wealth of the nation" would seem to have less to do with eradicating idleness than with helping his charges learn middle-class American ways. While he conceded that some immigrants were worthy, he feared that those who had taken up residence in New York City, their port of disembarkation, must lack the energy and enterprise necessary to make a positive contribution to their new nation. "Ignorant and shiftless," they were "the offscouring from the poorest, most degraded districts of the Old World" (qtd. Youcha 194). The solution, as Brace saw it, was to relocate the young of this degenerate species to the rural environment that their parents would have sought naturally had they possessed more gumption, and to exchange their "degraded" urban families for "kind-hearted farmers in the West" who would school their (initially) unpaid apprentices in Christianity and virtue (Brace, "Children" 552). Just as proximity to what remained of the American frontier was thought to encourage hardiness, residence in the heartland would encourage the acquisition of "American" values.

To be sure, the possibilities for reform were finite. For one thing, after the child reached puberty, its character might be set to such an extent that even farm life could not cure it. After investigating the progress of some of its alumni, the Society concluded that children placed out before age fourteen tended to do better than their older counterparts (Brace, *Classes* 241), and Brace gradually became convinced that beyond that age, girls in particular were "hopeless" (qtd. Holt 140).[12] A characteristic moment in *The Dangerous Classes of New York* (1872) recounts a talk with a prostitute's daughter whose younger sister he envisioned as an orphan-train recruit: "She seems glad and her face, which must have been pretty once, lights up, perhaps, at the thought for her sister, of what she shall never more have— a pure home" (145). Although this response suggests that the older girl, too, still has a softer side, no one offers to reclaim her.

Shaping Brace's vision of the redeemability of the younger child was his understanding of heredity. A devoted reader and eventual acquaintance of Charles Darwin (Holt 42), he held beliefs on the inheritance of character that echoed both the theories of pre-Darwinian child-rearing experts such as Bushnell (who, reports Wishy, contended in his influential 1847 parenting manual *Views of Christian Nurture* that "a proper nurture could counteract mere 'tendencies' to depravity if nurture began . . . in infancy" [23]) and the popular science of the 1850s and after. Vice, Brace wrote in *The Dangerous Classes of New York,* tends not to be transmitted through many generations because the vicious often die without surviving issue. Thus even among "the worst-endowed families . . . the 'gemmules,' or latent forces of hundreds of virtuous, or at least, not vicious, generations, lie hid in their constitutions. The immediate influences of parents or grandparents are, of course, the strongest in inheritance; but these may be overcome, and the latent tendencies to good, coming down from remote ancestors, be aroused and developed" (45).[13] In other words, the bad heredity that makes the "dangerous classes" dangerous is itself vulnerable to the inherited virtue underlying it, which may be activated by judicious manipulation of environment. In this formulation, couched in authoritative and technical-sounding language, the social reformer becomes a genetic engineer to the nation, suppressing bad traits and bringing out good ones in partnership with adoptive homes.

Orphanages, in contrast, used the power of environment in a mistaken way. Brace charged that they bred

> a species of character which is monastic—indolent, unused to struggle; subordinate indeed, but with little independence and manly vigor. If the subjects of the modern monastery be unfortunates—especially if they be already somewhat tainted with vice and crime—the effect is a weakening of true masculine vigor, an increase of the apparent virtues, and a hidden growth of secret and contagious vices. (*Classes* 76–77)

The phraseology here bears a striking resemblance to turn-of-the-century diatribes complaining that the unfit were breeding faster than the fit and that modern life was sapping national vitality. But as the derogatory way in which Brace uses the term "monastic" suggests, his stance was affected less by scientific than by religious considerations. Part of his objection to orphanages was that they were the favorite child-saving mechanism of the Catholic Church, which sought, by segregating its displaced youths in foundations where their religious and moral training would be in the hands of priests and nuns, to prevent precisely the assimilation into mainstream Protestantism that Brace and his cohorts were attempting.

Indeed, Brace's activities (both rhetorical and practical) spurred Catholic counter-efforts such as the 1863 founding of the Society for the Protection of Destitute Roman Catholic Children in the City of New York, known as the Protectory. This organization, staffed by members of the Sisters of Charity and the Christian Brothers, sought to retain within the fold children who might otherwise fall into Brace's clutches, go to Protestant families, and be lost to the faith. While it made its own foster placements (using Catholic homes) and from the outset took a stand against the "serious evil of weakening the family tie by unnecessar[ily] separating children from their parents" (qtd. Carp 14), the Protectory was preeminently a gated community housing its own industries, schools, and fire company; it even slaughtered its own meat (Crenson 71–80). By the end of the century, it was the nation's largest orphanage, housing 2,500. While the Protectory and similar institutions could not, in fact, accurately be described as "monastic," they bore enough resemblance to the monastery model to inspire Brace's use of the term. More importantly from Brace's perspective, Catholic orphanages were what Crenson describes as "a vehicle of resistance against the dominant culture" (41), and Brace took a dim view of such resistance.[14]

Brace and his Catholic rivals agreed that children removed from their original families could easily be diverted from their cradle faiths; the malleability of younger children, a quality stressed by theorists of childhood from John Locke (1632–1704) onward, suggested that environment would always dominate over heredity. Even so, heredity, in the sense of ethnicity, seems to have been a factor in placement. Although Schwartz remarks that Brace deemed African Americans "superior in virtue to the Irish" (163) and thus potentially more easily redeemable, few blacks—or, for that matter, Slavs or Asians—rode the orphan trains.[15] The Society remained particularly interested in recruiting children of Irish or German stock, perhaps an indication that Brace was trying to stack the deck by shipping out only children whose racial heritage would, he thought, assist them in blending into their new communities. A shrewd selection of candidates would both generate favorable publicity for the Society's efforts (thus increasing the chance of finding foster homes for future shipments) and benefit society.

But if Brace was correct that rural America was not ready to absorb displaced children whose ethnic difference from the new community was too marked, we may hypothesize that displacement itself represented a quasi-ethnic "otherness." It is noteworthy that foster children of any ethnic background were often compared in the 1850s and after to African Americans because of their association with a particular kind of work.

Consider an editorial published in the Belleville, Illinois *Weekly Democrat* on 17 April 1858, on the occasion of the visit of a placement officer employed by the Society and by the Five Points Mission, which scolded,

> There are a great many good Christian families . . . [who] are not partial to colored servants—are very religious: could not bear the thoughts [*sic*] of slavery. Oh, mercy, no! not for a moment, that find it very convenient to open their hearts to the poor creatures of the Five Points and give them *so good a home*—How benevolent! And yet the whole truth told, it is to fill the office of servants [that] they want them. The unfortunate poor who, are doomed to that species of *family equality,* in those fashionable circles of society are not half [as] respected and beloved as the black man and his children. (Qtd. Holt 100)

This editorialist's point that foster children should not be treated as "colored servants," but given a good home in a true rather than an ironic sense, may be balanced against an 1857 proposal made to the Boston Children's Mission by a resident of Missouri, then a slave state. As Holt reports, "The man . . . reasoned that if enough children were sent out to serve as laborers, there would be no need for owners to keep their slave property. Thus, slavery might cease to be a point of contention in the region" (84). Or take the 1882 remark of another Southerner, North Carolina orphanage superintendent J. H. Mills, who in criticizing the Society for careless placements asserted, "Men needing labor, their slaves being set free, take these boys and treat them as slaves" (*Orphan Trains*). As late as 1940, one Roman Catholic orphanage in Boston engaged in an informal system of foster-child placement established in 1890 and known as the "parish slave auction" (Holloran 103). In short, although Brace reiterated that his charges should work in order to be independent, other writers had a tendency to see such children in terms of chattel. The slave metaphor suggests that labor often operated as a barrier rather than a unifying force for placed-out children and the families with whom they lived. The children's youth potentially encouraged the formation of emotional ties, but it also allowed adults to focus on the dependency and helplessness that slaveholders had ascribed to African Americans. Finally, the idea that displaced children were property awaiting the manumission that would come with age may have contributed to child-savers' desire to place out only those of "superior" racial stock, on the ground that some groups were better suited to grow into "freedom" than others.

Such distinctions between what reformers saw as the salvageable and the unsalvageable, the deserving and the undeserving poor, were common in the nineteenth century. The movement to send needy children to orphanages or reform schools rather than to almshouses or jails was itself an attempt to sequester the young, who might be rehabilitated and whose inability to function in adult society was not culpable, from adults who were beyond help. As the Puritan conviction that children who had not yet developed a mature religious faith were mired in original sin gave way to the Romantic vision of childhood as inherently innocent, dependent children could be reclassified as meriting nurture instead of condemnation. The question then became that of the meaning of "nurture." Did orphans require loving care, or merely the chance to prove themselves by earning their own way respectably? And what might "respectable" labor consist of?

Brace's efforts would influence the thinking of other American child-savers, from the New England Home for Little Wanderers (established 1865) to the placing-out efforts of the New York Foundling Hospital (established 1869 as the New York Foundling Asylum). Consider the Rev. Willard Parsons's Fresh Air Fund, which was founded nearly a quarter-century after the Society but framed the problem of slum children similarly. A *St. Nicholas* article by I. N. Ford published in 1883, by which time the Fund's beneficiaries had grown from 60 to 5,599 children annually,[16] emphasizes the brutality of tenement parents, the "cruel bruises [on the children's] haggard, sickly faces, bearing witness of a father's intemperance or a mother's ungovernable temper" (617). It then traces the children's journey to the country; the civilizing process begins even in the city when the children receive their first baths and respectable garments and "are gradually bleached into comeliness and decency" (619). While a brief stay will not always turn "sickly," "puny" slum children into "brown-faced," "sturdy" country lads and lasses (though some leave "ruddy with health" and carrying a broody hen or caged squirrel [625]), it at least proves the ease with which emotional assimilation occurs: "Before the first breakfast came to an end, the waifs of the New York streets were like members of the farmer's household, and from that moment until it was time to go back to the city they were contented and happy. The number of genuine cases of homesickness among the six thousand children taken into the country last year could be counted on the fingers of a single hand" (621). Parting leaves the visitors sobbing (623).[17]

To be sure, as a writer of the 1880s rather than the 1850s, Ford is more likely to focus on evidence of emotional bonding between foster parent and child. Thus this article describes the pleasures and pastimes arranged by the former for the latter in much more detail than is accorded to the description of any chores the children might perform. Indeed, we hear at the article's end that some children have had their vacations extended or have been "adopted by a farmer's family" because "The pathos of neglected childhood softened many a heart" (626); this is not typical of the rhetoric of the 1850s.[18] As we shall see, the Society, too, came to emphasize sentiment and de-emphasize work in its discussions of child placement. But in a larger sense, both work and sentiment were always only different means to the same end. The real "work" of child placement, from the child-saver's point of view, was the salvation of America itself.

❀

When we consider *The Wide, Wide World* and the rhetoric of the New York Children's Aid Society side by side, several common elements emerge. First, we have seen that for all the importance of the cult of domesticity, the concept of "family" was problematic in the 1850s. Warner's novel examines multiple families, from Ellen's birth family to her adoptive families to the families of neighbors, and in almost every case scrutiny reveals flaws so great as to be incapacitating. Parents and parent-surrogates fail morally, emotionally, and physically; they set bad examples for their children, lack interest in them, prove incapable of understanding them. Even Mrs. Vawse, so admirable that the estimable Alice takes her as a model, cannot establish a significant bond with the granddaughter she is raising. While Warner takes the standard position that it is within a family that we learn morality, she suggests also that this family will typically not be composed of our blood relations. The very informality and tenuousness of adoption in 1850 permits the aspiring Christian to trade one set of family ties for another—and, if necessary, for another and another and another, until a suitable spiritual environment is found.

Brace and his colleagues at the Society clearly agreed that the blood tie was not paramount and that it might well be to the moral benefit of the child and the nation to transplant the child. But while Warner implies that the wealthy and the comparatively impoverished mingle freely (if not altogether easily), Brace assumes that the divide between the upper or middle class and the very poor is, and should be, immense. What goes on in the tenement home is often morally dangerous: parents of the lower working classes are probably abusive, distanced from their children by overwork or drunkenness, and incapable of providing Christian nurture. Move the child from the slums to a farm or some other middle-class setting, and the environment will become morally as well as socially decent. Despite the absence of a blood relationship or a legal adoption, the new guardians will be better able to nurture the child than its impoverished parents were—even when the original parents loved the child and the replacement parents do not—because the effect of extreme poverty is to shatter the family's "natural" defenses against the evils of the outside world, to turn the private into the public. What such assumptions help to reveal is that although the rhetoric of the cult of domesticity insisted in the mid-nineteenth century that families, and especially mothers, were the fount of all virtue, in fact there was a strong suspicion that money and social class might be the true source of good. To save a child in the 1850s, one did not need to find it a new mother in any emotional or sentimental sense; what the child really required was respectability.

But Warner's novel and the Children's Aid Society writings also have something else in common, namely an intense interest, even at this early date, in the emotional experiences of the dependent child. *The Wide, Wide World* charts Ellen's every mood, measuring her passions and her success in repressing them, recording her thoughts with absorbed attention. That

Captain Montgomery's failure to understand (or care about) his daughter's feelings is his greatest sin warns the reader not to follow in his footsteps: being poor, solitary, young, female, and powerless does not render Ellen unimportant.

As for Brace, if he was not primarily concerned with the feelings of his orphan train riders, he was still heavily invested in their characters. His was not simply a slum-clearance project, under which New York City would gradually rid itself of the excrescence represented by its poorest inhabitants. Rather, he proposed a rehabilitation for his protégés that would embrace personal finance, livelihood, class, diet, hygiene, wardrobe—in short, all the accoutrements of respectability. Most importantly, he believed that as the exteriors of the children exported by the Society changed to fit their new environments, their interiors would change as well. The right kind of work, the respectable households in which the children found themselves, would bring out the buried virtue that he was sure lurked inside the most unpromising. That he encouraged the children to write to him of their experiences in their new homes, addressing him as "Dear Friend," suggests his understanding of the need for emotional connection on a one-to-one basis, his acceptance of responsibility for their well-being and their characters. In a sense, he offers himself as the ultimate replacement for their birth parents, a distant but kindly father who both models accountability for his charges and demands it from them in return.

This interest in the dependent child as an individual formed one crucial strand in the changes that occurred over the next several generations within American representations of the orphan. It did not, however, form the whole. As subsequent chapters of this study will argue, adoption and foster care were seen both in generalized, abstract terms as responses to the problems of the mass and in particularized terms as solutions hand-tailored to unique problems—problems that finally came to be located not within the child, as was asserted in the 1850s, but within the adult. The eventual sentimentalization of adoption, the perception that the adopted child might wield real spiritual power within its new home and the larger community and that the child's true "work" is emotional rather than practical, depended to a significant extent on this interplay between the many and the one.

2

Money Talks

The Displaced Child, 1860–1885

Many of the profound changes that the Civil War wrought upon American life directly affected postwar attitudes toward adoption and foster care. Most obviously, the conflict created countless displaced children, as fathers' temporary or permanent absence straitened family circumstances. Wartime poor relief was minimal, and most soldiers' aid bureaus ended benefits for families when the soldiers left the armed forces, even when the cause of their departure was death. As a result, the population of almshouses—where mothers and children could go together—boomed; in New York State alone, the number of minors in such institutions tripled during the war years (Clement 16). In the North, the postwar enactment of federal legislation providing generous benefits to disabled Union veterans and to the families of the dead eased the situation; in the South, which had proportionately more war orphans because Confederate soldiers died at a higher rate, states were only gradually able to offer scanty pensions, many established as late as the 1880s. But in North and South alike, the scarred nation was newly aware of displaced children as a major social problem. Shortly after the cessation of hostilities, just as almshouses began to leave the business of caring for the young, more than a hundred institutions opened their doors to house the bereaved dependents of soldiers (Holloran 56).[1]

That war orphans could belong to any social class encouraged their sentimentalization. Prosperous veterans or unwidowed wives confronting a fatherless child might well reflect that but for good fortune, their own offspring might have found themselves in the same position. Between 1865 and 1873, a wave of epidemics involving diseases from smallpox to cholera and occurring in at least seven major cities (Baltimore, Boston, Memphis, New Orleans, New York, Philadelphia, and Washington) extended the cataclysm, again creating orphans in all walks of life. Moreover, the war temporarily stemmed immigration, so that while some child-savers continued to frame their project as one of assimilating aliens—as in the 1865 report of the board of the Massachusetts State Primary School, which promised that the "habits and character [of placed-out children] must become radically changed; they will be no more foreigners, but Americans" (qtd. Crenson 52)—the figure of the foreign street waif could briefly be replaced in the popular imagination with that of the native-born child whose father had died for his country.

Then too, adults were increasingly prone to idealize childhood in general. The rapid industrialization of the second half of the nineteenth century changed work patterns so that more labor was performed outside the home and fewer jobs required skilled artisans. Mechanization not only contributed to cities' growth and dominance, it also helped to sharpen the distinction between public and private spheres, encouraging what Christopher Lasch has famously called "the concept of the family as a haven in a heartless world" (6). This new vision of domesticity, in turn, contributed to the gradual romanticizing of childhood as a time of innocence and purity, an idea that was to have major consequences for dominant attitudes toward displaced children.

We see this romanticizing at work in many Reconstruction-era texts. Thus Northern children's writers of the late 1860s might attribute abolitionist beliefs to young Southerners, on the assumption that children's political insights are purer than adults'. Typical is Dolly Dixie's heroine Mary, raised by a "colored Mammy" after her mother's death, who becomes the partisan of all African Americans on the ground that "My good old Mammy . . . has been the most faithful friend I ever had. She has a great warm heart, and I love her" (140). When Mary's father dies, she frees his slaves, so that the original readers of this 1868 "true story" could reflect that if Southern political power had been vested in middle-class orphan girls, there might have been no war. Conversely, some commentators found that associating youth with pathos lent special urgency to child placement. Virginia Smith, who began directing public mission work in Hartford, Connecticut in 1876, proposed that the halo with which bourgeois parents crowned the memory of a lost son or daughter would extend to the waif as well. The dead child "become[s] our inspiration. . . . Warmed through all our nature with the tenderness of this world and with radiations from the world to come,—how can we fail to work unceasingly and to our utmost to give neglected children the homes and friends they need!" (212).

Even so, Smith's remark indicates that the real focus of tenderness is the dead middle-class darling; the war by no means extirpated anxieties about displaced children. Smith herself noted that without intervention on the part of the respectable, the "neglected" would

> grow up into lives of iniquity and crime and shame. Their sweet faces will grow coarse and hard with the brutalities they will learn to practise; and

their hands will reach out into every immoral phase of life, and soil themselves hopelessly by the thousand impurities of the world. The dear,
gentle eyes that fill with tears at unkindness now will by and by flame
with the unrestrained fires of passion; and their happy, prattling tones
will one day voice the maledictions of their sires. (219)

Noticeable in Smith's rhetoric is that the wrongs that she envisions the
children committing in later life stem from a lack of self-control; they are
"unrestrained." Moreover, her word choice allows readers to infer that
these crimes are associated with sexuality ("passion," "impurities,"
"shame," "immoral[ity]"); propagation or copulation evidently become
aggressive and antisocial when perpetrated by the submerged tenth. What
is necessary here is the imposition of middle-class discipline, standards of
conduct, and inhibition, since although little differentiates the "dear,
gentle" child of poverty from its bourgeois counterpart, destitute adults—
as Charles Loring Brace had argued before her—are another matter.

If some conditions encouraged a sentimental approach to youth, others
pointed to a more purely utilitarian focus. One such factor was a sharp
uptick in child labor between 1861 and 1865, particularly in the North, as
the shortage of adult males in field and factory was remedied by the recruitment of women and children. The war also hastened industrialization,
which meant in the short run that there were potentially more jobs for
children than ever before. Machinery was reducing the need for strength
and skill on farms and in workshops, and the working child (or child sol-
dier, drummer boy, or battlefield messenger) was an important figure during the war years. Thus fiction published in children's magazines such as
Our Young Folks in the 1860s might profile heroic thirteen- or fourteen-
year-olds who took up arms beside their elders, escaped from prisoner-of-
war camps, or guided detachments through enemy territory to win crucial
battles. Images of such protagonists shouldering adult burdens and facing
adult dangers furthered the idea that society could expect parentless youths
to be self-sufficient.

The twenty-five-year period that this chapter examines, in short, experienced deep conflict about the proper approach to the displaced child. Sentimental visions of the child as cherub warred with the contention that to
leave the destitute to help themselves would improve their characters and
winnow out the weak, to the ultimate benefit of society. Some commentators used coldness toward displaced children as a basis for cultural and
domestic criticism, while for others such children embodied delinquency
and degeneration. Social-service workers argued the relative merits of placing out, institutionalization, and paid foster care, while fiction writers exposed the discrepant attitudes toward orphans rich and poor, male and
female. And in practice, displaced children were sometimes mistreated,
sometimes exploited, and sometimes nurtured; if one Massachusetts in-
vestigator of 1867 discovered a number of guardians who had enrolled

their indentured boys in the army and pocketed the enlistment bounty (Crenson 173), and other foster children were overworked or starved or abused physically and sexually, many found loving homes even before sentimental adoption became the dominant mode.

But one element that united images as disparate, and as common, as the deserving poor boy with his fortune to make, the parentless Southern belle in a transformed society, and the orphan-train rider who threatens to bring big-city sin into bucolic life was that all these figures exposed, albeit in different ways, the instability of social class and custom. Modeling middle-class values without the advantage of a middle-class upbringing, poor but virtuous orphans communicated to wealthier readers that class was at once all-important and potentially meaningless, since in these tales even the indigent might speak, act, and feel with refinement. Elsewhere in fiction, aristocratic girls, trained within an ethic of leisure and consumption, might experience a precipitous social fall if orphanhood meant the loss of their natural protectors. And if society sometimes menaced the individual, the converse was also true; many commentators expressed their fear that the contamination represented by displaced working-class children might sabotage the apparently solid morals of Midwestern farming communities.

Given this fixation on class, it is not surprising that the debate surrounding displaced children was often couched in financial terms, although the questions being discussed differed. Proponents of placing out often viewed it as a mechanism whereby unproductive children—unproductive not because they were luxury items but because they lived in a sphere too degraded to have accepted the work ethic—might be made productive, learning to pay for their own upkeep not only during their minority but also as adults. Proponents of sentimental adoption, in contrast, saw children as consumers of a loving charity; they believed that adoptive parents should not demand work from their child, insofar as the child's labors would taint the adults' benevolent impulses with self-interest, an emotion that by the mid-nineteenth century seemed inappropriate to parenthood. Proponents of paid foster care sought at once to save the state money (since fostering could reduce the number of orphanages, whose physical plants were costly, and since foster parents might develop into unpaid adoptive parents) and to spare the child drudgery, at least during its extreme youth. In order to justify early and sweeping intervention, reformers cited the presumed cost of permitting indigent youngsters to give rein to their criminal impulses. Legal commentators warned that adoption would blur socioeconomic boundaries that might better be preserved.[2] And fiction follows Brace's lead in dwelling obsessively on how parentless children of the lower orders earn their livings and lay out their cash; both getting and spending are presented as important clues to character.

This chapter, then, will begin by illuminating a typical pattern in the orphan fiction of this period in order to establish a context for the nonfiction debate over what to do with the displaced child. Before 1885 we see relatively few of the idealized orphans, so remarkable for virtue or talent or charisma, who flock through the stories and novels of the turn of the century. Like Brace, whose writings contain many prose sketches of ragamuffins whose appeal lies in their vitality, authors such as Mark Twain, Horatio Alger, and Louisa May Alcott create a composite portrait of a displaced working-class child whose energy compensates for his (or her) lack of refinement. Susan Warner's Ellen Montgomery, with her pious strivings and earnest wish to master her baser side, is not the prototype for the protagonist of the postwar orphan tale. That protagonist shares more with Capitola Black, fatherless heroine of E.D.E.N. Southworth's comic novel *The Hidden Hand* (published serially in 1859, 1868, and 1883, and in book form in 1888), a lost heiress who variously appears as the ward of a black laundress, a news"boy," a rescuer of damsels in distress, an apprehender of desperadoes, a duelist, and a wealthy young woman "bored to death" by her guardian's demand that she stay safe at home (173).

The Hidden Hand dwells obsessively upon imprisonment, a theme that comments on the strictures normally governing middle-class female life; it also contemplates the probable (or improbable) sources of women's income. As Nina Baym argues, it performs "a severe criticism" of the cult of domesticity, even while superficially it may seem to ratify that ideology (116). Similarly, orphan fiction between 1860 and 1885 keeps returning to the issue of money in order to engage, like texts of the 1850s, in criticism of those twin Victorian icons, respectability and the family. Just as commentators questioned the motives, decency, and parental competence not only of the indigent biological parent but also of the affluent foster parent, novelists and short-story writers used orphans to express their own suspicions of family life, both among the marginalized classes and among the bourgeoisie. Whereas fiction of the 1920s often suggests that children enter adoptive families with ease, and fiction at the turn of the century shows children reviving the withered hearts of the adults who take them in, this earlier fiction typically focuses on the self-supporting orphan or on the problems that adoption poses when class differences divide the parties concerned. And if these problems are sometimes traceable to the roughness of the child, many authors attribute them to the cold heart of the "respectable" adult.

Thus Twain's Tom and Huck, like Alcott's Rose Campbell and Phebe Moore, serve on one level to illustrate the callousness with which a culture that sentimentalized children could treat youngsters who lacked worldly goods. Middle-class Tom can rely on his aunt to fill the void left by his parents' deaths, and heiress Rose has her pick of prospective homes. In contrast, Huck is a pariah to the adults of St. Petersburg until he comes into money,[3] and Phebe's worthy employers initially overlook her need for an education in *Eight Cousins* (1874) and object to her marrying into the family in *Rose in Bloom* (1876). Between 1860 and 1885, both canonical and noncanonical orphan fiction uses money as a way of distinguishing the adoptable from the unadoptable child. And in this context, it becomes the more possible to see financial arguments as a fundamental thread within nonfiction. While historians have documented the evolution of utilitarian child to "priceless" one and the tensions between institutionalization, adoption, and foster care, it is illuminating to examine an aspect of this topic that has received less attention, namely the extent to which the rhetoric surrounding these issues relied upon a fascination with money, and the purposes that this orientation served.

The Rich and the Poor in Fiction

Before 1885, orphan fiction for the young often suggests that what distinguishes the child who requires nurture from the child who may be expected to support itself is not age, ethnicity, or even gender, but social class. In children's stories, the orphaned sons and daughters of the respectable slip easily into new families as equal members. Their adoptive mothers or fathers typically had ties of blood or friendship to the biological parents, so that prosperous children can expect to inherit a stable family along with their patrimony; gentility apparently guarantees domestic happiness. That such adoptions, which are invariably represented as informal, do not involve the children of strangers also ensures that all parties are familiar with each other (at least by reputation) before the transfer occurs, so that assimilation into the new family will be comparatively painless for both sides. Texts that show wealthy uncles taking the father's place, such as A. Hartlie's playlet "The Birthday Box" (1866), can concern themselves not with the difficulties of establishing new affectional bonds but with the question of how a father—whether by birth or by adoption—may improve his charges morally. Hartlie minimizes adoptive angst: "Uncle loves us because we are his good brother's children," muses young Fred, and hence "The blessing of a good father still rests upon us" (743).

In contrast, waif fiction suggests that while sentimental adoption (again informal) is a possibility, it is neither a probable fate for the destitute child nor an emotionally easy process. When such texts feature adoptive families at all, the families are usually well-to-do: these are adults who can afford sentiment, but the class barriers between family and child complicate the bonding process.[4] Even a false perception of class difference can cause anguish, as in Mary Mapes Dodge's *Donald and Dorothy* (1883), in which the title characters were orphaned in a shipwreck as infants. This loss is much less traumatic than their discovery, at age fourteen, that perhaps Dorothy is not really Donald's twin and thus the blood niece of the kind uncle who has reared them; she may be the daughter not of her uncle's brother but of his adopted sister, Kate, who came of "homeless, destitute" stock (82). In that case, asserts the narrative, she must go to Kate's dissolute blood brother (who was adopted by a different set of parents) to be "handy about the house" (91). Only Donald's detective work can save Dorothy, since he finds proof that she is his twin by birth as well as by rearing. The implication here is that class membership is at once arbitrary and dispositive. Whether or not Dorothy is Donald's biological twin, the narrative asks us to see them as equals. Still, one adoption is evidently all that a bloodline can stand. Dorothy's discoveries, first that "I have n't any Aunt Kate at all" because Kate was not a "true" Reed (173), and later that she may not be a true Reed herself, pain the entire family; the happy ending requires the restoration of both class status and blood ties.

Alcott, too, often uses the orphan to suggest that class differences may have an important effect on family life. While having too much money makes for shaky parenting in cases such as those of Laurie and his grandfather (and many minor figures) in *Little Women* (1868), the Shaws in *An Old-Fashioned Girl* (1870), and Charlie and his mother in *Rose in Bloom* (1876), poverty is clearly dangerous as well. When Alcott's waifs attempt to enter the families of their social superiors, the process is fraught with tension, ruffling the interaction of loving kin. Thus in *Under the Lilacs* (1878) we find a society both democratic, in that there is amicable interaction among all levels, and stratified, in that class strongly influences this interaction. Both ends of the economic spectrum are occupied by parentless young people: at the top are Miss Celia, the local Lady Bountiful, and her fourteen-year-old brother, Thorny, while the bottom is represented by twelve-year-old Ben Brown, who has fled the circus in which he grew up and turns up, starving, in Celia's coach-house. But while Thorny and Celia's orphanhood creates no social difficulties, Ben's lack of money and position is the mechanism that exposes the ethnic, class, and familial tensions beneath the surface of the fictional society.[5]

Ben initially finds a temporary home with Celia's lodgekeeper, the widowed Mrs. Moss, and his entrance into this poor but respectable family is smooth. Joining Celia's family, however, is fraught with emotional problems. While Celia feels empathy toward him because "We are orphans, too" (it is she who breaks the news of his father's death) and proposes that "this shall be your home, and Thorny your brother" (106), what she intends is not sentimental adoption but employment: Ben will live with her but will be her groom and Thorny's "man-servant" (213). Celia rapidly becomes Ben's "dear mistress" (131), in part because he admires her Arab mare.[6] Thorny, though, is irked both by Celia's desire to move beyond the brother-sister bond (nearly ten years his senior, she has raised him) and by the requirement that he treat Ben civilly; he "had decided beforehand that he wouldn't play with a tramp, even if he *could* cut capers" (87). Thorny's personality matches his name, but it is Ben who brings out the other boy's unpleasant side and occasions comments from Celia and the narrator about his failings, his physical frailty, and the overindulgence that he has received because of his ill health.

That one of Ben's chief narrative tasks is to exacerbate Thorny's "domineering and petulant" deportment (130) is connected to his position as indigent orphan, which enables him to be inserted into the family as a temporary placeholder. Near the end of the novel, we officially learn what has long been hinted, namely that Celia is engaged to a clergyman, George, who spends all but the final pages in Europe. George's profession means that Celia plans to spend her married life reaching out to "our poor people" (265), so that Ben's adoption/employment allows the rehearsal of later philanthropy: "If I can bring one lost lamb into the fold, I shall be the fitter for a shepherd's wife, by-and-by" (278). More subtly, that Ben precedes George in distracting Celia's attention from Thorny makes the waif a lightning rod to attract resentment that Celia would not wish to see directed against her fiancé. By the time of the wedding, when we first hear Thorny's views on George, the latter can be described as "regularly jolly. . . . I didn't care [when they became engaged]" (288–89). But given Thorny's dislike of outsiders, his fondness for being the "head of the house" (197), and his difficulty in loving anyone but his sister, we may suspect that Ben's real work is not his job as groom-cum-manservant, but his role as disposable surrogate brother-in-law, within which he can defuse Oedipal tensions. Since Thorny can despise Ben as uneducated and poor even while he envies his physical superiority, he can learn to stop seeing other males as rivals for his sister's affections—even when they are.[7]

Moreover, Ben's equivocal position within a society in which all other roles are clearly demarcated means that once he has served his function in Celia's household, he may be removed.[8] The novel's last excitement is the discovery that Ben's father is still alive, a narrative move that finally permits Ben's absorption into a family as an equal when Brown senior marries Mrs. Moss. Alcott thus performs a juggling act that allows her both to soften and to purvey her era's party line on the evils of displaced children's families of origin. If Ben's flight from the cruel Smithers gets him a stable home and benefactors who later help him reunite with a parent whom he loves, readers may nonetheless conclude that a father who abandons his twelve-year-old in a touring circus while he himself goes to seek new work, leaving no forwarding address, has his faults. The narrator invites criticism of Brown senior's conduct via Sancho the circus poodle, whose "intense interest" in Ben's story culminates in "a little whine which said as plainly as words: 'Cheer up, little master; fathers may vanish and friends die, but *I* will never desert you'" (45). As Sancho is Ben's closest friend and confidant throughout, exhibiting skills akin to the boy's and serving as the mechanism through which Ben forms most of his human ties, we may deduce that he functions to express resentments that Ben himself is unwilling to confront.

We may also see implicit criticism of the elder Brown in Alcott's handling of the class rise that Ben enacts during his separation from his father. Just as the clientele of the New York Children's Aid Society *must* leave home to learn American ways, it is Celia, not Mr. Brown, who civilizes the boy. The narrator notes that "merely living near such a person [does] more to give him gentle manners, good principles, and pure thoughts, than almost any other training he could have had"; while Ben does not yet realize this, he is "conscious that it [is] pleasant to be there, neatly dressed, in good company, and going to church like a respectable boy" (114). By the time that Ben dons his circus attire for a last appearance as "Master Adolphus Bloomsbury," he has learned to feel shame: "I *want* to take [my costume] off; for somehow I don't feel respectable," he admits (277). And Ben's father becomes correspondingly genteel. He gets a job at a livery stable, prevents Celia's house from burning, and finally gains a wife and two more children.

Hence Alcott manages to endorse the visions both of Brace and of his rivals who argued for propping up, rather than destroying, the destitute family. Like Brace, she suggests that the children of the socially marginal must leave their brutal lower-class caregivers—here, Smithers, who like his counterparts in other fiction of the day wields an illegitimate power—in order to join the more innocent environment of the petit bourgeoisie. But we nonetheless gather also that the original family's vulgarity may be repaired because the poor can form ennobling emotional ties. For father as for son, the spurious glamour of the entertainment world gives way to the real attractiveness of domesticity on a shoestring. While Brace complained at about this time of the selfishness of destitute mothers who refused to send their children away to be socialized, Alcott hints that the newly acculturated child may be the salvation of his father.

But both in fiction and in real life, working-class families were presumptively more fragile than their well-to-do counterparts, partly because making a living was expected to take up more time; if for the rich domesticity was deemed more necessary than work, the reverse was true for the poor. Thus in some states, common law held that a father's social standing helped to determine the extent of his claims over any children: as *Albany Law Journal* contributor Philip Joachimsen wrote in 1873, an affluent man had more hope of gaining custody of a minor than did a poor man, whether or not the former was the biological parent (353–54). Adult indigence was often considered either the cause or the symptom of a failure in character, so that then as now, society assumed that poor children were more apt to be abused and neglected by their natural protectors. One may also detect a perception that middle-class children, purportedly more civilized than their penniless peers, were more deserving of domestic bliss. And, of course, children already schooled in the social niceties could more readily be absorbed into a middle-class home. Moreover, orphaned middle-class children usually possessed relatives or friends who were financially able to care for a nonproductive youngster; they did not need to be supported at public expense or, later, bound out to strangers.

Children's fiction about orphans demonstrates, then, two separate systems of values, one for the rich protagonist and one for the poor. In emphasizing the upward mobility to be achieved through industry, stories about poor orphan boys partake of the Bracean belief that none but the lazy are beyond reclamation. Apparent also in prewar texts such as *The Wide, Wide World*, productivity, competence, and the cheerful completion of monotonous tasks are recommended particularly to the working-class child in the postwar era, as if the reconstruction of the nation might be mirrored in the reconstruction of the formerly degraded self. Predictably, good work habits permit protagonists to rise. But significantly, orphan stories do not present these values as universally necessary; upper- and middle-class orphans (especially girls) fallen on hard times may have to earn their own livings for a while, but the denouement will rescue them from toil and restore them to a leisured domesticity.[9] In such cases, work usually does not improve the character, but rather offers a contrast to the comfort of home, functioning primarily to indicate the extent to which the parents' deaths—or, in Dodge's and Alcott's novels, the adoption or fostering of a déclassé child—may have temporarily shattered the natural order.

Hoeing for Dollars:
Work vs. Family in the "Bootstrap" Story

The affluent literary orphan of the 1870s and 1880s, frequently a lost heir, thus prefigures what Warren Susman identifies as a turn-of-the-century movement away from the nineteenth-century "culture of character," involving a diminished emphasis on "producer values" and an increased valorization of consumption (274). For the destitute child of fiction, conversely, work is often surrounded quite late in the period with a quasi-domestic halo. If class rise, represented as the improvement of one's financial position, is more likely than adoption, represented as the formation of emotional ties, we also find that in the classic poor-boy-makes-good story, economic self-sufficiency is equated with emotional satisfaction.

Similarly, most orphan fictions of this era do not indulge in extensive criticisms of society's treatment of the displaced child, even while they criticize society on other grounds. Respectability may be shown to cover selfishness and cruelty, "sivilization" may be excoriated as provincial and smug, but not until the 1890s do we encounter many children's books that suggest that poor orphans deserve as much nurturing as their richer counterparts. The independence that orphan tales between 1865 and 1885 attribute to their protagonists is less a subversive literary device than a reflection of what society required of penniless young people in real life. In a nation largely without child labor laws or welfare benefits, orphans without class standing had to be prepared to "light out for the Territory" or to earn their bread as servants.[10]

Thus orphan fictions with poor heroes often describe the protagonists' work lives in the kind of detail that other genres might lavish upon courtship or adventure. Here, authors intimate, is the appropriate emotional and spiritual center for a young person who has his way to make in the

world. I use the masculine pronoun advisedly, as the heroes of these romances of endeavor are almost always male. Orphan girls are more likely
to be players in a kind of chutes and ladders game in which they first prove
their worthiness and then are exalted, in a single swoop, to riches through
marriage or new family membership, as happens to Phebe in Alcott's *Rose
in Bloom* and to Capitola Black. Phebe progresses from maid of all work to
paid companion to professional singer to *un*paid nurse (and thus surrogate
daughter to her patient and benefactor) to wife, after which any further
rise will depend on her husband's efforts, not her own. Capitola acquires a
wealthy guardian in chapter 7 of *The Hidden Hand* and finds also, by the
novel's end, a mother, a fortune, and a genteel husband. Both young
women are enterprising, energetic, and well able to take care of themselves, but even so, both must retire from the public sphere; Capitola's
happy ending puts her, literally, in "the Hidden House" (Southworth 485).
For girls, achieving domestic satisfaction mandates the abandonment of
the effort—if not always the desire—to be self-supporting. Orphan boys, in
contrast, are not eligible to found a family until they have demonstrated
their earning capacity, so that domesticity must wait on job training. Family and work, then, often become antithetical, and of the two, work is to be
preferred.

Moreover, poor boys may attract the patronage of a benevolent adult,
but adoption is not part of the package. Often fiction shows them becoming orphans at a more advanced age than do their wealthier peers; age
brings with it expectations about independence, laying to rest questions
from middle-class child readers about why no kind parent shows up to
adopt these protagonists. Characteristic is an 1860 column in *Merry's Museum* that describes the encounter of one of the magazine's editors with a
disabled sixteen-year-old peddler who has lost both mother and mobility
in the train accident that left him responsible for three younger sisters.
Struck by the boy's "deep, unutterable grief" and "filial affection, which
was the highest possible eulogy of a faithful, affectionate mother," the editor pays for his medical care and notes that he has since "prospered in
business, and has educated his sisters to be, like himself, ornaments to society" ("Uncle Hiram's" 37). Adoption is neither offered nor needed.

Children's magazines contain many such tales. When Eula Lee's crossing sweeper Mike Riley saves the life of an upper-class baby in an 1867
Merry's story, the grateful mother promises that "he need never be homeless again, for in future baby's home should be his"—but not on equal
terms: Mike is given a job and eventually works his way up to coachman
(175). While Lee highlights Mike's honesty, heroism, industry, and love of
golden-haired infants, no one hints that he should be promoted to son.[11]
And in an 1860 narrative by "Fritz," teenage violinist Paul Goldschmeid
supports his widowed mother until her death and then attracts the interest
of the leader of the Dresden orchestra, who "would establish him in that
[group] as soon as he had mastered the musical exercises which were

necessary to prepare him for so high a place" (165). In six months, he has become "one of the most promising members of the Royal Orchestra" (166); when his patron dies, Paul wins his position. As Paul's triumph comes when he improvises a meditation that describes in music his father's death and his mother's despair and decline, we may deduce that in his case, adoption would have been counterproductive: to mature as a musician, he needs the lonely struggle of orphanhood and poverty. Success in work depends upon *not* being sheltered. Indeed, because pulling oneself up by one's bootstraps is part of the American mythos, making good without help may be more desirable (and better proof of one's assimilation into the national mindset) than finding powerful new parents.

Such is the message of Edmund Morris's *Farming for Boys,* serialized in *Our Young Folks* between January 1865 and April 1866 and published in book form in 1868. Part agricultural primer and part tract on upward mobility, *Farming for Boys* describes life on the Spangler farm, a small and unprofitable operation whose hands include Mr. Spangler's two teenage sons; a hired man; an elderly Spangler relative known as Uncle Benny; and Tony King, a fifteen-year-old indentured orphan. Sentiment, interiority, and plot are all minimized so that the narrator can focus on issues deemed more important to characters' and readers' later lives: the tale revolves around the lessons that Tony, in particular, learns from Uncle Benny, the farm's chief moral force and an advocate of a scientific approach to cultivating both land and boys.

For boys, Morris makes plain, are the real crop to be produced here, and there are right ways and wrong ways to "farm" them.[12] Characteristically, these approaches are described in terms of economics. Mr. Spangler's technique with adolescents mirrors his method of farming, a dogged and unthinking application of muscular effort that results in waste and stunted crops. Tony's parents are worse models still, since they died "miserably poor, and [left] no relations to take care of him," allowing the narrator to comment that "when parents are so idle and thriftless as to expose their children to such a fate as his, they leave them a legacy of nothing better than the very hardest kind of bargains" (I:64, 65). Both foster parents and birth parents are found wanting not because of the flaws in their emotional relationship to their children—this issue is inconsequential—but because of those in their relationship to work.

In contrast, Uncle Benny sets an example of cheerful industry, intelligence, optimism, and interest in his juniors that steers a middle course between the drudgery of Mr. Spangler and the laziness of Tony's parents. As such, it will turn a profit both metaphorical and actual. While Mr. Spangler "had been taught that hard work was the chief end of man" and that farmers need "hands, not heads" (I:64), Uncle Benny prefers that boys learn "how and why the work should be done" (I:97). His lessons cover not only the best way to feed hogs and the value of timely repairs, but also the American dream. Fortune, he preaches, "is an open common, with no hedge, or fence, or obstruction to get over in our efforts to reach it, except such as may be set up by our own idleness, or laziness, or want of courage in striving to overcome the disadvantages of our particular position" (I:238). Tony needs no family. Only the "dozen of friends" represented by his two hands and ten fingers are necessary if he is to "[carve his] way up" in the world (I:748).

Tony's orphanhood makes him the ideal recipient for Uncle Benny's homespun wisdom, since he must make his own fortune. By implication, inherited wealth, and even middle-class domestic security, is for sissies; Uncle Benny insists that the man who will be President in the year 1900 is surely, at the time of the story, a poor boy, or at most in "moderate circumstances" (I:99). Orphans cast upon their own resources develop initiative, while "Boys that grow up in idleness [perhaps because their parents are supporting them] become vagabonds" (I:99). Hence *Farming for Boys* pullulates with exemplary orphans, from its major inspirational story, the wealthy Mr. Allen, to the courageous newsboy-turned-peddler John Hancock (whose patriotic name makes parentlessness a metaphor for Americanism), to Mr. Allen's nephew Frank Smith, whose misfortunes in the city prove the superiority of rural over urban ways. But in all cases, the challenge facing the orphan is not establishing emotional ties or adapting to domesticity, but rather learning how to earn an honest penny. Success in the public sphere is success in life, for one of the orphan's advantages is that he is exempt from the sentimental demands of family.

Such narratives suggest that most authors of orphan fiction during this period agreed with those commentators who held that penniless children should expect to earn their keep (without being exploited, abused, or sweated) and that work of the right sort is morally as well as financially beneficial. Orphans of the pre–Civil War period, such as Susan Warner's Ellen Montgomery, do not typically change the adults around them, but rather adapt themselves to adult society. Their immediate successors, similarly, are less likely to transform their environments than they are to better their own lots in a material sense. The quest for prosperity takes on heroic proportions, since it entails living out the American dream. As representatives of the nation, literary orphans are often represented in the postwar decades as infinitely flexible, upwardly mobile, innately decent, potentially useful—and enviably free. Such works reassure readers not only about orphans' worth and salvageability, but also about their ability to survive in an era in which children had little legal protection: like America itself, they are fighters.

Thus waifs in fiction are treated more positively than their counterparts in nonfiction commentary, which often views the displaced child as a threat to the country, a carrier of crime and lack of enterprise. To novelists, the waif may rather look like a national asset, and again, financial images and themes loom large in these texts. While he had many imitators, the doyen of fiction of this type was, of course, Horatio Alger, Jr., author of some 120 books whose sales totaled at least 17 million volumes (Fink 7). Alger's career took off with the 1867 publication of *Ragged Dick,* which recounts a bootblack's initial progress toward membership in the middle classes. Among his early readers was Charles O'Connor, superintendent of the Newsboys' Lodging House that Brace had founded in 1853; O'Connor's approval of the novel was such that he made the acquaintance of the author and invited him to use the Lodging House as a source of material. Alger identified himself closely with the institution (not only donating time and money, but also, according to some biographers, becoming a permanent lodger himself), with O'Connor, and with the mission of the Children's Aid Society, all of which his books occasionally advertise. One way to read these works, then, is as narrativized versions of the reportage associated with the Society, both endorsing the organization's efforts and augmenting its appeals for financial support. Thus Alger's preface to *Julius or The Street Boy Out West* (1874) notes the novel's debt to Brace's *The Dangerous Classes of Society* [*sic*] and calls the earlier work "instructive and entertaining" (n.p.); within the narrative, we find O'Connor shepherding Julius aboard an orphan train bound for Wisconsin and gratefully accepting on the Society's behalf $100 from a fellow passenger, a moment that suggests the novel's possibilities as a fund-raising tool.

Ragged Dick established the typical formula for an Alger novel: a street boy glimpses respectability and decides to strive for middle-class comfort. Aided by a rich patron whom he has been able to assist (usually by returning lost property or averting a family tragedy), the boy scrapes up an education and a job with prospects of advancement. While Alger heroes do not aspire to the presidency, they reach at least the lower middle class through good fortune and good character. But not all Alger stories fit this formula, and it is instructive to contrast a novel with a boy hero, such as *Julius,* with one of Alger's rare fictions with a female protagonist, *Tattered Tom; or, The Story of a Street Arab* (1871). Not only do the two make rather different points about domesticity, family, and money, but the differences in plot also help to illuminate cultural understandings of the different possibilities for male and female displaced children.

Julius fits the paradigm; *Tattered Tom* diverges from it in making its protagonist a lost heiress whose climb into the middle class is interrupted by her reunion with her wealthy biological mother. Whereas Alger insists upon the orphanhood and consequent independence of his boys, who act as their own parents by bringing themselves up and teaching themselves industry and application, he finds it harder to imagine a genteel career for a female. "Tom" (AKA Jane Lindsay) may labor as a street Arab or lead a leisured existence as an aristocrat, but she cannot advance too far by her own efforts. Alger's insight that respectability for girls requires that they be someone's daughters helps to explain the gender divide apparent within orphan fiction of this period, in which boys work and girls variously inspire remunerative labor or escape it via marriage, reunion with family, adoption, or death.

While Tom's gamine vitality and liveliness will keep her from degenerating "into one of those average, stereotyped, uninteresting young ladies that abound in our modern society" (274), the acquisition of even a little money and status, and of even the legally insignificant family ties associated with informal adoption, forces her into comparative passivity. By gaining value, she becomes an object rather than a subject. Far from serving her enemies as they deserve, she is first framed for theft and later kidnapped again, and the villains are punished not by Tom's efforts but by Captain Barnes and fate, respectively. Significantly, too, it is always family that threatens Tom: the girl who brands her a thief is a kind of wicked stepsister trying to protect her own standing as Captain Barnes's heiress presumptive, while the kidnapper, a tool of Tom's uncle, poses as Tom's grandmother. While the major characters want the emoluments that accompany kinship (money, status, custody rights, and—a distinct also-ran—affection), family would appear to have its dangers, in that family members must wear price tags.

For boys such as Julius, in contrast, class rise means acquiring power rather than losing it. A former bootblack who has spent his childhood in thrall to the burglar Jack Morgan (who, we learn early on, is en route to Sing Sing after nearly murdering the boy for foiling one of his jobs), he is going West not only to seek respectability but also to evade Morgan's wrath. O'Connor places him with Ephraim Taylor, the town's richest man and the head of the local committee greeting the orphan train; while Julius is glad of this placement, he has no say in it.[13] Moreover, Julius solidifies his position with Taylor by a virtue of omission, not one of commission: that is, he decides not to run off to California with his benefactor's well-stuffed wallet when it drops out of Taylor's pocket. Julius's beginning, like Tom's end, is comparatively passive.

But for Julius, mere passive respectability gives way to forcefulness, rather than the reverse. Strengthened by farm life and clean air, he gains muscle and grows three inches; outdoes his effete Eastern schoolmaster in learning; saves little Carrie Taylor from a drunken Indian kidnapper; and finally thwarts the attempt of Morgan's accomplice to murder him and steal $600 belonging to Taylor. By the end of the story, Julius is "treat[ed] in all respects like a son" by Mr. Taylor (135), has betrothed himself to Mrs. Taylor's niece, and can return to the Lodging House in order to make an inspirational speech to its street-urchin inmates. We also learn that he owns a house and land worth $4,500, and this financial information seems morally inextricable from the emotional information provided alongside it.

Unlike the heroine of *Tattered Tom*, Julius must earn his way into a family unrelated to him by blood, and while his rise is less high than hers, it may be more gratifying to the reader because his route to success, unlike Tom's, is theoretically open to all. Moreover, belonging to a family will apparently augment rather than sap Julius's strength. Still, despite the differences attributable to their protagonists' genders, and despite their shared

assumption that respectability is the only happy ending, both novels make
it apparent that the home life of the prosperous is fragile, precisely because
the presence of money brings vulnerability. Tom was kidnapped as a young
child by the crone she knows as "Granny"; the crime reveals the perfidy of
the servant class (Granny worked for, and resented, Mrs. Lindsay), but also
exposes the fault lines within the upper class, as the man who hired
Granny to steal the little girl was Tom's father's brother, who stood to inherit $100,000 in Tom's absence. And Captain Barnes's sister, although "a
good woman" and "really a kind-hearted woman" (122, 186), resents her
brother's selection of a street waif as his daughter-elect. When she discovers that her own child has stolen a valuable ornament and allowed the
blame to fall on Tom, she does nothing to right the situation, even though
her brother has paid her to look after his protégée. As for Mr. Taylor in
Julius, he is unable to defend himself against the lower orders, who steal
his watch (a gift from Taylor's dead son, and thus symbolic of a vulnerable
family affection), kidnap his daughter, and menace his adopted son and his
cash. Julius's superior competence in thwarting these efforts implies that
only poor boys are tough enough to become money's masters rather than
its victims. Because waifs have neither possessions nor social value, they
are individuals rather than commodities; let them acquire bank accounts,
and they will nonetheless retain their native energy and initiative.

To be sure, like the child-savers with whom he associated, Alger is more
scathing about the home life of the poor than he is about the failings of the
prosperous. While his novels usually contain a token poor family marked
by the same decency that his wealthy citizens display, such families are in
the minority. In his formulation, children of the respectable classes usually
have at least one parent, while waifs have no known kin. He suggests that
the very poor often clump together without regard to biological ties, a
middle-aged or elderly person becoming the fellow-traveler of a youth of
the same sex. But while the bond between two surrogate siblings is idealized when no adult is present,[14] the bond between "parent" and child draws
sharp criticism. Such imitation families are characterized not by mutual
regard or by the adult's protective behavior toward the child, but by the
mature partner's abuse and/or exploitation of his or her smaller companion. For Alger as for Brace and the Children's Aid Society, the destitute
child must be saved from its adult associates, extracted from "families" that
are authorized neither by sentiment nor (in the Algerian paradigm) by
blood. And this salvation is measured by money.

Empty at the Heart:
The Elusive Family in Morse and Twain

But other authors suggest that money and class may confer comfort
without solving central emotional problems. Here adoption may occur, but
it does not by itself constitute a happy ending. Consider first Lucy G.

Morse's twin stories "The Ash-Girl" and "Cathern," published in *St. Nicholas* in 1876 and 1877. Far from conventional sentimental tales designed to endorse the status quo, these narratives merit attention for both their overt criticisms of impoverished families and their covert criticisms of the wealthy: just as Twain aims his barbs at both the down-and-out Pap and the privileged Grangerfords, Morse suggests that domestic perfection is hard to come by. The first story begins when Cathern, despite her professions of scorn for rich children who need a mother to look after them, decides to find her own "reel [*sic*] mother"—that is, an elegant woman of the upper classes who will turn her into one of the well-cared-for children she has affected to despise. To prepare herself for this quest, she washes her face and combs her hair as token that she is ready to leave her station, since she anticipates that "my mother'll put me on [*sic*] a nice, pretty dress an' things" (387). After an extensive search, she locates an aristocratic widow who has just buried her last remaining daughter; caught in a moment of weakness, the bereaved Mrs. Percy does indeed cry, "Come! come to me! It is as if my child cried out to me from heaven! Put your little head, so, upon my breast, and I will be as true—as true a mother to you as I can. Yes, I will, my darling!" (392). Sentiment, and the need for a family on the part of both adult and child, would appear to be transcendent.

But while like Brace, Morse denigrates the maternal capacities of slum women, who are not to be considered "real mothers," the interaction of waif and society woman challenges as well the claim of the wealthy to possess feeling hearts. Despite the note of affirmation on which "The Ash-Girl" closes, so reminiscent of Virginia Smith's comments (quoted at the beginning of this chapter) on grief's role in softening middle-class hearts, "Cathern" addresses the difficulty of integrating its rough title character into a genteel home. Morse suggests that this difficulty arises in part from the aristocracy's emotional limitations. Conscious that her "impulsive" promise to take in Cathern is potentially "a difficult one to fulfill," Mrs. Percy feels doubt and ambivalence as she nurses the child through a fever (302). When, months later, she finally allows her informally adopted daughter to accompany her on a walk, Mrs. Percy is horrified to see Cathern jeer at a homeless child on the ground that "he's got rags an' patches, an' I aint!" (304). When Mrs. Percy offers the consoling words, "Remember that your rags cannot make you a bad boy any more than her clothes can make her a lady" (304), it is apparent not only that class rise is more complicated than Cathern has supposed, but also that Mrs. Percy has been ignoring her protégée's moral training. Like the former ash-girl, she has concentrated on appearances.

To be sure, Mrs. Percy's reformation is not the issue here. Morse's stories show that the acquisition of a "real mother" demands work on the part of the child, who must shed all lower-class markers, interior as well as exterior. But this circumstance is at least partly attributable to the coldness associated with wealth. Only after the girl, now known as Kathleen, confronts her own inferiority ("I was n't never good in my whole life, not till this mother showed me how; an' then I was on'y good a little" [308]) and "adopts" a tenement child can she legitimately join the order to which she has aspired. This lesson, however, appears to be aimed primarily at the well-to-do. Charity and virtue may be upper-class luxuries, but many who can afford them do not manifest them. And it is suggestive that Kathleen's adoption of Trudy is motivated by guilt (she has knocked the toddler down and injured her) rather than by precocious maternal instinct. Still more than a feeling heart, Morse implies, the wealthy need a sense of responsibility.

One result of this stress on duty above emotion is that the child is less sentiment's object than its source. Morse presents the girl as feisty as well as pathetic; it is Cathern/Kathleen's vision of the "real mother" that is idealized to the point of near-divinity. In other words, the story focuses not on a quality intrinsic to its protagonist but rather on something external that the protagonist lacks: an absence, not a presence. This central void creates tension through unfulfilled longing, but it also militates against the deification of the orphan herself, who cannot become the focus of longing because she is too corporeal. And for the same reason, it is hard for readers to accept Mrs. Percy as the embodiment of the child's longing for the maternal.

Thus Kathleen's transformation improves her social status without providing her with the "real mother" she has sought, if we accept her premise that "real mothers" are wholly wrapped up in their offspring. For neither as Cathern nor as Kathleen can the base-born girl wholly fill the place of the lost Mabel Percy. Addressing the portrait, Mrs. Percy says, "I had too much love for you to bless me alone,—it runs over to bless these little helpless ones too!" (309). Her comment hints that at best, the adopted child can expect only surplus emotion. Only once in each story is Mrs. Percy "touched . . . to the heart" ("Cathern" 303), and readers may conclude that instead of forging new family ties, Mrs. Percy has merely acquired a therapeutic occupation and Kathleen a kind patron. To be sure, Kathleen has no complaints; she has assumed from the first that the material goods associated with maternal love, such as the pretty clothes that "real mothers" bestow upon their children, are equivalent to the thing itself.

Still, even if we take Mrs. Percy as an ideal adoptive mother—and Morse's focus on her ambivalent reception of Kathleen discourages such a reading—to identify the affectionate family as a product of money rather than of human nature permits the reader to notice that middle-class families too may be unhappy. In this sense, Morse's stories join those by Alcott, Alger, and others in hinting that what we now see as the radical antidomesticity of canonical authors such as Twain is in fact a hallmark of the period. As we have seen, the invitation to doubt the very foundations of the cult of domesticity is a common feature of orphan fiction for both boys and girls during and after the Civil War, just as we will also see it at work in nonfiction texts. Both poor and middle-class orphans frequently point to the limitations of the parent-child bond, while children who demonstrate an ability to succeed without the advantage of formal membership in a family excite the admiration of narrators and readers.

Twain's representation of families is a case in point.[15] While love clearly exists between Tom Sawyer and Aunt Polly, Tom's real emotional life centers on his friends rather than on his aunt or siblings; the peer group, it seems, offers a far better outlet for a muscular imagination than can mere domesticity. Indeed, it is Huck's escape from family respectability that excites Tom's envy in *Tom Sawyer* and, in *Huck Finn*, helps Huck to move from identity to identity until he "becomes" Tom Sawyer, a transformation that suggests that we may find among society's flotsam a fluidity and resilience denied to the privileged.[16] After beginning his series of impersonations by posing first as a girl and then, more successfully, as a bound-out foster child running away from "a mean old farmer in the country" (80), Huck pulls the wool over the eyes of his various auditors by manufacturing assorted families for himself, all headed by Paps who, we may presume, are superior to his own despite—or because of—their tendency to succumb to shipwreck, smallpox, bankruptcy, and death (see 96–97, 117, 127, 158–59).

One crucial trait of the invented Paps is that they permit mobility: they run family trading-scows, house their children on rafts, shrug at the breakup of their households, and plan 1,400-mile moves. Gregory Marshall finds that "Huck is unable to invent lastingly effective blood ties" (44), but perhaps "unwilling" is a better word, given that, as is also the case with an earlier picaresque protagonist, Southworth's Capitola Black, the keynote of Huck's experience of real families is imprisonment. The widow's rules and strictures leave him feeling "all cramped up" (12), while Pap not only insists that his son is not to learn skills (such as literacy) or acquire habits (such as cleanliness) that his relatives have lacked, but also kidnaps Huck and places him in close confinement in order to assert his own right to custody (33, 38–39).[17] As for Huck's other two potential families, the Grangerfords are slaves to a meaningless feud that has turned their home into a "locked" and "barred" and "bolted" fortress under siege (125), and the Phelpses first come to his attention because they have chained Jim to a bed in a locked cabin.

Tom's attempts to take on other identities are far more limited. His role-playing games in the first novel are always only games (that is, his auditors never mistake him for the outlaws he mimics), and in the sequel he masquerades as his own half-brother, an impersonation that does not require him to put his family behind him.[18] That Tom can stage a return from death but cannot become someone else hints that family ties encumber one with an identity too solid to be eluded—a handicap, from Tom's point of view. Thus a sensation of being "cramped" by family may help motivate Tom's construction of new multiple roles for Jim, whom Tom forces to trace inscriptions commemorating not his genuine grief at being separated from his family but his "bitter captivity" as a "natural son of Louis XIV" (313). In a slave-holding society, a servant's identity is subject to his master's whim, and Tom is clearly using Jim to live out fantasies of noble alienation that cannot be realized within Tom's orphaned but unalienated existence.

That Huck must operate within the adult world rather than the child's play-world reflects, in part, his lack of social status—in a sense, he is too poor to have a childhood—and the absence of the kind of family ties that would enable him to postpone confronting reality. Although, following a 1958 article by Kenneth S. Lynn, one school of thought has long held that Jim is Huck's spiritual father (see, e.g., Shulman, Segal, Marshall, and Wirth-Nesher 264),[19] and Mark Altschuler has contended that Mary Jane Wilks is an idealized mother-figure, these quasi-parental roles are recognized neither by society nor, consciously, by Huck himself. To Huck, what Randall Knoper sees as the raft's domestic qualities, the "quietness, intimacy, tenderness, emotional transparency, [and] sympathy" that link it with the bourgeois home (127), appeal not because they connect him to family life but because they let him escape it. Huck, after all, sees the moral education instilled by his voyage with Jim as antidomestic and antisocial, an introduction to *im*moral acts such as transgressing his culture's racial codes. Tom's family life is far easier for both critics and participants to identify.

The distinction that the narratives draw between the two orphans Tom and Huck, in providing only the former with a permanent caregiver and a defined social niche, finds its mirror in the king and duke's behavior toward the wealthy Wilks orphans and toward Huck, whom they believe to be penniless as well as recently bereaved. And here, as in other episodes in the novel, financial considerations rise to the surface. When the king proposes fleecing the Wilks girls not only of the $6,000 that has already been given into the confidence men's keeping, but also of their house and slaves, the duke demurs, saying that "the bag of gold was enough, and he didn't want to go no deeper—didn't want to rob a lot of orphans of *everything* they had" (216). The king, however, points out that the girls will recover their property, minus the gold, as soon as the imposture is exposed. Indeed, since even the gold is finally returned to the girls, including $415 that came from the tricksters themselves, these orphans end up profiting from their association with their "uncles." Yet the men feel no compunction about selling Jim (for a paltry $40[20]), even though they suppose him to be the only piece of property belonging to the much poorer orphan Huck, who has been both servant and benefactor to them. There is no suggestion that the law will intervene on behalf of a boy without family; the best that the duke can offer is an unconvincing "some idiots don't require documents. . . . maybe he'll believe you" (263). The rich are insulated from disaster even when they have lost their parents; the poor are on their own.

Although family and social position limit the mobility and freedom that the narratives treasure, then, they afford a security valuable within the chancy world that Twain describes. Just as Huck is ineligible to join Tom Sawyer's Gang unless he can name a family member to act as hostage for his loyalty to his fellow highwaymen (19),[21] kinfolk—even imaginary ones—are necessary if he is to navigate within a society that holds that identity should be stable; that home, family, and schooling are privileges rather than shackles; and that it owes the waif nothing. Similarly, despite narrators' skepticism, the criticisms of parent-child relationships that we encounter in other Gilded Age orphan fiction are sometimes revealed as merely temporary, inasmuch as domesticity is often presented as the happy ending even for children ineligible (because of their social class) for full membership in a family. Authors, it would seem, could identify the ways in which families might fall short of the ideal but were hard put to it to propose alternatives to the domestic model. Huck and Jim's idyll on the raft is too socially unstable to last, and must give way to one of the most notoriously problematic endings in fiction; even *Tom Sawyer*, larded as it is with observations about the narrowness of small-town Southwestern life, offers as a triumphant conclusion Huck's adoption into the bourgeois family, though *Huckleberry Finn* rejects that apotheosis as unsatisfactory.

Placement and the Balance Sheet

While fiction about orphans published during and after the Civil War critiqued some of the assumptions that governed nonfiction commentary on the subject, it shared others. Perhaps the chief point of agreement is on the impoverished family's fragility, although even here we find writers who insist that such families may be shored up, redeemed, or reconstituted. Less predictable, given our stereotypes of Victorian America, is the tendency of both forms of writing to use the displaced child to enable attacks on an institution that we may believe to have been considered sacrosanct in the late nineteenth century, namely the aristocratic family. Such children, then, might function as the canary in the coal mine to indicate the early stirrings of what would later become a full-fledged social trend, what Peter Holloran identifies as the "literary convention" of the "declining family" in America (22).

Even so, whether it focuses on poor children or on wealthy ones, orphan fiction asks us to see the child's welfare as the major issue. But during the period discussed in this chapter, the real-world placement debate often hinged rather on which solutions would best serve society. An issue of perennial interest at conferences within the nascent field of social work was the long-term cost-effectiveness of any one method of dealing with the poor. Traditionally, raising the indigent orphan or deserted child had frequently entailed a form of indentured servitude so that the child's sponsor would not be out of pocket at the end of the transaction. Indenturing—

a contractual arrangement whereby the child was obligated to serve its master until it had reached a certain age—was still widespread in the 1880s, although it would look old-fashioned ten years later, and some working-class children became indentured servants in their first month of life.[22] Even in the absence of legal documents, most foster placements during this era involved the exchange of the child's services for board, lodging, and the promise of some minimal schooling. Children who remained in orphanages, similarly, could expect to earn their keep, a principle illustrated by Mrs. M. E. R. Cobb's 1884 comment that at Milwaukee's Industrial School for Girls "our real, heavy work . . . is all done by the inmates. . . . Our girls are trained for domestic service and home-making, but they have done a great deal of outdoor work. . . . We even made our own wire fences the first year I was there" ("Discussion," 1884 *Proceedings* 356).

In contrast, children's fiction asks readers to consider what work does for the orphan rather than for society; industrious protagonists, as we have seen, avoid the further fragmentation of their families or rise to the middle class. Nineteenth-century newspaper coverage of the orphan trains likewise frames the children's search for employment as necessary and desirable from their own point of view. Like the advertisements placed by the Society and quoted in Chapter 1, such articles stress the children's attractiveness and intelligence and certify that there are no delinquents among them, rhetoric obviously aimed at prospective foster parents. At the same time, the writers present work as inherently beneficial to the worker. For the New York *Tribune*, reporting on the departure of thirty-five children for Iowa in 1880,

> there was reason to believe that all who were old enough to form plans in life realized that they were leaving a scene in which struggle was well-nigh hopeless for a future in which success required only their own honest efforts for attainment. They had tried life in the large city and had found it very hard; they expected to find hard work and hard living in the homes in which they were going, but believed that at the end there was a reward which no efforts here could gain for them. ("Rescued" 16)

Similar comments may be found in newspaper articles at journey's end. We find the Ravenna, Ohio *Republican-Democrat* describing another 1880 group of exiles as follows: "Many of them were orphans, all were poor, but none of them had been beggars and all who were of sufficient age, had made honest endeavors to obtain a livelihood through their own efforts" ("Child Emigrants"). Like the Alger hero, in short, these children are represented as already imbued with the work ethic; they are primed for success, whether or not they find loving homes.

In practice, most placements of poor children required the children to work, although the amount of labor varied. In theory, though, this custom increasingly aroused anxiety and outrage, particularly when the children in question were young. If, for the majority, social class was the chief factor determining how a displaced child should be treated, there was a growing minority for whom the status of *child,* putatively innocent and worthy of nurturing, trumped all else. The newspaper articles' focus on the characters of the orphan-train riders, like fiction's emphasis on the admirable qualities of the independent orphan, is child-centered without attacking dominant social practice. But other commentators and child-placement agents were beginning to decry the idea that displaced children of any class might be sent off to lives of toil rather than to loving families. Some orphanages, such as the New England Home for Little Wanderers (founded in 1865 to serve war orphans, freed slaves, and immigrants), specified that the children they furnished were to be treated as full-fledged family members, not servants.[23] Increasingly, the expectation that dependent children should earn their keep was a measure of society's unconcern.

Yet during the heyday of Social Darwinism, when poverty seemed to hard-liners to be nature's way of signaling an imperfect bloodline, rescue efforts were sometimes denigrated as misguided attempts to help the individual at what was literally posterity's expense. Critics often charged the Children's Aid Society, with its mission of relocating at-risk youths and its inability to supervise such placements closely, with unfairly burdening the taxpayers of the heartland by exporting delinquency; both Marilyn Holt and LeRoy Ashby cite complaints on this score from 1874 onward (Holt 121; Ashby, *Children* 52). As a Mr. Coffin of Indiana, a common destination for the orphan trains, editorialized in 1880, "Children so thrown out from the cities are a source of great corruption in the country places where they are thrown. . . . Very few such children are useful. . . . I am the last person to question the conscientiousness of these agencies, yet the remark is true which I heard from a gentleman in Massachusetts: 'It may be good for New York, but very bad for the West.'" Even so, Coffin also expressed concern about what would befall the children at the hands of foster parents who "are apt to look at a boy or a girl just to see how much they can get out of them. . . . The idea of home life is beautiful, is grand; it is God's plan; it is the place for the most healthy development of manly qualities,—and yet there are very many homes in the West unfit for children to live in" ("Debate" 238). That even the abused child is described as a "source of great corruption" suggests that Coffin was responding, in part, to a sense that placed-out children represent a commercialization of the home.

It is difficult to know how much connection this strand of rhetoric had to reality. Some contemporaneous investigations found little, as in the case of an 1884 inquiry conducted by the Minnesota State Board of Corrections and Charities after complaints that the orphan trains were "swelling the ranks of pauperism and crime" by importing "vicious and depraved children" and, conversely, that the children were often abused by their foster parents. This inquiry turned up only a few instances of incorrigible delinquency and still fewer cases of abuse (Hart 143–44), and in this regard it was typical; while delinquency and abuse undeniably existed, abuse in particular received little publicity (Crockett 65–66), just as placement agencies minimized reports of delinquency. But if indeed unfounded accusations were more common than revelations of genuine problems, we might conclude that displaced children sometimes functioned symbolically as the embodiment of adult fears about the fragility of civilized order, fears that are embodied in a different way by fiction about wealthy children—Dodge's Dorothy is one—whose orphanhood threatens their rightful social status. Similarly, concern that urban hooligans are besmirching the countryside's moral purity inverts the tales about working-class orphans who manage, against all odds, to construct a stable domestic situation for themselves.

The rhetorical mode most closely associated with the hooligan conceit was melodrama. But it was often a melodrama strangely inflected by scientific and/or economic "facts," designed to uncover the hidden social costs of what a given commentator deemed either an inadequate or a too vigorous intervention in the lives of the marginalized. This mixture of the exaggerated and the painstaking is apparent in the study produced in 1874 by Elisha Harris, secretary of the New York Prison Association, launching what the twentieth century would christen the "germ theory" of eugenics, in which a single criminal is identified as the source of an epidemic of misbehavior in later generations. Harris's "Margaret, Mother of Criminals" had moved from the Old World to New York State, where she and her sisters became the ancestors of 709 persons who were disproportionately convicts, prostitutes, inmates of poorhouses, and beneficiaries of the county's nascent welfare system. Margaret was followed most immediately by Richard Dugdale's 1877 work *The Jukes,* but the argument flourished well into the twentieth century: a notorious similar study of 1912 is H. H. Goddard's *The Kallikak Family, a Study in the Heredity of Feeble-Mindedness,* which contrasts the upstanding descendants of an intelligent man and his Quaker wife with the moronic and delinquent line springing from the same man's irregular union with a subnormal barmaid.[24] For all that these studies bristle with purported facts, they rely upon familiar and emotion-packed tropes: for Goddard the Madonna/whore dichotomy, for Harris the image of the fallen woman whose further sins may be laid at society's door.

These melodramatic images helped to imbue the figure of the working-class displaced child with a special urgency. A major conclusion of Harris's study, he pointed out at the 1875 Conference of Charities, was that "in any of the generations, most of the individual members in it could have been rescued and saved from vice and offences by a prompt and reasonable care and training of the children" ("Discussion of Miss Carpenter's" 79). But the urgency was again often presented as a practical matter of social costs. As what the English reformer Mary Carpenter called "the cause of an inconceivable amount of expense, inconvenience, trouble, disgrace and crime," Margaret's greatest errors were not her own misdeeds but those of her descendants (Carpenter 67): the sins of the children were visited upon the parent. In this formulation, every waif left on the street might be a source of major financial outlay for generations to come.

Whether its audience took it as a call to intervene in the lives of disadvantaged children or as a warning that such efforts were often wasted, Harris's study had substantial impact; it was repeatedly cited in commentary on child-saving and shows up as late as 1915 in Jean Webster's orphanage novel *Dear Enemy,* which treats it as representative of the latest eugenic thought. Among the many authorities quoting Harris's findings was Brace, who reported in 1880 that "the whole cost of this vagrant child and her sisters to Ulster county and the State of New York, in the property stolen and destroyed, and the public expense of maintenance and trial, is carefully estimated by Mr. Dugdale at $1,023,600" ("Method" 227). In contrast, he noted, the Children's Aid Society spent $4,194.55 in 1853, when it placed 197 youngsters, and $205,583.25 in 1880, when it placed 3,360; of 700 relocated to Kansas over two decades, "only *four* children had turned out badly" (233, 237). This balance-sheet approach counters and thus legitimizes the melodrama inherent in the Margaret origin myth; Dugdale's calculations of the exact social cost of this family's depredations—calculations reminiscent of Archbishop Ussher's manipulations of Genesis to show that Creation took place in 4004 B.C.—"prove" Harris's central premises.

Criticizing the Middle-Class Home

Whether framed as a budgetary question, as melodrama, or as sentimental fiction, rhetoric about the failings of the impoverished home is plentiful. The assumption that indigent urban parents were latter-day Fagins who had apprenticed their offspring to crime was common enough that orphanages might be viewed, officially, as reform schools for delinquents who had not yet had the chance to break the law. Cobb noted in 1884 that because girls were sent to her Milwaukee Industrial School by the courts, they arrived "technically as criminals," although some were as young as two weeks old ("Discussion," 1884 *Proceedings* 357). While she averred that the school did not view the children in this light, it was still a reformatory, and "those committed to us are, if not themselves offenders, mostly the children of delinquent and wicked parents" (356). Thus, in one sense, infants and toddlers were being imprisoned for their parents' crimes. The system's injustice struck Smith, who complained that "it seems a blight upon a child's character to be thus placed. It cannot be otherwise, when, to become eligible to enter [an industrial or reform school], one must be duly arrested and committed thereto by law." She nonetheless noted that for "the unfortunate little sufferer," a childhood in a reformatory was preferable to "the vile and squalid life in which it was being reared[, which] would be its sure destruction" (214).

Such formulations come as no surprise; we might expect to see childsavers contrasting the "vile and squalid" den of the destitute to the morally uplifting middle-class home and arguing that the former fosters sin, the latter virtue. And, indeed, many child-savers, including Brace, presented the middle-class home in this sentimental light as the best solution to the (melo)drama of crime and punishment that would otherwise cost society so much. But after the Civil War we also see a growing tendency to suggest that a system that allowed the indigent child to become a source of profit for its foster parents might expose a canker at the root even of the middle-class family. If fiction lauded the pluck and virtue of the economically productive displaced child, social workers increasingly represented such children as threatened by adults who held the same Yankee values (labor, profit, thrift) that the child was supposed to be absorbing.

Binding out children to earn their keep was not the only form of foster care during this period; after 1880, we also find foster parents being paid to house children who might otherwise be consigned on a long-term basis to orphanages.[25] Supporters lauded the system for offering a simulacrum of home life at moderate cost, accustoming the child to a noninstitutional milieu while still keeping it under state control. And Matthew Crenson points to another advantage: like placing out, paid foster care discouraged children from associating not only with their undesirable parents but also with other displaced children, allowing the kind of moral quarantine and "adult scrutiny of their characters and conduct" for which Brace was calling (203).

Nevertheless, subsidized foster care attracted criticism. Some commentators were irked to see taxpayers' money spent to buy homes for children who might be supporting themselves. Others found such care risky from the child's standpoint. Of the practice of paying foster parents $2.00 a week—later $1.50—to provide homes for children whose extreme youth or mental or physical disabilities disqualified them for work, Anne Richardson observed in 1880 that "the sum, though small, is enough to tempt the cupidity of the unworthy, and the character and age of the children so placed will render them more liable to wrong than more fortunate or older ones" (198). Still other commentators deemed paid foster care unseemly on symbolic grounds: as Coffin had implied of placing-out, it seemed to profane domesticity, to prostitute motherhood. Thus in his 1888 history of Pennsylvania's Bethany Orphans' Home, established in 1863 to benefit war orphans aged six through thirteen, superintendent Thomas M. Yundt wrote that "to us the plan of 'farming out' children for a stipulated sum appears to be radically wrong. The temptation is great to make money by the transaction, and evil results follow" (14).

For commentators often implied that displaced children and potential foster parents were natural adversaries. While we have seen that sometimes the assumption was that the children were social outcasts liable to damage the decency of their new environments, as time passes we are more likely to hear that the seemingly respectable people who took them in were grasping, cold-hearted, or ill equipped to raise a child. Typical is

Richardson's plaint that

> the families that would receive . . . those who, if not themselves offend-
> ers, were yet the offspring of incapable, unworthy and often criminal par-
> ents, were few, and these few were seldom of a character to recognize the
> great responsibility, or to ensure any help in the reform of the one or
> wholesome training of the other. Seldom were they taken but as helpers
> in daily toil. The idea that the work begun in the institution was to be
> carried on,—that they were to instruct, to counsel and to warn, or to do
> aught beyond feeding and clothing,—seems, in rare instances, not to have
> been entertained, while the ignorance shown of real duty, proved in
> many cases, that the indenture was only understood as securing their
> own, with no reference to the child's rights. (189–90)

Like orphan fiction, the National Conference of Charities and Corrections became a venue for criticism of the lay world. The conference was
named for the state administrative units that oversaw both dependent children and delinquent adults, a juxtaposition reflecting the attitude that led
to the placement of infants in reformatories—but most participants in the
annual meetings rejected the equation of displaced children with criminals. By the 1880s speakers were voicing anxiety about the exploitation of
children by demanding taskmasters and (as in fiction) about the emotional
barriers that social class might place between child and adoptive parent.
Here again, a major focus of the discussion was the role of money in enabling children to be placed in homes.[26]

A representative paper is "The Shady Side of the 'Placing-Out System'"
(1885), a defense of orphanages presented by Lyman P. Alden, superintendent of the Rose Orphan Home and former superintendent of the Michigan State Public School. Although he considers most dependent children
ragged and unmannerly waifs, products of "the streets and slumholes of
society," Alden finds that the chief drawback of foster care is the character
of prospective foster parents, who are seldom genuinely charitable. In his
diatribe, Alden argues that what animates the foster parent is not a love of
children but a love of money:

> It is well known . . . that the great majority of those who apply for chil-
> dren over nine years old are looking for cheap help; and while many,
> even of this class, treat their apprentices with fairness . . . a much larger
> number of applicants do not intend to pay a *quid pro quo*, but expect to
> make a handsome profit on the child's services, and, if allowed one, will
> evade, as far as possible, every clause in the contract,—furnishing poor
> food, shoddy clothing, work the child beyond its strength, send it to
> school but a few months, and that irregularly, and sometimes treat it with
> personal cruelty. (203)

To support his remarks, Alden quotes numerous colleagues across the
country. And like Alden's own criticisms, most of his source texts address
the would-be foster parents' approach to money. An Illinois orphanage

superintendent remarks that "the greater number of applicants for children have no other aim in view than to secure cheap help" (qtd. 203); the president of Girard College for Orphan Boys (a private Philadelphia institution founded in 1831 and still extant) agrees that farmers "are not considerate for the child's welfare, caring only to use him for their profit" (qtd. 204); and an Iowa children's-home director concludes, "The average family with us wants a child for what they can get out of it in the way of work" (qtd. 204).

Such complaints put "the average family" in a poor light. To be sure, Alden also contends that most foster parents are simply not competent to meet the challenge posed by the unsocialized child of the slums, who needs orphanage discipline to counter his or her bad habits, "inherited tendencies to wrong," or "complicated moral maladies" (205). But if the children are not at first respectable enough to enter middle-class households, the charges that Alden levels at the foster parents suggest that respectability is only a veneer masking serious character flaws in the adults. In this equation, respect for domesticity is hard to come by; the children lack it because of their unfortunate upbringing, while the adults see home as a sweatshop where profits take precedence over working conditions and good employer/employee relations. The American family, we may assume, is in sad shape when its functions are best assumed by the institution, and Alden's implied criticisms are early examples of what would develop by century's end into widespread anxiety about what Lasch calls "the crisis of marriage and the family" (8).[27]

If Alden and his allies expressed dismay about the excessive utilitarianism of many foster placements during this period, other speakers raised concerns about sentimental adoption. Participants in the 1884 Charities and Correction meeting heard a paper by Alden's successor at the Michigan State Public School, John N. Foster, on the school's experiences with various forms of placement. Between 1874 and 1884, Foster noted, the school admitted 1,672 children, 70 percent of them between three and ten years old and almost all of them white. Boys outnumbered girls by two to one.[28] The fate of the great majority—894, with another 56 "on trial" and anticipating a similar disposition—was indenture. Another 278 children were still in the school as Foster spoke, their future unclear. But since only 95 were legally adopted over the course of the decade, most probably did not acquire loving parents.[29]

Certainly, that so many children committed to orphanages still had parents made adoption less likely. As historian Judith Dulberger (who calls the late-nineteenth-century orphanage "the poor man's boarding school") notes, many parents sent their children to institutions temporarily and collected them a year or two later when times had improved (11, 10). Nor would adoptive parents rush to accept children whose presumably disreputable relatives might resurface to claim them or embarrass the adoptive family. Even so, Foster hints that indenture might be preferable to adoption, precisely because it is not family life. He claims, for one thing, that children placed out to work are often blissfully happy, asking him "to be sure and not let their father or mother know their whereabouts, lest they might try to get them away" (141). But when they are less contented with their placement, one advantage of indenture is that it can be temporary. While most children are apprenticed but once, some have gone through four, five, six, and even seven foster homes, until each "divinely wrought statue" finds its "fitting niche . . . no matter how much soiled and bruised it may have been by its rough contact with life" (139).

Class seems to be at the root of Foster's distrust of legal adoption. While he concedes that some caregivers want "a child simply with reference to its commercial value" and mete out "unjust and inhuman" treatment (141), he also suggests that a working home may be a more fitting haven for the displaced child than an affluent and emotionally involved adoptive family:

> Kind-hearted, well-meaning people, in comfortable circumstances, desir-
> ing a child to help "mind" the baby, run errands, prepare vegetables, etc.,
> allow the children to go more carelessly dressed and not always as "clean
> of face" as might seem orthodox; yet they are trained in good ways, are
> sent to school, are treated in every way as members of the family in which
> they live, are taught to work, and are really in good homes, and, if
> adapted to the home, are more happy than they would have been in one
> of finer mould. (141)

The proper balance, it seems, is being struck—and struck because the child is not being removed too far from its natural level. Still dirty and disheveled, still required to earn its own living, the indigent foster child becomes respectable without upsetting the natural order: like Alcott's Ben Brown, it is a "member of the family," but it is also a servant. A richer family, interested in the child as child rather than the child as maid-of-all-work, would expect too much emotionally and not enough practically. One cannot, Foster implies, make a silk purse from a sow's ear; the children of the lower orders *must* work because work is what they are fit for.

Not all commentators shared Foster's feeling that adoption might not be a fitting solution to the problem of the indigent child. The rhetoric employed by John C. Ferris, a Nashville probate judge, criticizes neither adoption nor the child, but the snobbery and ancestor worship that may prevent the bourgeoisie from embracing their class inferiors. Ferris's adoption work began during the cholera epidemic of 1873, when, he reported eleven years later, he had to find homes for forty newly minted orphans within a single week. Advertising for adoptive parents, he found that applicants outnumbered the available children, and hence he began to seek recruits for placement in and beyond Tennessee, feeling that "the best place on earth for little children is the home" ("Discussion," 1884 *Proceedings* 360). By 1884, some 500 of his 1,300 protégés had been legally adopted.

Cholera epidemics, of course, are no respecters of persons. Placement workers who dealt only with destitute slum dwellers often found it hard to take a sentimental stance; in contrast, Ferris's clientele, at least originally, presumably included the children of the "deserving poor." Moreover, Nashville's population was ethnically more homogeneous than that of New York City, so that Ferris would have perceived fewer differences between himself and the children he sought to aid. Thus he stressed the ease with which his protégés could be integrated into families and the "pure love" with which the families would greet new members (Ferris 340).

Ferris clearly saw adoption as a matter of emotion, not expedience. Although he undertook to find homes for children as old as fifteen, he presented even these children as "young and helpless" (Ferris 338), adjectives that ask us to see them as unproductive by rights. For Ferris, in other words, all orphans were honorary members of the middle class. Not only did he report with gratification that one of his placements had recently inherited an estate worth seven or eight thousand dollars, but he scoffed at would-be adoptive parents who asked that he be "very particular about the blood" of the child he furnished to them: his response to one such plea was, "Its eyes are blue, its hair light, and its blood is *red*" ("Discussion," 1884 *Proceedings* 360).

Ferris gave short shrift to adults whose request for a child was motivated by a need for additional household help. His standard reply in such cases was, "I am not furnishing drudges" ("Discussion," 1884 *Proceedings* 360); the applicant seeking "a good strong boy or girl from 12 to 15 years old" was sent away unsatisfied, having revealed a lack of interest in "gladdening his or her home by the presence of childhood made happy by kindness" (Ferris 337–38). But the applicant concerned about a child's family background comes in for just as much criticism, even though the chances are good that such an adult is offering legal adoption and responsible care. Respectability here appears in a negative light. If adoption, to Ferris, is "the love of God at work in the hearts of good people . . . the spirit calling and telling them to work, to do something for Him who will not forget even a cup of cold water administered to one of these little ones" (Ferris 340), excessive concern about a child's background can only inhibit charity.

Predictably, some of Ferris's contemporaries objected to understanding placement in this eleemosynary way. Representative is Elizabeth Cabot Putnam, a trustee of the Massachusetts State Primary and Reform School and the organizer of the corps of volunteer social workers assigned to visit "state girls" in their foster homes, who spoke at the 1884 Charities and Correction meeting on the foolishness of a King Cophetua approach to adoption. Her words make explicit what Foster's only hint at, namely that adoption cannot succeed where there exists too great a social gulf between parent and child. Too often, she argued, "children of the unfortunate classes" adopted "by persons of ample wealth and higher station . . . are complained of as they grow up as unworthy of and ungrateful for the benefits bestowed upon them." Blame in such cases was not to attach to the children, but rather to the placement officers, who should have known that youngsters of "humble" background "[are] not by nature fitted" to luxury:

> Had these very children been reared among plain, hard-working people, they might have found the discipline of hardships necessary to bring out their powers. A child with a respectable inheritance of energy and industry might thrive under any reasonably favorable conditions, but those who inherit sluggishness of mind and body from their pauper parents cannot too early be taught to rely upon their own exertions. In many cases, our natural teachers, cold and hunger, are needed to rouse them to effort. (128)

Putnam's views invert those of Ferris. His cavalier assertion "Its blood is *red*" dismisses heredity; similarly, the report of a discussion held at the 1885 conference quotes his complaint that meddlers "begin by saying, 'Why, Mrs. Jones, do you know the history of that child?' What does it matter to Mrs. Jones what its history is, so long as it is God's child? That is enough for her to know, and to know that it needs her love and protection. The least we can do is to give these innocent children a good character" ("Discussion," 1885 *Proceedings* 461). Putnam, however, whose specialty was the care of delinquent girls (Crenson 177), perceives indigents as fallen: they are not infinitely malleable, and hence they are not infinitely redeemable. For her, the poor are poor because they are "sluggis[h] of mind and body," a taint that is passed on from parent to child. Whereas Ferris believes that children need love above all else, Putnam finds that "cold and hunger"—as an antidote to sluggishness, a reminder that those who do not work may perish—may be more salutary. He implies that any child is adoptable by any adult of good feeling, rich or of modest means; the success of the placement appears to depend exclusively on the adult's character. In contrast, she intimates that the *child* will be unable to respond suitably to an adoptive parent, however loving, who has too much to offer in the way of material goods; one may expect to climb only so many rungs of the economic ladder before finding oneself out of one's element.

Finally, Ferris notes that "a home without a baby is a poor home" ("Discussion," 1885 *Proceedings* 461) and likens himself to a merchant dispensing goods to "cash customer[s]," a simile implying that the "goods" are desirable. Putnam, though, wants orphans to be "boarded at an early age in country families where, by the time the payment is withdrawn, they may find permanent homes free of expense" and gain "a practical knowledge of the kinds of work by which they are likely to have to begin to earn their living" (127–28). This system assumes that they are unwanted; at least at first, no adult will provide care without recompense, and the state in turn hopes to find foster families who will forgo payment if the child comes to be "of use in the household or so well beloved as to be legally adopted" (128). Putnam clearly considers the latter eventuality unlikely.

The differences between Ferris and Putnam are emblematic of the division between social workers who supported sentimental adoption and those who supported orphan labor during the period discussed here. It is therefore all the more telling that both speakers organize so much of their discourse around money; financial preoccupations seem pervasive no matter what one's ideological stance. Even so, the emphasis on money that we see during these years in fiction and nonfiction alike would seem to have multiple causes and functions. On a purely pragmatic level, money is obviously important both in establishing and maintaining a certain degree of comfort for the individual (the focus of much of the fiction) and in funding social-welfare efforts. Observations such as Brace's remarks about the comparative cheapness of saving children via orphan trains reflect a sense that philanthropic largesse is usually limited and that if one wishes to help a large number of individuals, one's methods must be reasonably priced. Similarly, revealing the immense hidden costs of failing to help a "Margaret" in timely fashion is a useful fund-raising technique, whether one is dealing with private benefactors or with state legislatures.

But money has its symbolic meanings as well. Within the Victorian ideology of separate spheres, it sometimes stood for the values associated with Mammon, connoting an unchristian willingness to forgo tenderness and compassion in order to amass ever-greater wealth. This sensibility appears to underlie the criticism of aristocratic adoptive homes found in stories such as Morse's, and the anxiety, expressed by many child-welfare workers, about placements that promise the foster parent material gain. The blending of private and public represented in the idea that one's home might be a source of profit or (as in Alger tales) a site of display to excite the hostility of the unscrupulous, was often deeply dismaying, and this dismay certainly contributed to the rise of sentimental adoption.

Even so, the idea that displaced children might be encouraged to generate and manage income in appropriate ways also had other, more positive connotations. In 1866, Brace described his encouragement of habits of saving on the part of inhabitants of Children's Aid Society lodging houses as a way of "break[ing] up the gambling and extravagant habits of the class" (qtd. Schwartz 48). Put another way, what Brace and his colleagues were attempting to do was to instill self-discipline and to train working-class youths out of the desire for instant gratification. Early in this chapter, I quoted Smith's comment that without intervention, poor children would grow up to display the "unrestrained . . . passion" of their sires. Thrift, the opposite of the "extravagant habits" cited by Brace, rests upon self-restraint, perhaps the preeminent middle-class virtue in the mid-nineteenth century. Hence, of course, the plethora of fiction aimed at affluent readers but focusing approvingly upon the saving ways of impoverished young orphans such as Alger's Julius. The ability to handle money sensibly promises the ability to handle other things well too; Julius will not grow up to be a drunkard, a brute, or an unmarried father.

In focusing so much rhetoric on the financial aspects of the displaced child, in short, whether by compulsively calculating costs or by detailing how inmates of orphanages or lodging houses earn and dispose of their money, child-savers often indicate that the central issue is one of control. What I have termed the balance-sheet approach to philanthropy clearly aims to persuade its audience that matters are fully in hand, that efforts are being conducted on a sound business footing, and that the business is not about to fail. (Conversely, critics who charge that agencies are sending children to the hinterlands oblivious to the social costs of the practice are challenging this model of organizational competence.) But in a larger sense, associating the displaced child with money furthers the representation of that child as someone who can, quite literally, be "saved"—if not also banked, tabulated in ledgers, and generally brought out of chaos into order.

3

Melodrama and the Displaced Child, 1886–1906

Turn-of-the-century nonfiction aimed at social-service workers, like that of earlier decades, frequently represented displaced and at-risk children as the objects of reform. But mass-market texts, which had always tended to put such children in a more positive light, became more optimistic about their virtues than ever. Much contemporaneous fiction, in particular, cast them as the embodiment of goodness—not as the target for reform, but as the motivating force behind it. Indeed, fiction often presented them as reform's most effective agents. Paradoxically, their effectiveness was shown to lie in their pathos, and specifically in the discrepancy between their innocence and sweetness and the threatening world surrounding them. The feisty fictional orphans of the 1860s and '70s grapple with challenges, certainly, but challenges that they can readily master by demonstrating their energy and grit. Their descendants in the next generation have more in common with Susan Warner's prewar Ellen Montgomery, in that they too are thrown into environments that seem bleak and loveless, in which their principal task is to manufacture the emotional climates that they need for their very survival.

Thus the rhetorical mode that animates many orphan narratives of this era is melodrama, in an expansion of strategies that we have earlier seen operating in both fiction and nonfiction. And there were sound commercial reasons why this should have been the case. The 1890s marked the birth of a "new journalism" that emphasized human-interest anecdotes and a sense of personal connection to large events (Ziff 146–48). Upstart magazines such as *Cosmopolitan, Munsey's,* and *McClure's,* which depended largely on newsstand sales, challenged the hegemony of older and more highbrow monthlies such as *Scribner's* or the *Atlantic,* which relied on subscriptions. For the popular magazines, emotionalism was an important merchandising technique through which to attract the impulse buyer, especially the less educated (and larger) segments of the reading public. Similarly, newspaper tycoons such as Joseph Pulitzer and William Randolph Hearst battled for readers not only by recruiting star reporters and instituting crowd-pleasing innovations such as colored comic strips, but also by emphasizing sentiment and promising to expose social wrongs.

A reporter who could show the effects of such wrongs on children could link outrage to sentiment, increasing sales. Thus the first of the great muckrakers, Jacob Riis, campaigned for better housing for the poor by publicizing the lives of young slum dwellers, as in *Children of the Poor* (1892) and his 1903 collection of fictional and semifictional pieces, *Children of the Tenements*. In the mid-1880s New York City housed (often under appalling conditions) 290,000 people per square mile; from the beginning of his career, Riis seems to have hypothesized that focusing on children might be the most effective way of ameliorating this situation. His first book, the influential *How the Other Half Lives* (1890), contained four chapters on displaced children and other young victims of abuse, complete with heartrending photographs, and used issues such as baby-farming, foundlings, infanticide, and efforts at child-saving to advance its larger project. Indeed, many of the journalists who followed in Riis's footsteps in the early 1900s found that child labor or malnourished schoolchildren—discussed respectively in *Cosmopolitan* and the *Independent*—made perfect spearheads for critiques of the selfishness or wrongheadedness of particular groups of adults. For as Martha Banta writes of feminist muckraking, "the sentimental tradition was . . . the most effective weapon the woman journalist possessed. . . . What mattered was that the seemingly sentimental (a soft, fantasy form) be revealed as the ultimate realism (strong, brutal, true)" (148).

These techniques helped make the United States a nation of magazine readers. Turn-of-the-century publisher Frank Munsey estimated that in this era, the audience for periodicals tripled to 750,000 (Regier 20), and the number of magazines rose dramatically as well. The expansion of the literary marketplace created an increased demand for fiction and nonfiction designed for mass consumption. Many of the new publications targeted women and were thus particularly likely to address children's issues. But for men and women alike, displaced children were a popular subject, inasmuch as the melodramatic mode allowed them to be presented either as pathetic figures to elicit tears or as indictments of the social practices that had brought about their misery. In an era that held, in Anne Scott MacLeod's words, that "the best books for children were also good for adults" because "the best adults retained much of the child" (*Childhood* 120), orphans appealed to a multigenerational readership, thus boosting sales.[1] Moreover, they provided the human face that enabled reporters to explain complex issues as simple matters of justice, allowing emotion to substitute for abstract thought for a mass readership.

For novelists, they also served as a mechanism for critiquing certain child-rearing practices, both because orphans might plausibly occupy multiple homes with contrasting philosophies and because attacking foster parents was (and is) less risky than attacking "real" mothers. While we have seen this technique on display in *The Wide, Wide World* and even earlier, it became especially common at the turn of the century, an era that combined reformist zeal with an experimenter's fascination with child development. Increasingly, as well, the displaced child was idealized in order to strengthen the didactic thrust of such fiction, a circumstance that both drew upon and fed the late-century tendency to sentimentalize the child.

Novelists sharply criticized utilitarian placements in which the child was expected to spend most of the day working for the foster parent, although such placements were still common in real life. But the displaced children who populate turn-of-the-century children's fiction were nonetheless commodities, just as those who serve as the objects of readerly identification in journalistic nonfiction were used to sell magazines. The orphans of fiction were, in effect, advertising agents for a new kind of parent-child relationship, one that benefited the adult in an emotional rather than a practical way. Such fiction presented the effort of understanding, helping, and sympathizing with orphans as one that would uplift those orphans' adult patrons; adoptees, it seems, were still expected to earn their keep, although their job description had changed from farmhand or mother's help to moral exemplar and cultivator of the affections. Free to move into new families, fictional orphans, in Gillian Avery's phrase, "bring warmth and light where there has hitherto been cold and dark" (178).

In short, while the virtuous orphan was no new phenomenon in American literature, the turn of the century witnessed a boom in sentimental tales about parentless children who reform their new milieus, not now through hard work and self-discipline but through charm. In order to merit reclassification as leisure articles, they display the "fascination, magnetism, [and] attractiveness" that Warren Susman considers intrinsic to mainstream American culture's "new interest in personality" as opposed to "character"—an interest manifest in the advertising rhetoric designed to promote more overtly commercial transactions than adoption (280–81). At this time, as children's-literature specialist Perry Nodelman writes, orphan stories followed a clear formula: the protagonist "shocks, and then delights, repressed or unhappy grown-ups . . . makes them more natural" (32), so that the adults themselves may develop as much "attractiveness" as their natural limitations permit. In a variety of ways, this redemptive energy helped to fuel Progressive Era reforms and transformed adoption literature.

Reportage and the Selling of the American Foundling

This chapter will focus on the ways in which the orphan literature of this period exploits melodrama in order to promise redemption—sometimes that of the orphans themselves, but more generally that of the adults who surround them. As such, the chapter's primary concern will be stories and novels by writers whose commercial and critical success demonstrates their understanding of the public's needs and desires. But before we proceed to a discussion of the fiction, we might pause to contemplate two representative magazine pieces on foundlings. Together, these articles help to illustrate rhetorical techniques common in nonfiction mass-market representations of displaced children during this period, techniques that have relevance within fiction as well. They also suggest the extent to which such children functioned as commodities within the literary marketplace of the Progressive Era, a rhetorical trope that offers insight into the less commercial contemporaneous representations as well.

The title of Anne O'Hagan's contribution to *Munsey's Magazine* in June 1901 sums up the article's contents: "The Biography of a Foundling: The Story of a New York Waif, Telling How He Got a Name and a Religion, and How He Passed through the Dangers That Are Fatal to Most Babies in the City Institutions." Focusing on a foundling whose name, William McKinley Bryan, seems intended as a satirical indictment of the system through whose cracks he has fallen, O'Hagan fluctuates between exposé and tribute. Thus we begin with an indictment of the infant mortality rate in the foundling hospital on Randall's Island, where "In 1895, out of a hundred and twenty nine foundlings received, four were immediately reclaimed by their parents, and one was adopted. The remaining one hundred and twenty four died" (313). These appalling statistics, however, which were cited (with minor variations depending on the year under discussion) by many reporters and social-service workers during this period, give way to an encomium to the New York Foundling Asylum. O'Hagan is particularly pleased that the Asylum not only offers loving care to abandoned babies but also manages to persuade many unwed mothers who have "every intention of deserting their babies . . . to stay and be true mothers to their children" (313).[2] The practice of paid foster care is then condemned; state-supported boarding-out (as a preliminary to adoption when the child is strong enough) is praised. Finally, after commending various institutions by name, the article ends with an impassioned plea against institutionalization: "When the dulling, dwarfing life of the institution does not lead to the viciousness which is akin to stupidity, it leads to the unenterprising state which is the parent of thriftlessness. . . . There is reason to believe that [the frequent criminality of erstwhile foundlings is] due rather to the effect of long continued institutional life than to the inevitable inheritance of weakness and viciousness from irresponsible parents," since other illegitimate children, from Nancy Hanks and Alexander Hamilton to William the Conqueror and Leonardo da Vinci, have made important contributions to society (316).

The point on which we might focus, however, is O'Hagan's decision to use "William McKinley Bryan," whose name suggests that he is a fictional construct, as the focal point for her fact-oriented mixture of muckraking and uplift. Her article depends on reportage as much as on editorializing, in that it presents the reader with statistics, historical details, sociological theories, and the like. But from the title onward, the piece relies on suspense and emotion to drive home the factual aspects of the argument. William is the spoonful of melodrama designed to make the medicine go down, to extend the "circles where statistics are scanned" (313) enough to raise a public outcry over scandals such as Randall's Island or the boarding-out system, which puts our token infant at the mercy of a washerwoman who feeds him alcohol in order to still his cries. In the newly mass-market world of periodicals, we must have a human face by means of which the author may tinge mere information with an appealing mixture of shock, sentiment, and inspiration. This "Biography of a Foundling" is many things besides a biographical sketch of an invented character, but it is evidently as the drama of a pathetic infant that it is most marketable.

Ada Patterson's "Giving Babies Away" (*Cosmopolitan*, August 1905) similarly hinges on the commodification of the child. Ostensibly a profile of the Guild of the Infant Savior, a benevolent society established to aid in the care and placement of foundlings, the piece opens with a bizarre anecdote that—at least for today's reader—points up the connection between consumerism and sentimental views of children. In this narrative, a widow loses her two young children to diphtheria and to dull her grief "adopts" a pair of wax dolls whose faces remind her of her offspring, caring for them devotedly for the three years before her death. The widow's solution presumably works because the passivity of the dolls, "her comforting companions" (406), makes them the perfect objects for an otherwise thwarted maternity. Since they lack personalities of their own, the grief-stricken mother can endow them with the attributes of her lost baby and toddler: they are "an almost exact reproduction of the children who had died" (406). Sentiment and reality are uneasy bedfellows; by choosing to adopt fantasy children rather than flesh-and-blood beings, the widow is ensuring that her devotion will never meet with the obstacles that may trouble motherhood in real life, be these diphtheria germs or any other evidences of human frailty. Patterson does not, of course, approve the widow's choice: a "wholesomer path" for her to follow, she remarks, would have been to take in a living child from the Guild. But this article goes some way toward suggesting that adoptable children display many of the qualities that attracted one bereaved mother to artificial offspring. In a sense, both the idealized children who populate Patterson's article and those who flock through the orphan fiction of this period are also wax dolls, marketed and understood as safer vehicles for sentiment than real children can hope to be.

One important question in this regard is that of provenance. As we shall see below, Progressive Era fiction typically identifies the displaced child as one born to affluence, although in reality there was little chance that being orphaned would render such a child dependent upon the kindness of strangers. Because Patterson is writing nonfiction, she cannot, like some novelists, ignore the twin stigmas of illegitimacy and institutionalization, social shames that the Guild attempts to address by placing foundlings for adoption and admonishing the new parents "to conceal the origin of the infant" (408).[3] But she can nonetheless downplay them. Thus she suggests that a birth mother often does not know that her child has been abandoned until retrieval is impossible, or is wont as she deserts the infant to hide "in the shadows . . . until she knows her little one is safe" (409). Either scenario allows the reader to conclude that these children's pasts are far from shameful, as they have been born to loving and caring parents. After all, we learn, "Forty-five per cent. of the women who surrender their children to the authorities or abandon them to chance, do so from necessity"; and moreover, their children have been born in lawful wedlock (412). The source of this statistic, as is typical of this romantic style of article, is unclear, but like the elaborate financial information used to buttress commentary on "Margaret, Mother of Criminals," even an invented datum lends the narrative an air of authority and provides a semblance of pedigree to the foundlings that it describes.

Lavishly illustrated with photographs of attractively dressed, chubby-cheeked infants and toddlers (a striking contrast to the stark pictures of poor children in Riis's *How the Other Half Lives*), the article stresses "the marvelous sunshine of a baby's presence in the house" (409). Like the wax dolls nurtured by the widow of the anecdote, adopted children's function is often "to fill the empty place, the great void, left by the baby who died" (411), and Patterson has no doubt that they will do just that. Hence the cherubs of the illustrations highlight the foundling's role as desirable commodity, just as they have a job to do for the magazine: they are eye candy designed in part to persuade the newsstand browser to select this periodical over another. At the same time, however, Patterson also addresses the sordid, as when she mentions the "pinched little face" of one "piteous little figure. . . . worse than orphan" whose "father killed his mother in a drunken frenzy, and . . . would have killed the child, but the mother saved it" (408). Similarly, would-be humorous reports of the strangely couched requests for babies received from children and from "a colored woman of Baltimore" jostle descriptions of the fabulously wealthy homes to which some foundlings have been translated ("When she was fifteen months old she owned three Brooklyn houses") and pathetic tales of other children who have died in infancy (410). Whether the reader is looking for sentiment or sensation, amusement or tales of high life, the article can furnish what is desired, thanks to the rhetorical adaptability of the foundling.

And, of course, we get information as well. Thus Patterson outlines the standards for becoming an adoptive parent: one must be a married church member of good character and adequate means, able to withstand a year-long probationary term punctuated by "frequent visits of the Guild committee" (410). Again, the implication is that adoption is a desirable plan not only because women who fill the void in their lives with children are emotionally healthier than those who mother wax dolls, but also because foundlings share two crucial characteristics with such dolls. One is an agreeable plasticity; Patterson assures readers that according to the Guild, "a child under two years may be entirely remolded . . . it even turns [out] to look like its foster-parents" (412). The other, still more important, is that unlike one's biological children, foundlings are *acknowledged* to be commodities, subject to the usual rules governing consumer satisfaction. A major advantage of the Guild, we learn, is that it adheres to a policy that we have earlier seen advertised in connection with the orphan trains: its wares "may be brought back and exchanged if their dispositions or habits do not suit" (412).

That articles such as Patterson's and O'Hagan's pulled in so many different directions suggests the degree of conflict and doubt about adoption that remained at the turn of the century. The issues that these Progressive Era writers raise recall those that we have seen debated in the social-work conferences discussed in Chapter 2. Which is more powerful, heredity or environment, and is illegitimacy always a sign of bad heredity? Are adoptable children social problems or desirable merchandise? But by the same token, Patterson and O'Hagan agree on some key principles. Not only do both consider public institutions deplorable places in which to rear children, but, more significantly, both assume that the motivation behind adoption is the longing for a child to love, not the need for household help or even the desire to ease social ills. And whatever the circumstances of its birth, any child is to be deemed potentially lovable—although the option of trading in an unsatisfactory acquisition nevertheless continues to receive publicity.

The sentimentalism and melodrama that infuse Patterson's article extend far beyond the borders of *Cosmopolitan* magazine. We may perceive them also in landmark nonfiction such as *How the Other Half Lives,* in which Riis claims, "It is one of the most touching sights in the world to see a score of babies, rescued from homes of brutality and desolation . . . saying their prayers in the nursery [of the Five Points House of Industry] at bedtime" (151). Together the two modes are both cause and effect of an increased respect for displaced children. Wishy points out a theological flip-flop that reflects a nationwide cultural shift toward a belief in the preciousness of all children: at the dawn of the twentieth century, even the fiercest Presbyterian churches abandoned the doctrine of infant depravity, replacing it with the notion that "all dying infants would be saved" because children are made in God's image (109). Adults received no such free pass into heaven. Young children, in other words, were now to be deemed the moral superiors of their seniors, whatever their heredity or social class, which in turn made them suitable focuses for melodrama. And it was precisely the triumph of sentimentality and melodrama that made the figure of the displaced child so successful as a way of attracting readers within the mass-market periodical. For the new journalism, such children could advance merchandising schemes not despite their angelic qualities, but because of them.

The Case of Frances Hodgson Burnett:
The Fictional Orphan as Royalty in Disguise

Within the value system of sentimentality, orphans were increasingly presumed to be the moral superiors of children with parents, since the orphan (at least in fiction) stood for the child untrammeled by close ties to adults—an unusually childlike child, then, what Nodelman calls a "pure manifestatio[n] of qualities that would be muddied in less detached children" (34). In part, this redefinition of the orphan seems to have been a response to larger social and economic conditions. By the turn of the century, argue historians Susan Downs and Michael Sherraden, America was feeling the effects of an "oversupply of child labor" (274), an important factor in the passage of state laws against the employment of the prepubescent in the 1890s and 1900s. Even more than most youngsters, displaced children needed a new social function, one more symbolic than utilitarian. Fiction thus became increasingly likely to distinguish acceptable labor from drudgery and to condemn adults who equate orphans with slaves. To be sure, some authors, especially early in the period, highlighted the therapeutic value of work in retraining spoiled middle-class children who have an inflated idea of their own value.[4] But others saw displaced children as members of a higher order than their caregivers, marked by unusual talent (such as Rebecca Randall's poetic gifts in Kate Douglas Wiggin's *Rebecca of Sunnybrook Farm* [1903]), strength of character (as with the heroine of Carolyn Wells's *The Story of Betty* [1899]), and/or aristocratic credentials (as when Tip in L. Frank Baum's *The Marvelous Land of Oz* [1904] turns out to be the land's rightful ruler, Princess Ozma). Far more uniformly than the nonfiction of the day, the fiction insists that it is the adoptive parent who ought to work for the child, not the child for the adult. Natural aristocrats, orphans "should" belong to the leisured class.

One of the most influential creators of this version of the iconic orphan was Frances Hodgson Burnett, whose best-known works remain her three major adoption narratives, *Little Lord Fauntleroy* (1886), *A Little Princess* (1905), and *The Secret Garden* (1911). While the protagonist of the last-named novel diverges from the pattern, in that she needs productive employment and contact with the wholesome poor in order to overcome her incapacity and sour personality, the first two books update the Cinderella story to contrast childish virtue with adult unpleasantness. Fauntleroy, a half-orphan separated from his surviving parent and given over to his paternal grandfather, the Earl of Dorincourt, reforms the old man's selfishness and hardness of heart by his guileless innocence and natural generosity. A harsh father to his own offspring, the Earl nonetheless cannot resist the naive purity of this boy raised in humble circumstances in New York City by an impoverished but saintly mother. Like many of the orphan novels that would follow it, the narrative thus reverses Brace's assumptions in guiding the New York Children's Aid Society: here the vice and coarseness once imputed to the déclassé urban child are the traits of the wealthy foster parent, and the moral rescue is performed by, not on, the boy.

If *Fauntleroy*—one of the most successful melodramas of the late nineteenth century, both in book form and on stage—critiques the bigotry and callousness of the aristocracy, *A Little Princess* indicts the representatives of middle-class respectability. Young Sara Crewe goes from riches to rags to riches; her hitherto wealthy father dies an apparent bankrupt, leaving her to the dubious mercies of Miss Minchin, the proprietor of the London boarding school that Sara has been attending. In the name of charity (but actually to gain an unpaid servant and to preserve her own reputation for decency), Miss Minchin forbears to turn Sara out into the street. Instead, she provides inadequate food and unheated sleeping quarters, forcing the child to labor as a maid-of-all-work from dawn to darkness. But Sara's pitiful situation, contrasted with her upper-class demeanor and fluency in Hindustani, attracts the attention of the school's wealthy neighbor Tom Carrisford and his Indian servant, who bestow numerous comforting luxuries upon the little girl before discovering her identity as the daughter of Carrisford's dead business partner. The narrative ends with Sara's informal adoption by Carrisford and the assurance that unlike Miss Minchin, she will devote a suitable portion of her wealth to philanthropy.

The novel merits extended discussion at this juncture because Burnett wrote it twice, once at the beginning and once at the end of the period covered in this chapter, and thus it offers a snapshot of certain significant developments in the orphan tale over time. In its first incarnation in 1888, it appeared as a long short story under the title of *Sara Crewe, or What Happened at Miss Minchin's;* after the success of a stage play based on the tale, Burnett expanded it into *A Little Princess,* incorporating material added to the dramatization. But length is not the only difference between the two versions. While the latter has a significantly larger cast of major characters, used to enable more dialogue and more episodes, it also rewrites the protagonist in important ways, heightening the melodrama by heightening the pathos. In 1888, Sara starts out spoiled and willful. We learn that "the instant she had entered the house, she had begun promptly to hate Miss Minchin," solely on the basis of the latter's appearance and "large, cold hands" (11). She forms no emotional bonds to other children until after she is orphaned, and must be reacculturated into childhood by a stay with the jolly Carmichael family, "learn[ing] to play and run about" like the Carmichael daughters (69), before she can embark upon her new life with Carrisford. This Sara is not presented as an attractive personality, full of the winning ways that endear Fauntleroy to all who know him. Her travail is the making of her, inasmuch as it demonstrates to her the importance of family and friends and causes her to expand beyond her father the circle of people in whom she takes an interest.

In contrast, the 1905 Sara shares her predecessor's imagination and "old-fashioned" ways, but uses them even before her bereavement to ameliorate the lot of the downtrodden, befriending the school dunce, the school baby, and the school slavey. The protagonist of *Sara Crewe* uses her gift for "pretending" exclusively for her own comfort; she is both author of and sole audience for her stories, except when she tutors her erstwhile classmate Ermengarde in order to gain access to the books she covets. For the protagonist of *A Little Princess*, however, storytelling is a means of reaching out to others, from her schoolmates to the young scullery-maid, Becky. Her penury does not change her personality; rather, it gives her an opportunity to uphold her principles even under unfavorable conditions. Hence, although in his capacity as solicitor Carmichael facilitates the custody transfer from Miss Minchin to Carrisford, Sara needs no extended sojourn with the Carmichael family in order to reacquaint herself with the rules for appropriate behavior. As soon as she realizes that Carrisford has been her secret benefactor and thus shares her belief that the rich have a duty to "scatter largesse" to the poor, she is ready to "kneel down by him, just as she used to kneel by her father when they were the dearest friends and lovers in the world" (56, 222).

The contrast between these Saras of different generations suggests a shift in the popular rhetoric of orphanhood over two decades. Arguably, the first Sara is more true to life than her successor, who despite her overindulgence at the hands of an inexperienced and doting father is "a very fine little person" who feels a natural imperative to be kind to her social or intellectual inferiors (21). It is telling that by 1905 Burnett apparently cannot bear to envision flaws in her protagonist. While the narrator informs us that the second Sara, at age seven, "did not care very much for other little girls" (9), this tendency toward unsociability (enforced by her consuming passion for her father) does not manifest itself in contempt for her peers, as it does in the earlier story. Rather, "there was something nice and friendly about Sara, and people always felt it" (28); known for her good nature, she is unfailingly patient and loving toward her satellites and forbearing toward her rivals. Burnett gives us no grounds on which to criticize the later Sara. Whether as heiress, as despised orphan, or as adoptee, she is an intellectual, moral, and emotional phenomenon, a child born to instruct and delight her comrades and caregivers alike. What child reader would not view her with awe? And what adult reader would not wish to take in such a child and shower her with love rather than with chores?

But the criticism that Burnett withholds from the "princess" Sara has become finds other targets. If the fiction discussed in Chapter 2 generally concentrates its fire on the very poor and the unusually wealthy, by the turn of the century middle-class authors are readier to address the faults of their own kind. Specifically, Burnett charges that the merchant class is often so spiteful and smug as to be impervious to what a natural social healer such as Sara has to offer. The most significant characters added in the 1905 version are Becky; Lavinia Herbert, Sara's chief rival within the school; and four-year-old Lottie Legh, the youngest of the boarders. All function to identify the inadequacies and failings of the bourgeoisie. Fourteen-year-old Becky, herself presumably an orphan, has apparently been hired not merely to carry coal scuttles but also to provide a vent for the collective ill-temper of the school staff, from Miss Minchin to the cook. Sara's kindness to her, which turns into a truer fellow-feeling after her father's death and her own precipitous slide down the social ladder, points up the coldness and callousness displayed by Miss Minchin and the "dull, matter-of-fact young people" she teaches (95).

Moreover, while Becky has neither beauty nor intellect to offer, she has the insight to see instantly that the proper response to Sara is "a sort of adoration" (54) and the loyalty to remain true to her idol, even to the extent of jeopardizing her own position. We see these marks of emotional promise in neither Miss Minchin nor the vast majority of the pupils; accordingly, Becky is permitted to join Sara in the Carrisford ménage, while Miss Minchin and her young ladies lose access to the ideal child whom they have failed to appreciate. And Becky is "delighted" by her new role as Sara's maid (237). If Carrisford will never adopt her because she drops her aitches and lacks Sara's aristocratic charisma, her rise from dogsbody to trusted upper servant nonetheless provides her with a domestic comfort and emotional satisfaction not vouchsafed to her wealthier contemporaries at the Select Seminary. It would seem that the lower classes and the upper—the very groups criticized by earlier fiction—may make common cause, while the once-virtuous middle may deservedly be shut out from Paradise.

Functioning as a demi-Minchin within the ranks of the schoolgirls is Lavinia, the oldest and least likable of the pupils. Lavinia is intolerant toward her juniors, catty about Sara (of whom she is jealous), and class-conscious without being ladylike. Sarcastic and spiteful, she speaks priggishly of duty when she tattles to the headmistress in order to get Sara in trouble. In short, she shares Miss Minchin's worst qualities: hypocrisy, narrow-mindedness, snobbery, and malice. But Burnett hints that Lavinia's snobbery and faultfinding come from her mother, who (sniffs Lavinia) "wouldn't like *me* to [tell stories to servant girls]" (48) and "says that way of [Sara's] of pretending things is silly" and that "she will grow up eccentric" (37). The bourgeois school, in short, is not the only institution likely to perpetuate the failings of the middle class. The seminary's shortcomings are the more distressing because the bourgeois family works the same way. It is no surprise that Sara devotes herself to observing, voyeuristically, the happy domesticity on display within the Carmichael household: within this novel, family jollity is rare.

For Burnett continues the exposé of family inadequacies begun by the orphan fiction of an earlier day. If the kind of mother represented by Mrs. Herbert and Miss Minchin (who stands in loco parentis to her charges) is fatally flawed, Lottie's and Ermengarde's cases show that the bourgeois father is also not beyond criticism. After her mother's death, "Lottie had been sent to school by a rather flighty young papa who could not imagine what else to do with her. . . . As the child had been treated like a favorite doll or a very spoiled pet monkey or lap-dog ever since the first hour of her life, she was a very appalling little creature" (38–39). Since a similar point might be made of Captain Crewe's efforts at paternity, which have involved showering his daughter with luxuries and surrounding her with servants who "gave her her own way in everything" (8), it is a mark of Sara's virtue that she has not turned into just such an "appalling little creature" as Lottie. As Mr. Legh has washed his hands of child rearing, it is left for Sara to take care of Lottie, just as she has earlier taken care of her own father; Captain Crewe's pet name for her, "the little missus," acknowledges her status as the real adult in the family.

But Mr. St. John, who unlike Mr. Legh and Captain Crewe seems to have reached years of discretion, is also no paragon of paternity. A clever man, he finds his daughter Ermengarde's stupidity maddening, so that he has browbeaten and criticized her until she "would do anything desperate to avoid being left alone in his society for ten minutes" (33). While the protagonist of *Sara Crewe* shares Mr. St. John's disdain for Ermengarde's slowness—"'He will like it, I dare say, if you learn anything in any way,' said Sara. 'I should, if I were your father'" (27)—the protagonist of *A Little Princess* "always felt very tender of Ermengarde, and tried not to let her feel too strongly the difference between being able to learn anything at once, and not being able to learn anything at all" (172). Under Sara's tutelage, Ermengarde is able to acquire some of the information that her father has so signally failed to din into her.

Indeed, one of Sara's major functions in the later novel is to repair adult omissions and inadequacies. She provides for Becky, mothers Lottie, and instills in Ermengarde a modicum of both facts and self-esteem. During her father's lifetime, Sara takes her dead mother's place as his "comrade" and "companion" (16, 10)—even, as we have seen, his "lover": it is their plan that when she finishes her education, she will act as his hostess and housekeeper. Their parting, at which she tells him, "'I know you by heart. You are inside my heart.' And they put their arms round each other and kissed as if they would never let each other go" (17), has the same adult overtones that characterize the wardrobe he buys her, full of ostrich feathers, ermine, and Valenciennes lace (14). Finally, when she moves in with Carrisford, it takes her only a month to heal him of the invalidism imposed by the Indian climate and a guilty conscience. By the standards of this narrative, Sara's emotional competence is more than adult.

But while her other good works have required her to take the initiative and use her talents for creativity and maturity, her miracle cure of Carrisford demands only that she accept the gifts that he showers upon her. If Sara herself is more than a commodity, her worth is signaled by the number and cost of the commodities that she ultimately receives. And from Carrisford's standpoint, even Sara's personality matters less than her role as the object of his generosity and remorse for his part in her father's death. Carrisford's recovery begins when he first starts acting as Sara's anonymous benefactor, and escalates as soon as it becomes clear that he can devote his life to making her happy. Sara's greatest achievement, then, is not her ability to pinch-hit for absent or inadequate parents, but her transformation of one of these missing men into an ideal father. Note, too, that "ideal" has seemingly become identical with "indulgent," which is perhaps one reason why nabobs such as Carrisford and Ralph Crewe are portrayed more sympathetically than the merely comfortably off Mr. St. John. We are a long way from the ethos of *The Wide, Wide World,* in which good fathers devote themselves to disciplining and training their charges. Orphans such as Sara have no need of molding; they demand only love.

Thus the narrative, which devotes so much space to criticizing families that have gone wrong, suggests at the same time that family is the ultimate therapy. If the Select Seminary and its inmates stand for all that can go wrong with domesticity, the Carmichaels and the newly formed Carrisford family indicate what domesticity at its best can accomplish. What really ails Carrisford, arguably, is childlessness, and his adoption of Sara—his co-opting of the domestic duties of his own former schoolmate Ralph Crewe, which both men define as the unlimited indulgence and adoration of their "little princess"—is the only answer to his woes. In short, Burnett's point is not only that the dependent child has a right to domestic bliss even when cold-hearted respectability (personified in Miss Minchin) seeks to deny her claim, but also that the happy ending for both child and adoptive parent requires the child to live a life of leisure.

This ending dramatically redefines the usual role of the real-life orphan of this era. On one level, Sara's fall and rise symbolically represent both the emotional devastation felt by the child suddenly deprived of love and the possibility of healing that devastation via sentimental adoption. But just as few ten-year-old drudges outside the pages of fiction were lost heiresses, few could expect to be adopted for sentimental purposes at so advanced an age. To be sure, Burnett complicates her idyll by showing that the socially inferior orphans Becky and Anne (a street child) must continue to earn their own livings instead of undergoing transformations as fabulous as Sara's. Still, even Becky and Anne are assured of good treatment and stability at last, and it is Anne's future as much as Sara's that is the focus of the end of the novel. Moreover, they too make important emotional contributions to the families that expand to take them in. Even the flotsam and jetsam of urban society, evidently, may now hope not merely for congenial employment but also for affection—and affection received as well as affection given.

The differences between Sara as she was originally drafted and the transformed Sara of 1905 help to highlight the increased power that the sentimental approach to orphanhood gained in the interim. While Fauntleroy, a half-orphan, certainly functions to change the adults around him, much of the authority in this narrative belongs to his mother, who uses him as a stalking-horse in her effort to ameliorate the lot of the poor. The 1888 Sara has her philanthropic tendencies, instilled by her own ill-treatment and expressed in sharing her meager supply of buns with the beggar Anne when she herself is famished, but her effect on her environment is much less than that of her later namesake. Somewhat similarly, while the eleven-year-old protagonist of "Little Saint Elizabeth," published in *St. Nicholas* in December 1888 and January 1889, devotes herself to good works in an effort to follow the example of her first guardian, her Aunt Clotilde, Burnett presents Elizabeth's benevolence not as an indication of moral authority but rather as a sign of the orphan's difference from the child with two parents. Clotilde, a "marble saint" who engages in her charitable activities with cold fanaticism and who has no softness to give to her niece, dresses the little girl in quasi-monastic garb and pushes her into premature adulthood; from toddlerhood onward, Elizabeth has no recourse but to model herself on her aunt in a fruitless effort to extort affection from her (134). When Clotilde dies, Elizabeth finds herself still more adrift emotionally, as she must move from Normandy to New York City and from asceticism to sybaritic luxury as the ward of her playboy uncle, Bertrand. Alienated by Bertrand's "easy, pleasure-loving life" and conscious that her charitable interests bore him, Elizabeth dreads him, while he in turn laughs, "I am half afraid of her" (135).

But while the child was able to adapt to Clotilde's ways because she had grown up with them, she finds it harder as a preadolescent to bridge the gap between herself and Bertrand. Hence she clings to her former life, preferring her "quaint black serge robe" to the fashionable garments that her uncle provides, and pleading with him to send money to her former village to alleviate a plague of illness and failed crops that the inhabitants are suffering. When he refuses, she sees no alternative but to sell her jewels (without asking permission) and to bestow the proceeds upon the needy of New York, who, she has gleaned from the dinner-table conversation of one of Bertrand's more serious-minded friends, are even worse off than the average Normandy peasant. Not surprisingly, her search for a purchaser is fruitless, but she succeeds in finding a plenitude of poor people—whose speech marks them as Irish—when she wanders into a slum neighborhood. There she gives her fur cloak to a plausible beggar, collapsing minutes later from a severe cold just as Bertrand and Dr. Norris, his philanthropic friend who is showing him around the city's worst neighborhoods, encounter her. The cold develops into an illness of some weeks, and Dr. Norris is the attending physician, providing Elizabeth with a nurturing and sympathetic caregiver at last. Between them, the doctor and the child convert Bertrand to charitable giving, while the two men in turn persuade Elizabeth to lead "a more natural and childlike life" (208). Mutual affection springs up between uncle and niece, and everyone lives happily ever after.

Susan Gannon sets this tale in the context of *St. Nicholas*'s effort to "encourag[e] children to be generous to the poor, but . . . moderately and carefully under adult supervision" (279). In this sense, we might see it as a quasi-parable in which the fruits of Elizabeth's misguided efforts to sacrifice her jewels and cloak suggest both that giving up the commodities that mark her as an aristocrat risks her very life (in a way, these possessions are her identity) and that she cannot have the love she craves unless she can convince Bertrand that parenthood requires spending more than money. But we might also consider it in the context of other orphan stories of the late 1880s, which typically exhibit less desire to idealize the parentless child than the tales that would become so prominent in the early 1900s. Elizabeth is sweet natured and virtuous, to be sure, but she is also warped and neurotic, made so not by nature but by her early bereavement and consequent unusual upbringing. If Bertrand needs her to inject seriousness into his "light, gay nature," she stands in at least as much need of discovering "that there were in the world innocent, natural pleasures which should be enjoyed" (208). Moreover, since Bertrand is as extravagant in his charity as in his luxuries, and even at story's end cares more for the latter than for the former, it is plain that the adoptive parent's effect on the child is greater than the child's effect on the adoptive parent. Elizabeth may be a "saint," but she is not the kind of saint who works miracles. Her task is less to remedy the failings of the adults than to adjust to them.

But although the Burnett orphan does not reach her full moral authority until 1905, we may nonetheless see significance in this author's fondness for writing about wealthy adoptees: the future peer Fauntleroy, the heiresses Sara and Elizabeth. For one thing, their fortunes contribute to their picturesqueness (always a plus for the creator of the Fauntleroy hairstyle and velvet suit), permitting Burnett to present them as luxury items, beautifully finished for public veneration. At the same time, the money symbolizes a certain social power, real in the cases of the charismatic Fauntleroy and Sara, longed for by the less potent Elizabeth.[5] It is significant that the figure of the orphaned aristocrat is rare in fiction before 1880. We have encountered it in Mary Mapes Dodge's *Donald and Dorothy* and in *The Wide, Wide World*'s revelation that Ellen Montgomery comes from a titled family, but not elsewhere; even Horatio Alger's Tattered Tom, like E.D.E.N. Southworth's Capitola Black, combines the inherited wealth of which she is ignorant with the manners of a street arab.

That the fictional orphan's socioeconomic status rises as we approach the Progressive Era suggests the increased value assigned to children at this time. Tales about destitute youths who turn out to be long-lost heirs proliferate after *Tattered Tom;* examples include the *St. Nicholas* serials "Jenny's Boarding-House" (1887), by James Otis [Kaler], in which a group of newsboys adopts a foundling later revealed as the future owner of "some fine houses and a lot of money" (784), and Wells's *The Story of Betty,* in which an Irish teenager moves from orphanage brat to servant to millionaire and uses her new wealth to buy herself a surrogate family, finally becoming reunited with her biological mother. Sometimes the acquisition of money precedes the acquisition of love, or vice versa, and sometimes the two occur simultaneously, but in either event narratives are newly likely to focus on the appreciation of the orphan, on his or her place at the center of a tangle of passionate emotion. No longer are displaced working-class children consistently depicted as social dangers to be made respectable by others' charity and their own hard work—even though such figures still abound in contemporaneous nonfiction.

Little Princes: The Orphan Boy as Savior

Rather, orphan tales of this period may suggest that working-class children are capable of carrying out reclamation projects of their own. This section focuses upon two representative boy orphans, both of whom serve the function recommended for the adopted child in articles such as Patterson's "Giving Babies Away": they fill the vacuum left by a death in the adoptive family. What distinguishes the orphan-train novel *Big Brother* (1893), by Annie Fellows Johnston, author of the popular Little Colonel series, and Kate Douglas Wiggin's *Timothy's Quest* (1890) from the foundlings Patterson advertises is that the protagonists are considerably older than the babies and toddlers so readily placed by the Guild of the Infant Savior. Both boys have younger siblings, identified within the texts as likelier prospects for sentimental adoption because of their age—an accurate observation, since then as now, prospective parents considered younger children more easily integrated into the family. The authors critique this view, however, making plain that the older children are not only more deserving than the younger ones but also better equipped (by virtue of their greater maturity) to provide the spiritual healing that the adults need. Unlike Sara Crewe, Johnston's and Wiggin's heroes come from modest or unknown stock; they are not the social superiors of their patrons. But the narratives use the fact that at first glance these boys appear entirely unsuitable for sentimental adoption to criticize not the boys, but the assumptions that cause observers to make such misjudgments.

Johnston's novel begins with a description of the passengers on the orphan train. While the entire carload of children is attractive, being "wonderfully merry and good-natured" (4), three-year-old Robin and his ten-year-old brother, Steven, are particularly taking: Robin has "a face so unusually beautiful" that two adult fellow passengers "utte[r] an exclamation of surprise" (2), while Steven is described as "grave and sweet," with a "finely shaped head" and a "sensitive mouth" (5). In the context of the 1890s, these physical descriptions are clearly intended to assure readers of the boys' good breeding. The oldest of the orphans, a Cockney girl, points out to the sympathetic Mrs. Estel that the other orphan-train riders need no pity because "The 'omes they're going to [will] be a sight better than the 'omes they've left behind" (10), sites of deprivation and abuse. Significantly, however, Steven and Robin are not the offspring of alcoholics and sadists but the sons of a father killed in a railroad accident and a mother who died of the shock (15). Their former home is no squalid tenement but a "little white cottage in New Jersey" noteworthy for "the peach-trees that bloomed around the house" and "the beehive in the garden" (19). The boys' good heredity, good looks, and good diction (no lower-class dialect here) identify them to Mrs. Estel and the reader alike as a peculiarly "safe" type of orphan, one in whom discerning adults ought to take an interest. Like Patterson in "Giving Babies Away," Johnston is establishing a desirable provenance in order to show that her subjects merit sentimental adoption.

But she also establishes that such placements are not readily come by. The rest of the story concerns Steven's struggle to find a suitable home for his brother and himself. Unlike the real-life Children's Aid Society, the "Aid Society" that has the boys in its care arranges homes for its wards before it puts them on the trains;[6] having rejected several foster parents because these placements would require separating the brothers, it has compromised by agreeing that both children will go temporarily to a farmer named Dearborn. While Dearborn and his wife intend to keep Steven to help with the market gardening, Robin is to go to the Dearborns' childless married daughter, who is "so charmed with Robin's picture that she want[s] to adopt him" as soon as her new house is ready (16). In other words, one brother is to serve a utilitarian function, the other an emotional one. This disposition of the boys becomes more complex after they have spent some weeks with the Dearborns. We learn that Robin has endeared himself to the elderly couple, who would like to keep him for sentimental purposes if they could afford such a luxury, while the "rough," "coarse" man who is Robin's prospective father "thinks it's all foolishness to get such a young one. He's willing to take one big enough to do the chores, but he doesn't want to feed and keep what 'ud only be a care to 'em" (45, 35). Meanwhile, while the narrator assures us that Steven is no drudge, his tasks include feeding turkeys, herding cows, picking vegetables, and—during the hired girl's vacation—"washing dishes, kneading dough, sweeping and dusting." Despite the Dearborns' representation to the Aid Society that Steven will receive an education, he does not attend school (34).

Steven himself does not object to the uses to which he is put. On the contrary, he is horrified when he overhears a conversation that suggests that he may be a "burden" to his caretakers, and he fantasizes about running away with Robin and supporting himself and his brother by becoming an itinerant chore boy (36). He fears, however, that the Dearborns' son-in-law Arad Pierson, "that black-browed, heavy-fisted man," will offer Robin cruelty in place of the love that is his due (45). Thus he accepts the premise that ten-year-old orphans are natural workers and three-year-old orphans natural pets. But Johnston's narrative denies the validity of this custom, at least in the case of such well-bred and desirable children as Steven and Robin.

Instead, Steven inadvertently wins himself, as well as his brother, a sentimental adoption. After Robin is sent off to the Piersons while Steven is briefly absent in town,[7] Steven seeks help from his erstwhile traveling companion. We learn that since their last meeting, Mrs. Estel's adored only daughter has died; she sees Steven as a potential substitute, and offers to adopt him. It is significant that it is Steven whom she wants, not Robin: "Steven, she felt, would be a comfort to her, but Robin could only be a care" (47–48). The older boy proves his unselfishness, and thus his desirability, by asking her to accept Robin in his place. Inevitably, the Estels determine to take both boys, "for little Dorothy's sake" (55), a decision facilitated by the Piersons' discovery that Robin is "so unmanageable and so different from what they expected that they were glad to get rid of him" and by the probability that Mr. Dearborn will be giving up his farm (56). For the poorer foster parents, in short, Robin turns out to have no sentimental value and Steven no use value. But for the wealthy Estels, who don't need a chore boy, Steven can be a "dear little comfort" (57) and Robin an amusement to lighten their grief.

Moreover, that Steven's future wealth is now assured guarantees as well the future of other orphans yet to come. The tale ends as Steven dreams "of the time when he should be a man, and could gather into the great house he meant to own all the little homeless ones in the wide world; all the sorry little waifs that strayed through the streets of great cities, that crowded in miserable tenements, that lodged in asylums and poorhouses" (58). The Estels' adoption of an orphan who shares their class standing (despite his lack of money) will thus enable the adult Steven to adopt other children who share his orphanhood, despite their more checkered background. Like Sara Crewe's largesse to the beggar girl Anne, magnified when Sara founds a permanent breadline in which Anne will take over Sara's erstwhile task of distributing buns to waifs, Steven's resolve suggests that erstwhile neediness encourages a philanthropic bridging of the divide between socioeconomic groups. In this equation, orphans will always have a moral advantage over more fortunate children. Small wonder, then, that even in childhood they are natural-born reformers, bringing happiness to any adult willing to open his or her heart to them.

By the 1890s, this premise had become an archetype in popular fiction. The plot of *Big Brother* is by no means unique; we find it in a number of sentimental novels of the period—novels that, like *Fauntleroy* and *The Wide, Wide World* before them, were not read exclusively by children. Hence

Wiggin's *Timothy's Quest* (1890) bears the subtitle *A Story for Anybody, Young Or Old, Who Cares to Read It*. A prolific author for both children and adults, Wiggin produced textbooks, manuals on Froebelism and the kindergarten movement, romantic novels, and girls' books. *Timothy's Quest* is unusual in her oeuvre in having a male protagonist, and one of the qualities that this novel shares with *Big Brother* is that both stories arrogate to the male orphan virtues, such as selflessness, nurturance, and sensitivity, that the gender stereotypes of the day usually assigned to the female. With its new connotations of pathos and moral superiority, however, orphanhood even for boys had taken on a feminine aura not present in the works of, say, Alger and Twain.

For in Wiggin's story as in Johnston's, we again have a noble and underappreciated ten-year-old boy, Timothy Jessup, who gives himself the task of finding a home for a more obviously attractive toddler, this time a girl named Gay. The two have been fellow inmates of a baby farm whose proprietor has recently died. To prevent the neighbors from sending Gay to the Home of the Ladies' Relief and Protection Society, Timothy improvises his own orphan train in order to get "to the 'truly' country, where . . . I can get a mother for Gay; somebody to 'dopt her and love her till I grow up a man and take her to live with me" (18–19). The threat of separation, the emphasis on emotion, and the vision of the child struggling with nearly insurmountable obstacles combine to establish *Timothy's Quest* as melodrama from the outset.

Timothy's origins are murkier than those of Steven in *Big Brother*; of his past life, he remembers only "a long journey in a great ship, a wearisome illness of many weeks,—or was it months?—when his curls had been cut off, and all his memories with them; then there was the Home [an orphanage in which he had been placed]; then there was Flossy [the baby-farmer], who came to take him away" (31). As for Gay, her antecedents are still less promising, as she was "Born in misery, and probably in sin, nurtured in wretchedness and poverty" (29). No matter; the two are natural aristocrats. Alone among the denizens of the novel, Timothy does not speak in dialect or drop his final g's. He also has "gentle manners, which must have been indigenous, as they had certainly never been cultivated; and although he had been in the way of handling pitch for many a day, it had been helpless to defile him, such was the essential purity of his nature" (27). To match the poetic, philosophical, and aesthetically refined Timothy, Gay is described as a Wordsworthian baby: "'with [sic] trailing clouds of glory' had she come, from God who was her home . . . heaven lay about her still, stronger than the touch of earth" (29–30).

Like Steven, however, Timothy defines himself as a worker and his charge as a luxury article. He expects to have to support himself, unless by some chance the "'truly' country" can provide enough mothers to go around, but sees Gay in terms of her attractiveness. Indeed, he seeks to enhance her marketability by making the most of her beauty: "I can never find a mother for her if she's too dirty. . . . And if I don't take the Japanese umbrella she will get freckled, and nobody will adopt her" (19, 23). Dirt and freckles, of course, had lower-class connotations, so that in preserving Gay's complexion Timothy is hoping to present her as an aristocrat among orphans, one who deserves a mother rather than a mere employer. He takes no such pains about his own appearance, and when he finds what looks like a suitable home for Gay at the residence of middle-aged spinster Avilda Cummins, he points out that while Miss Avilda "could n't find [another prospective adoptee] half as dear and as pretty as she is . . . you need n't have me too, you know, unless you should need me to help take care of her" (52).

Timothy's assessment of their relative chances of adoption initially proves correct. While Miss Avilda is proof against both the boy's salesmanship and the baby's charms, she agrees to take the children temporarily because the unused maternal instincts of her longtime servant and friend respond to "the wheedlesome bit of soft humanity" that is Gay: "At the . . . helpless, clinging touch of the baby arm about her neck . . . old memories and new desires began to stir in Samantha Ann Ripley's heart. In short, she had met the enemy, and she was theirs!" (59). Other townspeople also find Gay appealing, so that eventually she has multiple homes to choose from; still, no one seems to want her protector, even as a chore boy, and Miss Avilda resolves to keep Gay but to return Timothy to the orphanage. By this point in the narrative, however, Timothy's attractiveness, more subtle than Gay's, has worked its own magic. Samantha insists that he is so deserving that she will adopt him herself. Moreover, when Timothy runs away, leaving a note filled with kisses for all, because he fears being sent back to the orphanage, Miss Avilda's conscience revolts against her, and she finds Timothy and begs him to become her son. The household is instantly transformed for the better, as "a love of all things seemed to have crept into the hearts of its inmates, as if some beneficent fairy of a spider were spinning a web of tenderness all about the house, or as if a soft light had dawned in the midst of great darkness and was gradually brightening into the perfect day" (194). Samantha, indeed, patches up a rift with a former lover and marries him, abjuring spinsterhood under the stimulus of surrogate motherhood.

Wiggin's point is not that becoming a parent will always tap the dammed-up selflessness and tenderness in the adult heart, but rather that there exist particular children, rare and beautiful spirits, who will have this effect on their caregivers.[8] While she implies that Gay's infectiously blithe disposition is an accident of nature rather than a function of her birth or upbringing, Timothy's displacement appears to have intensified his native gentleness, sympathy, and sense of responsibility. In other words, his good qualities flourish not despite his low status and dubious origin, but at least in part because of them. This orphan is superior to the respectable child, and the narrator repeatedly comments upon the tragedy of such virtue being overlooked: "Plenty of wistful men and women would have thanked God nightly on their knees for the gift of such a son; and here he was, sitting on a tin can, bowed down with family cares, while thousands of graceless little scalawags were slapping the faces of their French nurse-maids and bullying their parents, in that very city.—Ah me!" (28–29). As Avilda's odd-job man says, adopting Timothy and Gay means that one "need n't resk the unsartainty o' gittin' married 'n' raisin' [one's] own; 'n' . . . would n't stan' no charnce o' gittin' any as likely as these air, if [one] did" (98).

As a misprized and stainless waif, "bowed down" by concern for others and "a natural 'kingdom of heavenite'" (22), Timothy is a veritable Child of Sorrows in a story that—like so many orphan tales of this era—is essentially a conversion narrative. Wiggin couches her narrative in a mixture of Down East dialect and biblical cadences. Phrasings suggesting the religious and mystical lard descriptions of Miss Avilda's state of mind as she draws emotionally nearer to Timothy. Thus when she offers to adopt him and he hugs her in love and thankfulness, "in that sweet embrace of trust and confidence and joy, the stone was rolled away, once and forever, from the sepulchre of Miss Vilda's heart, and Easter morning broke there" (188). Earlier, she has dreamed about climbing a mountain range while a child pleads to be carried; each time she refuses, and each time she finds another mountain in her path, until

> At last she cried in despair, "Ask me no more, for I have not even strength enough for my own needs!" . . . And the child said, "I will help you"; and straightway crept into her arms and nestled there as one who would not be denied. . . . And as she climbed the weight grew lighter and lighter, till at length the clinging arms seemed to give her peace and strength . . . and when she neared the crest of the highest mountain she felt new life throbbing in her veins and new hopes stirring in her heart, and she remembered no more the pain and weariness of her journey. . . . And all at once a bright angel appeared to her and traced the letters of a word upon her forehead and took the child from her arms and disappeared. . . . [A]nd the word she traced on Miss Vilda's forehead was "Inasmuch"! (73)

The New Testament references in both passages ("Inasmuch" is shorthand for Christ's teaching in Matthew 25:40, "Inasmuch as ye have done it unto one of the least of these my brethren, ye have done it unto me") are an important element in Wiggin's rhetorical strategy. Timothy represents infinite love and infinite forgiveness—not only his own forgiveness of Miss Avilda's "partiality" for Gay, which, after all, he shares (177), but also divine forgiveness of Avilda's rigidly righteous treatment of her beloved younger sister, Martha, after Martha gave birth to an illegitimate child. Martha's crime of love is ennobled within the narrative, as both the angel in Avilda's dream and Timothy himself have Martha's eyes (73, 177); hence Wiggin rehabilitates real-life foundlings, whose presumed illegitimacy, as

Patterson's article suggests, was often a source of anxiety for prospective adoptive parents.

A far graver sin than unsanctioned parenthood is that of coldheartedness, whether manifested by Flossy the baby-farmer, the social system that denies orphans parental care, or well-to-do spinsters who refuse to succor the orphan at their gates. What Beverly Crockett suggests of *Anne of Green Gables,* namely that it exposes and critiques adults' "lingering suspicions and prejudices against children who were placed out" (58), is equally true of *Timothy's Quest* and its fellows. As Samantha tells her employer, "the Lord's intention [in bringing Timothy to them] was to give us a chance to make our callin' 'n' election sure, 'n' we can't do that by turnin' our backs on His messenger, and puttin' of him ou'doors!" (164). Timothy's function, in short, is not the role that Samantha first assigns to him, being "handy round the house . . . pickin' up chips, 'n' layin' fires, 'n' what not" (103), but the salvation of Miss Avilda's soul. Under the circumstances, the question of who is benefiting whom is more complex than Avilda originally assumes.

The Job of the Adoptive Parent: Negative and Positive Examples

In the stories considered thus far in this chapter, adoption is the happy ending, just as conventional romances close with the heroine's acceptance of the hero's marriage proposal. We are to assume that all parties live happily ever after. But this trajectory is not the pattern of all Progressive Era adoption narratives, and thus it may be illuminating to conclude this chapter by discussing two novels in which informal adoptions, one based on ties of blood and the other on ties of sentiment, occur comparatively early in the story. Between them, Wiggin's *Rebecca of Sunnybrook Farm* (1903) and its near contemporary, Gene Stratton-Porter's *Freckles* (1904), display strikingly similar views of what constitutes an appropriate parental response to an older adopted child. The rhetorical strategies of the two works invert each other, however, not only inasmuch as Wiggin's title character is a ten-year-old girl and Porter's a young man of nearly twenty, but also because Porter's novel sketches an ideal adoptive father, while Wiggin's may be read as a cautionary tale about the consequences of being an inadequate adoptive mother.

Like a still more famous adoption tale, the Canadian *Anne of Green Gables, Rebecca* is the story of a talented, energetic, and charismatic preteen. Here, the heroine's widowed mother is invited to send one of her children to be raised by her two spinster sisters. Mrs. Randall selects Rebecca as a daughter who can more easily be spared than some; consequently, Rebecca moves to her aunts' austere home, some miles from her mother's dilapidated farm, to receive the benefits of an education and the expectation of an inheritance. Miranda and Jane Sawyer have extended this offer as a way of helping their sister, whose marriage to a fascinating but weak and feckless man has left her with more liabilities than assets. In other words, all parties initially envision the informal adoption as a practical measure. But in the event, Rebecca becomes the source of "warmth and strength and life" in the Sawyer home (307), bringing the acrid Miranda to a condign if unspoken sense of her own failings. When, at seventeen, Rebecca—who has long since become the chief comfort and interest of all who are close to her—inherits Miranda's house, land, possessions, and social position, her prayer, "God bless Aunt Miranda; God bless the brick house that was; God bless the brick house that is to be!" (309), implies that the once impoverished adoptee will fill her benefactress's shoes better than Miranda herself did.

Jerry Griswold argues that after Rebecca demonstrates that she is not "all Randall," but rather has inherited social poise and competence from her Sawyer grandfather, "the child's further successes come at the expense of her aunt." "The trajectory of Rebecca's successes," he continues, "seem [sic] inversely proportional to Miranda's own fate," so that Rebecca's greatest triumph, her graduation from Wareham, coincides with Miranda's crippling stroke (76–77). That no similar fate overtakes the more sympathetic Aunt Jane, who has made Rebecca a confidante and a delight, suggests that the narrative is punishing Miranda for her inability to express her love for and pride in her niece. While Miranda does right by her ward morally and financially, she never gives Rebecca her due emotionally. Under Rebecca's influence, "A greater change had come over Jane than over any other person in the brick house": the spinster has become maternal, acting as Rebecca's partisan and "taking pride in Rebecca's improved appearance" (158). In contrast, absorbed by financial worries and in possession of a heart that "she had never used . . . for any other purpose than the pumping and circulating of blood" (30), Miranda remains to the end "well-nigh as gloomy and uncompromising in her manner and conversation as a woman could well be" (233). The strokes that eventually kill her mirror an inner paralysis long indicated by her reluctance to acknowledge her feelings for Rebecca.

If adoptive parents are to draw a moral from *Rebecca of Sunnybrook Farm*, then, they might conclude that providing room and board and an education and forbearing to turn a child into a drudge is not enough: one's real task, Wiggin suggests, is to love. Other authors evidently agreed, since many of the adoptive parents in contemporaneous fiction seem much more alive to their emotional responsibilities than is Miranda Sawyer. Porter's Mr. McLean in *Freckles* is one. When the title character, a one-armed Irish teenager of unknown parentage who has grown up in a Chicago orphanage, asks McLean for a job guarding the trees in the timberland leased by a lumber company, the field manager is at first reluctant to give such work to a disabled boy. But after Freckles tells his life story—one of emotional deprivation and constant rejection because his missing hand, removed immediately before his abandonment on the orphanage steps as a newborn, has rendered him unfit for adoption—McLean relents. Indeed, when he asks his new employee's name and is told, "I haven't any name. . . . but I am going to be your man and do your work, and I'll be glad to answer to any name you choose to call me" (13–14), McLean bestows on Freckles the name of his own father, "my ideal man," whom the younger McLean "loved . . . better than any other I have ever known." The impromptu baptism, sanctified by Freckles's tears, seals an equally impromptu adoption:

> "Thank you mightily," said Freckles. "That makes me feel almost as if I belonged, already."
> "You do," said McLean. "Until some one armed with every right comes to claim you, you are mine. Now, come and take a bath, have some supper, and go to bed." (14)

Since Freckles's job entails solitary work, walking trails in a two-thousand-acre tract of the Limberlost swamp, McLean is necessarily an absentee father. Nevertheless, the acceptance of paternal responsibility implied in the gift of the family name and in the parental tone of the instructions to "take a bath, have some supper, and go to bed" signals real concern on McLean's part, one that will eventually ripen into something more than a job offer: "I intend to take you to the city and educate you, and you are to be my son, my lad—my own son!" (108). Moreover, the remainder of the narrative provides Freckles with more and more family ties. His landlady, Mrs. Duncan, appoints herself his "mother" within a few weeks of their first meeting. After Freckles faces her "with a trace of every pang of starved mother-hunger he ever had suffered written large on his homely, splotched, narrow features" and cries, "Oh, how I wish you were my mother!" Mrs. Duncan responds that after "a man-child has beaten his way to life under the heart of a woman, she is mither to all men, for the hearts of mithers are everywhere the same. Bless ye, laddie, I am your mither!" (27–28). Freckles subsequently finds romance with a beautiful and well-bred girl whom he calls his Swamp Angel. Finally, at the end of the novel he also discovers blood kin in his uncle and aunt (who turn out to be wealthy Irish aristocrats) and learns his origin story, a pathetic tale of star-crossed lovers who sacrificed their lives to save their newborn baby after the explosion and fire that claimed his hand.

What these adoptive, biological, and romantic relationships have in common is that all are founded on love. McLean is never merely Freckles's employer, just as Mrs. Duncan is always more than a landlady; indeed, the revelation of McLean's feelings for the boy is given nearly as much weight as the boy's successful wooing of his future wife:

> "But why should you be doing that, sir?" he faltered.
> McLean slid his arm around the boy's shoulders and gathered him close.

"Because I love you, Freckles," he said simply.
Freckles lifted a white face. "My God, sir!" he whispered. "Oh, my God!" (108)

Similarly, the titled O'Mores are desperate to find their lost nephew in order to redress the emotional wrong perpetrated by Freckles's deceased grandfather, who disowned Freckles's father and refused to retrieve the baby from the orphanage; they burn to make up the arrears of love and care. And Freckles's actual parents have nothing in common with the hideously abusive parents of his imagination, who "would take a new-born baby and row over it, until it was bruised black, cut off its hand, and leave it out in a bitter night on the steps of a charity home, to the care of strangers" (10–11). He has, it transpires, been wrong to assume that his unknown history might constitute a gritty naturalistic novel about lower-class vice. Rather, the uplifting melodrama of the lost heir of innate virtue and noble parents is what is true.

Porter's strategy, in other words, is to begin with what the casual observer might write off as singularly unpromising human material, and to demonstrate over the course of the novel that this material is not only lovable but unusually lovable. Thus Freckles's Irishness turns out to mark him not as a member of a despised ethnic group, stereotyped by real-life adoption workers such as Brace as hard-drinking and relentlessly lower class, but as a member of the aristocracy: he is Terence Maxwell O'More of Dunderry House, County Clare, a man "richer than McLean" (331). His missing limb, which has prevented the orphanage from placing him out because adoption and fosterage were reserved at that time for the physically and mentally normal, makes him heroic: as the Angel points out, he has taken on a difficult task "single-handed" and won (306). And before its revelation, his past is no cause for concern even though he himself assumes that he comes from the worst possible background. On the contrary, the fineness of his character reveals to his friends that his heredity must be impeccable: "Thistles grow from thistles, and lilies from other lilies. . . . You are a lily, straight through. You never, never could have drifted from the thistle-patch" (306). Thus while Freckles's employment enables him to gather a family circle around himself and to establish his self-respect by coping with what would be "a trying job for a work-hardened man" (9), it is merely an outward manifestation of his innate nobility. Unlike the Alger hero, who is usually a thistle making his way into lilydom by dint of industry and economical habits, Freckles has to work only because circumstances have conspired to disguise his worth. The novel is an extended penetration of that disguise, an unveiling that implies that other waifs may also turn out to be lost princes—if they receive the love that will discern the diamond in the ash-heap.

The orphan fiction of the two decades under discussion in this chapter has much in common with the orphan fiction produced between 1850 and

1885, but also has significant differences. The earlier orphans tend to lead more down-to-earth lives. Alcott's Ben Brown is reunited with a father he has believed dead, but neither has been endowed with a fortune in the interim; Phebe Moore proves her worth and her right to a good marriage but does not turn out "to be 'somebody'" in a social sense, as her employers have sometimes fantasized. Susan Warner's Ellen Montgomery becomes an exemplary Christian, but her spiritual effect on those around her is markedly less powerful than the influence that her own religious preceptors have on her. Tom Sawyer and Huck Finn discover a fortune and become a nine-days' wonder in St. Petersburg, but their sudden acquisition of status has remarkably little lasting effect. And Alger's heroes aspire to join the middle classes as respectable salarymen or, at most, prosperous businessmen; unlike some real-life riders of the orphan trains, they do not rise to the level of state or territorial governor. In contrast, the later narratives typically cast a mantle of glamour around the orphan, turning their protagonists into aristocrats by bestowing upon them titles, fortunes, charisma, and/or astonishing talent. If the earlier tales typically suggest that orphans may turn out a credit to their benefactors by becoming steady, respectable, hard-working adults, the later tales often suggest that an orphan—whether remarkable for liveliness or sweetness, imaginative power or generosity—is so great a blessing that any right-minded adult should be only too grateful to have the chance to take one in. Like certain nonfiction texts of the day, they thus effectively market the sentimental approach to adoption.

In establishing that devotion is the correct adult response to an orphan, the later melodramatic tales present the displaced child as a luxury item to be appreciated rather than used. To be sure, many also explore the flaws of particular adoptive families, which err either in rearing children or in loving them aright—but they suggest simultaneously that the orphan's presence might correct these mistakes or inadequacies. In all these messages, orphan fiction expressed attitudes also evident in contemporaneous nonfiction commentary and social action surrounding dependent children.

4

Metaphor and the Displaced Child, 1886–1906

For the reformers and activists who proliferated during the Progressive Era (roughly, the 1890s through 1918), social action centered on children was especially important. The belief that "catching them young" was the key to extirpating delinquency, degeneracy, and poverty and to speeding the assimilation of immigrants had long flourished, as the orphan trains illustrate, but it peaked around 1900. New journals and organizations reflected a growing emphasis on the scientific dimensions of child study, which promised to produce physically, mentally, and morally healthy adults; Harvard Medical School began teaching pediatric medicine. Buoyed by the assurances of experts such as John Dewey and his teacher G. Stanley Hall, both new-style child rearing and the theorization of childhood participated in the effort to reshape American society for the "American century."

But children were not only interesting to Progressives on their own account; they were also useful as a rhetorical stalking-horse, a way of justifying political moves that might not otherwise succeed. As Matthew Crenson argues, "Progressive leaders knew they stood a greater chance of promoting their broader social reform agenda if they started with children" (qtd. Keiger 4). Because voters who were inclined to protest adult-centered programs as socialist might accept child-centered programs as humane, children occupied a prominent position within the reformist platform. The years from 1886 to 1906 witnessed campaigns whose purposes included ending child labor, extending the benefits of public schooling, founding day-care programs and free-lunch programs and playgrounds and public kindergartens, improving infants' health and parents' child-rearing skills, and establishing a separate juvenile justice system.

Sometimes this focus on childhood created a kinship with reformist experiments that at first appear to have little connection to adoption and foster care. A case in point is that of the settlement-house movement. Designed to promulgate particular values and domestic practices by establishing middle-class enclaves in working-class neighborhoods where women and men could model bourgeois life skills, the movement reached the United States from England in 1886. It might seem that the principal point of overlap with the child-welfare agenda was that scientific child rearing was a particular interest at Hull House, the most influential of the American settlement houses. But more subtly and more importantly, the movement resembled earlier, more overtly child-oriented campaigns to assimilate the marginalized into mainstream society. As part of a burgeoning campaign to shore up the working-class family, seeking via day nurseries and parenting classes to offer beleaguered adults an alternative to placing their children in orphanages (Youcha 142), the settlement house participated in the eventual reversal of the trend toward adoption and foster care. At the same time, by allowing the respectable to stand in a pseudo-parental, advisory capacity to the poor, often acculturating immigrants at second hand by addressing their children, the settlement house also mimicked foster care. While its clientele did not have to leave home to be saved, the movement nonetheless shared key elements of its philosophy with practices that sought to disassociate youngsters from their original backgrounds and upbringings, such as the Fresh Air Fund and, more permanently, the orphan trains.

That reformist systems of child placement might have influenced social experiments primarily involving adults suggests the force and pervasiveness of the rhetoric surrounding phenomena such as the orphan trains. But the displaced child had another role within Progressive Era social-welfare rhetoric as well, and it is that role with which this chapter will concern itself. I refer to the frequency with which Progressive Era commentators made the displaced child serve as a vehicle for the discussion of cultural anxieties that, like the settlement house, might not seem immediately relevant to child placement. We have seen in the popular texts examined in Chapter 3 how value was gradually added to such children: far from being the financial burdens to society that the "balance-sheet philanthropists" of the Reconstruction years assumed, the displaced children of turn-of-the-century orphan narratives are represented as lost heirs, native geniuses, jewels (in a typical bit of rhetoric, the woman who is privileged to teach Rebecca of Sunnybrook Farm calls her a "pearl"), even saviors. The contemporaneous social-welfare texts do not, with some exceptions, assign this kind of value to the children they discuss. Yet we might indulge in a moment's wordplay and suggest that as metaphors, these children become ever richer in that they embody ever more numerous meanings.

It is important to recognize that the Progressive Era's tendency to discuss distressing social situations covertly via discussions of displaced children did not preclude conducting the same debate more openly at the same time. On the contrary, the commentators who one week warned of the debilitating effects of certain kinds of factory work on displaced children might the next week warn of the identical effects that identical work could have on adults—and inasmuch as it embraced a larger group of subjects, the latter argument might appear today to be the more important. The purpose of this chapter, however, is not to suggest that the arguments involving displaced children were minor, but to identify and explore the significant rhetorical uses to which these children were put.

What follows, then, will study four regards in which displaced children provided a forum for debating issues that extended well beyond the question of what to do with the offspring of deceased, absent, incapacitated, or unfit parents. Each of these cases deals with a separate set of children: inmates of orphanages, "graduates" of orphanages, residents of alternative forms of congregate homes, and children who were the objects of controversial placements. The first three groups, of course, consisted of children who were not, at the time in question, either adopted or in foster care. Nevertheless, the social-welfare rhetoric that surrounded such children is relevant here not only because the relative merits of institutional care and placement in private homes were hotly debated at the turn of the century, so that commentary on the one usually involves explicit or implicit commentary on the other, but also because the two groups of children overlapped. In many regions, a stay in an orphanage often preceded home placement; conversely, some young people who left the orphanage for the workforce would have been veterans of unsatisfactory foster-care situations as well.

The Child in the Age of Mechanical Reproduction

One important meaning for the child-as-metaphor had to do with Americans' relationship to their increasingly machine-oriented and corporate society. Chapter 3 notes that popular Progressive Era texts often appealed to the masses by invoking the individuality of the displaced child. Although in real life he or she might have parents and siblings, both orphan fiction and the new journalism played to sentiment and melodrama by representing the child as a waif without friends or immediate family; the acquisition of community ties is the source of the happy ending. But contemporaneous texts dealing with the *institutionalized* displaced child, the youngster entrusted to an orphanage or other form of congregate care while awaiting a foster home, full-fledged employment, reclamation by biological family, or (less frequently) legal adoption, take a different tack. Here we see not melodrama so much as a parable of the machine age. That the institutionalized child is obsessively discussed in terms of loss of initiative and the sapping of personality, so that membership in a community is not the solution but the problem, suggests concerns that go beyond the question of how best to care for the children of the state. In effect, denizens of orphanages are being represented as casualties of mass production, but also as extreme examples of a malaise that seemed to be affecting society as a whole, in this era of what Woodrow Wilson termed "submerged" individuality (qtd. Hofstadter, *Age* 225).

To be sure, not all observers considered mass production inimical to humanity. The assumptions of sentimental melodramas such as those described in Chapter 3 were by no means universal; prominent authors of realistic novels, such as Hamlin Garland, campaigned against romanticism and what they considered excessive emotionalism. Their narratives might exhibit a positive attitude toward the mechanization of society. Martha Banta, for one, discerns in canonical fiction of the turn of the century the ideological imprint of efficiency experts such as Frederick Winslow Taylor and pioneers of factory production such as Henry Ford, whose "sound management methods" were to be applied within the home as well as within the workplace (10). Over the objections of figures from Henry James and Henry Adams to Herbert Hoover, supporters of this ideal—a group that included many writers and social reformers as well as business leaders—demanded a smooth-running mechanism characterized by cleanliness and order and providing the best possible services to the largest possible constituency. "Principles of collectivism, standardization, and rationalization" informed the manufacturing of products from automobiles to ready-made houses (Banta 227), but also permeated visions of domestic utopias[1] and of the "assembly-line process intended to transform [immigrant factory workers] into good citizens and loyal workers" and to lessen friction between the classes (275). Such principles sometimes also informed understandings of the displaced child in real life.

For in its capacity as engine for furthering assimilation, self-control, productivity, and other middle-class virtues, the factory shared the goals, if not the methods, of earlier child-savers such as Charles Loring Brace and the values of novelists of working orphanhood such as Horatio Alger and Edmund Morris. Industrial welfare programs sought to increase output by inculcating in workers the self-discipline and acceptance of structure to which the typical Alger hero becomes a convert, a discipline that was expected to improve society at large (Banta 110). As Samuel Haber writes in his classic *Efficiency and Uplift*, "The factory . . . was not only an instrument for the production of goods and profits, it was also a moral gymnasium for the exercise of character" (2). If in its full-blown form America's "efficiency craze" extended only from 1910 to 1917 (Haber 74), it cast long shadows both before and after this period; Taylor began his motion-study work in 1882. Joining hands with other innovations of the day (notably scientific child rearing), the ethos of scientific management is already apparent in many Progressive pronouncements at the end of the nineteenth century and the beginning of the twentieth, not least in the commentary on orphanages and their inhabitants.

A commitment to efficiency might seem to demand support for the orphanage system, where experts could rear job lots of children under hygienic conditions while inculcating manners and sentiments designed to lessen tensions between youthful outcasts and the dominant society. And, indeed, contemporaneous accounts of orphanages emphasize their hygiene and order, their discipline, their attention to job training—their resemblance, in short, to the factories that likewise sought to assimilate a largely immigrant population into a homogeneous and theoretically more virtuous "American" mass. A characteristic 1903 encomium from Thomas L. Kinkead, chaplain of a Catholic orphanage in Peekskill, New York, praises the "habits of cleanliness" instilled in the children, the standardizing influence of "the military drill, teaching promptness, neatness, obedience, and activity," the calisthenics and music lessons, the vocational education, the avoidance of alcohol and tobacco, and "The regularity of the discipline enforced by trained disciplinarians" (394–95). Moreover, congregate institutions were at their zenith around the turn of the century. Public and private, religious and secular, they were becoming both larger and more numerous.[2] LeRoy Ashby counts 247 new orphanages incorporated in the 1890s and 214 in the first decade of the 1900s (*Waifs* 13); Timothy Hacsi observes, "During the first three decades of the twentieth century, more children were cared for in orphan asylums than ever before," a byproduct of rapid population growth and urbanization.

Even so, Hacsi adds, we may simultaneously discern "a national consensus . . . among almost all child welfare reformers other than asylum managers," to the effect that "asylums should be used only for temporary care and as a last resort" (13). As the editors of *Charities* put it in 1903, the orphanage's role was increasingly as "a training place for subsequent adjustment to family life" ("Editorial" 377). Hard-line commentators denied that orphanages could inculcate the skills necessary to family life, since the world of the congregate institution was so different from normal domesticity. To some extent, such criticisms reflect changes in American child-rearing practice, which increasingly valued individuality in the form of spontaneity, "naturalness," and even mischief—all traits that do not further the smooth running of an institution. Clare McCausland compares the child-rearing philosophy of the Chicago Orphan Asylum in the nineteenth century with that outlined in Lydia Maria Child's *The Mother's Book* (1831), which stressed "unquestioning obedience," accepting one's station in life, developing neatness and order, eradicating carelessness, and occupying oneself with useful tasks so as to keep out of mischief (McCausland 45). For reasons of institutional convenience, this approach remained current in orphanages long after it had become outmoded in homes, dismaying turn-of-the-century critics who felt that "scientific" child care should be on the cutting edge.

Such anxieties had been brewing for some time. The early 1880s saw many expressions of concern about the presumed tendency of orphanages to extirpate individuality and inhibit character formation in an era in which, as T. J. Jackson Lears notes, "personal identity itself [was coming] to seem problematic" (32). During the period discussed in this chapter, organizations such as the National Children's Home Society, which originated in Illinois in 1883 to advance home placement at the expense of institutionalization, were gaining power and influence (Ashby, *Waifs* 31, 38). And no observer could long have remained in doubt about the Home Society's anti-collectivism, which was crucial to its founding, organization, and mission. Its potentially misleading name betokened a loose confederation of autonomous state societies, clustered particularly in the Midwest, South, and West, rather than a centralized bureaucracy. Within each state were districts with city and village advisory boards who consulted on appropriate homes for the children within their purview and conducted post-placement supervisory work, so that each placement was arranged on a local level.

Part of the Home Society's success came from its manipulation of images calculated to resonate with people who shared its distrust of impersonality. The organization was the brainchild of Martin Van Buren Van Arsdale, a minister who drew his inspiration from Brace but who found the group aspect of the orphan-train placements disturbing. In the words of Charles Henderson, a sociologist who was the Home Society's president in the early twentieth century, "To Dr. Van Ardsdale [*sic*] every child was an individual soul too precious to be massed with others" (610). A typical slogan quoted by LeRoy Ashby, "There's a child outside our door" (*Children* 89), reflects this philosophy syntactically through its use of singular nouns. And the mythology of the Home Society's beginnings likewise stressed the individual, even the amateurish, even though by the 1910s it had developed into a massive federation placing some four thousand children a year (Fearing 193). Henderson described how "the plucky pastor was forced to sell a patent window-fastener from house to house" in order to finance his lifework and how he "took the first little girl in his arms and carried her one hundred and eighty miles to place her in a selected home" (610). The Home Society's emphasis, both rhetorical and structural, on the local and the personal, its conviction that the private home would always be superior to the institution, reflected its resistance to mass production, its desire to see each child as unique rather than as a representative of a class.

Elsewhere, too, the trend was away from the group home. The Boston Children's Friend Society, founded in 1833, switched over in 1900 from committing children to asylums to placing them exclusively in private homes, citing the difficulty "of properly knowing and mothering a family of fifty or a hundred children" (Kingsley, "Substitution" 388). Similarly, the Boston Children's Aid Society (founded in 1864) closed two asylums in 1896 and 1899 so that it could put more of its energies into foster-home placement (Holloran 57). *Municipal Affairs*, reviewing a work by Homer Folks (then New York City's commissioner of charities and later secretary of the New York State Charities Aid Association), listed the "great development of the system of placing children out in families" as part of the improvement discernible in the treatment of such youngsters between 1802 and 1902 (Devine 295). Folks was not alone in arguing that even the child residing in a cottage-type institution (designed to mimic the family home) "is never supremely happy until he is placed in some humble home in the country in which he receives the individual and personal attention and care of his newly-found mother and father" ("Institution" 546). The stress on the "individual and personal" touch, the dismay at mass-produced child care, questioned goals such as efficiency and high production figures as inappropriate to child rearing. Standardization, of course, undermined what Warren Susman identifies as the new national impetus "to be unique, be distinctive, follow one's one feelings, make oneself stand out from the crowd" (280), all qualities celebrated in the fictional orphan of the era.

Thus in nonfiction commentary as in sentimental tales for children or the article by O'Hagan cited in Chapter 3, orphanages were criticized precisely for their production-line virtues: they were too hygienic, too efficient, too likely to subordinate the individual to the smooth running of the whole. Because such institutions lacked the "human element," children could not learn about family life, develop their emotional capacities, or reach normal maturity. Under what Henrietta Christian Wright called "the reduction to mechanical routine of all the ordinary offices of life," children became "dulled in faculty, unthinking, and dependent . . . [mere] 'number[s]'" (112). Indeed, as inmates of child-producing "factories," they turned into mechanical devices themselves, and this and other industrial metaphors recur in rhetoric of this sort. Henry Smith Williams's 1897 lament is typical: the congregate orphanage, he charged, makes the child "a part of a great machine whose working is never duplicated in the outside world. He is gradually moulded to fit his niche in this great machine until at last all spontaneity, independence, and individuality are well nigh pressed out of him. In a word, the institution training tends to make its recipient an automaton rather than a flesh and blood mortal" (407).

In short, while some commentators praised orphanages' purported ability to manufacture disciplined Americans from unpromising raw material (institutionalized children were presumed to come from homes that were at least temporarily nonfunctional, and many had foreign-born parents), others used their discussions of congregate care to protest an industrial ethos whose influence was widespread at the turn of the century. It is no accident that the fiction discussed in the preceding chapter often features protagonists who have lived, invariably unhappily, in a group setting before finding fulfillment within a family. Freckles's orphanage, Timothy's baby farm, Sara Crewe's boarding school are miserable places run by tyrants incapable of recognizing the worth of their charges. With its emphasis on emotion and individualism—the latter symbolized by marks of unusualness such as Freckles's one arm, Sara's and Rebecca's literary talents, or Timothy's spiritual gifts—the sentimental melodrama rejects the ethics of the more canonical industrial novel and complements the anti-orphanage rhetoric (itself a protest against the status quo) of social workers such as Folks and Williams. Yet while it is true, as Ashby argues, that popular novels reinforced "the increasingly negative public perception of asylums" (*Children* 87), we should remember that social workers were already objecting to orphanages on psychological and character-training grounds some years before the boom in anti-orphanage best sellers. For once, the professional child-savers were ahead of the curve.

National Exhaustion: The Displaced Child in the Factory

If the rhetoric discussed above uses displaced children in orphanages to warn of the perils of standardization, other texts use displaced children in the workforce to warn of national exhaustion. The enervation of the orphanage inmates imaged by Williams and his cohorts inverts the liveliness of the protagonists of Reconstruction orphan fictions. But this enervation is still more severe—and proportionately threatening to average Americans—in writings discussing children who have left the orphanage not for homes but for factory work, so that the image of the displaced child in the factory becomes propaganda for adoption and foster care. The turn-of-the-millennium American perception that children consigned to Asian orphanages may graduate to sweatshops encourages adoption by arousing public sympathy for the child; in contrast, Progressive Era rhetoric describing displaced children in a similar situation seems calculated to arouse anxieties about the health of the nation at large, anxieties that adoption may alleviate.

Manufacturing was happy to accept displaced children, especially since such employees did not ask a grown man's wage. Indeed, many parents relinquished custody of their offspring to organizations such as the Children's Aid Society primarily because these agencies would find the children work, whether in factories or on farms (Zelizer 173). But while placement experts and other commentators often represented farm work in a positive light (not coincidentally, it was one of the last areas of child labor to be regulated), stressing the healthfulness of outdoor activity and the emotional importance of being bonded to the land, factory work received considerable negative press. Teenage farm hands could be said to be in foster care, having been placed with an individual farmer who stood in loco parentis; teenage factory workers were at once prematurely independent quasi-adults and child sacrifices to an impersonal Moloch. The farm was home as well as workplace, while the factory was home's antithesis. Thus the displaced children—and, by implication, the adults—who entered the latter arena were risking both body and soul.

The distinction between "good" and "bad" work was usually framed in terms of the work's perceived ultimate social effects, which often extended into delicate areas. Thus Jane Addams warned that too early an entrance into the workforce would debilitate children and render them unemployable as adults; hiring children was poor economic practice, since youngsters "subjected to premature labor are handed over to the future in an abnormal condition. They are deprived of education as well as depleted physically, and they enter the life of the community handicapped in every way" (120). The key words here, "abnormal" and "depleted," echo the proscriptions of the day against allowing children to participate in other adult activities, such as drinking, smoking, engaging in sexual behavior, or (in the case of girls) undertaking difficult intellectual tasks. Since turn-of-the-century medicine deemed the physical mechanisms of young people substantially different from those of adults, whose developmental stage was behind them, excessive activity of almost any kind—athletics, for boys, being one exception—could accelerate maturity in undesirable ways or place it forever out of reach. Work, then, could endanger not only the individual but also the society to which he belonged.

Florence Dale, secretary of the Children's Protective League, struck a similar note in her 1904 discussion of the glass factories of New Jersey. As Dale pointed out, the glassworks, like a number of other industries, were accustomed to use placement societies and orphanages as sources of child workers (343). Such workers might not last long:

> The disease causing [the death of the erstwhile "glass boy"] may . . . have gained its hold because of a lack of vitality, sapped invisibly, but surely, in the years when he was growing fast. . . . The hours spent walking in intense heat, sweating in the warm months, and exposed to sudden and great changes of temperature in the cold months, and the alternate day and night work . . . all these may not visibly injure the helper to-day or to-morrow, but the subtle sapping of his energies is none the less injurious. (345)

Certainly these strictures against unhealthy working conditions do not seem unreasonable today; at the same time, they are conditioned not only by demonstrable fact but also by particular anxieties of the Progressive Era from the 1880s onward. The "lack of vitality" that Dale adduced touched, like Addams's remarks, upon the fear that Northern European stock had already reached its peak and was now entering upon a long decline, a physical and moral degeneration that threatened the foundations of civilization and opened the door to the hegemony of racial "inferiors" such as Southern and Eastern Europeans, Jews, or Asians.

Thus Theodore Roosevelt linked the falling birth rate among the educated to "national death, race death" in 1903 (qtd. May 61; see also Kimmel 268–69); female college graduates who chose professions over procreation were criticized both for selfishness and for "nerve exhaustion" (qtd. May 73); psychologist G. Stanley Hall termed America "sterile and desiccated" (qtd. MacLeod, "Robin Hood" 44). Many such comments were motivated by fears about the nation's incipient takeover by the proletariat, as may be seen in Dr. James Weir's 1894 warning that "the lower classes, taking advantage of this moral lassitude [on the part of the "effeminate, weak" upper classes], and led on by their savage inclinations, undertake strikes, mobs, boycotts and riots" (qtd. Lears 30–31). But workers were also sometimes considered subject to the general loss of energy. The physical and mental exhaustion of youthful workers—what Folks terms the "sighs, fatigue, and strain of the 46,000 children employed" in producing fine fabrics, "the weary and haggard faces of the 7,000 children employed" in glass factories ("Under-side" 342)—portended, for Progressive Era science, the exhaustion of America itself.

To be sure, Dale noted, the boys sent to the glass factories by placing-out societies were not young children and not the cream of the orphanage crop, but sixteen- to eighteen-year-old "difficult cases, the rougher or lazier boys, who had not been contented with the work and form of life provided at the farm school of the society" (343). Even so, their very imperfections made the factory an unsuitable haven for them. Such boys, she warned, were "often homeless because of drunken parents," and were thus especially prone to succumb to "the tendency to alcoholism among glassblowers" (345). They needed more care and love than their fellows, not less. While the placement agents had considered glass production relatively safe employment for teenagers, since the work did not entail heavy lifting and the workweek was shorter than that in other industries, Dale concluded that the threat of further degeneration and debilitation of a class already at risk was such that hiring displaced boys for such positions was "no real and permanent betterment to society" (346). In this regard, factory work stood in stark contrast to adoption and foster care, which had long promised precisely this kind of permanent social improvement.

Thus if the apostles of efficiency insisted that properly managed industry was the key to improvement for such other "difficult cases" as immigrants, Dale and her fellows were equally sure that displaced children should be left out of the equation. Such children, after all, were especially vulnerable because they lacked what S. Y. Tupper, chaplain of a federal prison in Atlanta, described in 1903 as "the home influences . . . that mould [children] into a true character and that enable them to retain that character. . . . After a day's labor in the factory the child who is weak by nature and is exposed to all sorts of temptations, who has not had proper home training, is easily led into a criminal life" ("Discussion," 1903 *Proceedings* 544). Adopted children could take it; the unplaced could not. If the less specialized work of the 1870s had allowed child workers to learn a trade in comparatively pleasant surroundings, Addams concluded, the assembly line had made factories inimical to development. She argued, "It is because modern industrial processes are so monotonous, and because the routine is so deadening to the unenlightened mind, that we must keep the children out of it" ("Discussion," 1903 *Proceedings* 548).[3] Even Frederick Hoffman, who assured his audience at a 1903 Charities and Corrections meeting that child glassworkers "are as healthy and as happy a body as one is likely to

meet with anywhere" (146) and thought that setting the worker's minimum age at sixteen was an unwarrantable "interference with the natural
and rational development of the child as an effective element in the general social economy" (141), found it cause for anxiety that most children
were employed in Taylorized industries: "Whatever serious effects this extreme sub-division of labor has had upon the minds of adults, it is quite
safe to concede that the effects . . . must be more serious on the more
plastic mind of the child" (140).

In one sense, then, the tendency to view factory work as "bad" work for
displaced children relies upon the assumptions that the child is biologically
different from the adult and that the displaced child is emotionally different from the child with "proper home training"; such criticisms are, in part,
pleas that children be placed out in domestic settings rather than left in the
care of various institutions. At the same time, that the child afforded an
opportunity for sharp criticism of the factory system exposes turn-of-the-
century unease about the effects of mechanization not only on the young,
but also on adults. Emphasizing the undesirability of factories employing
orphanage graduates, who lacked the ballast that family and maturity
might provide, was one way for social critics to suggest that "national efficiency" and industrial efficiency were sometimes at odds. As Leslie Frost
has commented of the thousands of photographs of working children that
Lewis Hine began to take in 1906 at the behest of the National Child Labor
Committee, the depressing factory pictures in particular enabled "the child
[to embody] the dark side of the American celebration of technology—the
fear that indeed its celebrants are not ubermensch engineers designing and
implementing their rationalized system of control, but rather the dehu-
manized matter upon which systems are imposed" (4). Later, such rhetoric
could be extended to adults as well, so that in supporting the federal Child
Labor Law passed in 1913, Senator Robert F. Wagner could suggest, "The
isolated worker today is a mere connection link in an impersonalized and
heartless machine. He is powerless to defend himself" (qtd. Frost 4). Implicit in the situation of the displaced child in the factory—without family,
without status, without the freedom and delight and vitality supposedly
inherent in youth—was what some reformers saw as the powerlessness
and exhaustion of the working-class adult.

Re-creating the Frontier:
The Cottage Plan as "Good Orphanage"

But if displaced children were sometimes used as a focal point for reformers' protests against soulless efficiency and the eradication of individuality, it is also important to recognize that reformers as a group were often
inclined to embrace Taylorism. The latter, after all, stressed virtues attractive to Progressives, such as "character, competence, energy, hard work,

and success," and promised to raise wages and bring about "material abundance for the multitudes," another goal to which Progressives were committed (Tichi 81, 78). Peter Conn points out that "Progressives in particular wanted to . . . bring to politics the efficiencies of scale and good management" that formed the basis of this second industrial revolution (11; see also Crenson 40); Richard Hofstadter writes that Progressives "were trying . . . to keep the benefits of the emerging organization of life" even while they also sought "to retain the scheme of individualistic values that this organization was destroying" (*Age* 217). Some theorists who were not themselves orphanage superintendents, then, found ways to justify congregate care while still stressing the importance of the "individualistic values" to which Hofstadter refers.

For many reformers, the institutions that best combined the emphasis on discipline and productivity with the emphasis on personality were the "cottage-type" institution and the "junior republic," whose very names evoke associations that these reformers found attractive: the small, modest, rural family home in the former case, patriotic and civic-minded Americans in the latter. Both were linked in the rhetoric of this period with the frontier (or sometimes the bucolic life) and with the artisan-oriented values of a bygone era. And both often seemed to promise an alternative to the passive and conformist youngsters said to be (mass-)produced by the older style of asylums. By the late nineteenth century, most social workers agreed that children raised under such systems ran less risk than orphanage children of becoming institutionalized and thus would be better fitted both for placement in private homes and for raising families of their own later on.

The cottage system, a prominent feature in orphan care from the 1880s onward, was intended to be less uncompromisingly institutional than its predecessor. Instead of mass dormitories in which dozens of inmates slept side by side, it made use of smaller, detached buildings housing perhaps ten or twelve children. Cottagers were assigned to the care of housemothers or housefathers, whose duties included instilling appropriate moral values in their charges. Although most cottage plans grouped children by age rather than mixing teenagers with younger children and infants in a true mirroring of family experience, the number of inhabitants of each cottage was calculated to approximate the number of children that might occur naturally in a family—significantly, a family that did not suffer from the tendency to "nervous exhaustion" and "race suicide" so feared in America's middle class.

Meanwhile, the junior republic, precursor of Father Flanagan's famous Boys Town, featured self-government: boys (for this system, with some exceptions such as Pennsylvania's Carter Republic, was predominantly single-sex) passed the institution's laws, held down jobs on the premises, and determined rewards and punishments, theoretically learning both how to cooperate with their fellows and how to lead. States that housed junior republics included New York, Michigan, California, Connecticut, Pennsylvania, Maryland, Georgia, and Ohio, whose "Boyville" near Toledo specialized in newsboys; William R. George, who founded the best known of these sites in New York State, formed the National Junior Republic Association in 1908. Junior republics drew their inmates, who were usually in their early teens, both from orphanages and from reformatories. Typically, they stipulated that children "must be committed to the guardianship of the Republic, which makes impossible on the part of the parents interference with the boy" ("Jail" 250; see also King; "Town"; Ashby, *Waifs,* especially 19, 112–13). This requirement not only addresses an issue that was (and is) of great concern to prospective adoptive parents, thus implicitly equating the republic with other kinds of homes; it also follows the lead of the orphan trains by establishing the republic's "citizens" as individuals without legal families, turning children with living parents into imitation orphans.

Both plans featured not only pseudo-domesticity but also very genuine labor. In the seventh of a series of articles detailing his experiences in transforming a congregate institution in Manhattan into a cottage-plan institution in the Hudson Valley, R. R. Reeder, superintendent of the New York Orphan Asylum, described his wish "to develop industrial and economic power in each child" (187): "Each cottage," he assured his readers, "is a hive of industry" (188). Inmates raised poultry, cultivated tomato plants, and worked as "janitors, storekeepers, gardeners, house-cleaners, cooks, etc.," the better to learn "that a wholesome amount of work lies at the very foundation of things" (188–89). In Taylorist fashion, inefficiency, "wastefulness, carelessness or neglect" were to result in financial hardship in the form of fines or lost wages (188).

Still, Taylorist principles were invoked cautiously, not wholeheartedly. Reeder insisted that the work performed in the Asylum was not a matter of assembly lines, standardization, or routine, for "The factory type of industry . . . does not answer the purpose. . . . Such labor does not bring the independent and self-reliant spirit we are seeking to develop" (187). While Boys Town was later to follow other Roman Catholic asylums (such as the New York Catholic Protectory) in instituting the mass production of everything from magazines to personal hygiene, the New York Orphan Asylum was more Deweyan in its focus. Just as Dewey's pedagogical theories emphasized hands-on experience and the relation of lesson plans to children's daily lives, Reeder argued that "The boy that can draw a picture of an incubator knows something about it, but the boy that can run the incubator and get a seventy percent hatch out of it knows the incubator itself. The former may learn his lesson in school, but the latter must go to the poultry yard and develop an experience" (187). At junior republics, too, the emphasis was upon the Deweyan formula of "learn[ing] by doing" (Ashby, *Children* 91).

The turn of the century witnessed a boom in "manual training" in public schools across the United States, and we may see the cottage institution's reliance upon practical skills as a variant of this phenomenon, just as it also belongs to the American tradition that displaced children should have to work. But we should also bear in mind that the cottage rhetoric insisted that such institutions were designed to imitate not the home in general, but the farm home in particular. Supporters of the cottage plan pointed not to efficiency and quasi-military conformity but to the benefits of country living, citing clean air, healthful outdoor pursuits, and the absence of big-city temptations. Cottage asylums thus become metaphors not for the American factory, but for the American past. For the sake of convenience, congregate orphanages were often located in cities; cottage institutions and junior republics distanced themselves from the urban milieu, tapping into Romantic notions about the moral value of nature for the developing mind.

Descriptions of work in such institutions were likewise redolent of American frontier life, not of the modern assembly line, as we may see from H. L. Crumley's 1903 description of the Decatur Home, a cottage asylum outside Atlanta. Here, Crumley noted, "The children do all the work of the farm—raising seeds for the seed dealers—of the dairy—the butter commanding a fine price—of the bakery, the kitchen, the laundry, the blacksmith and carpenters' shops, tending the hogs and poultry, housekeeping and sewing, and nursing the babies and sick, and all else that pertains to a farm home" (566). The emphasis was on the cottage home's economic self-sufficiency; like the fabled frontier, it was supposed to create competent generalists, not the efficient but narrow specialists of Taylorist production methods. And because the Home was rural rather than urban, a cottage institution rather than a "barracks" institution, this labor could be celebrated as building initiative rather than eradicating it. The same claim could be made of the junior republic, with its emphasis upon self-government and personal responsibility.

Progressive Era discussions of cottage institutions and juvenile republics invariably spend time distinguishing them from conventional orphanages, which are firmly identified as inferior. Fiction and nonfiction alike, in other words, use the orphanage to embody the faults of the social-welfare system. But simultaneously, they offer covert criticisms of the expanding nation as a whole. Celebrations such as Reeder's make their argument in terms strikingly similar to those used by certain commentators writing in the ever more urbanized society of the Progressive Era, who, as historian T. J. Jackson Lears points out, "increasingly idealized farm life" even though they themselves were city dwellers. Lears sums up the "conventional wisdom" by quoting an 1888 article in the *North American Review* whose author claimed, "Once let the human race be cut off from personal contact with the soil, once let the conventionalities and artificial restrictions of so-called civilization interfere with the healthful simplicity of nature, and decay is certain" (28). The "anti-institutional institution[s]" of the turn of the century (the phrase is Ashby's; see *Children* 90) suggested that the converse might also be true: transplanting the "decayed" child, the delinquent or the product of a failed home, away from "civilization" into the "simplicity" of a preindustrial era, would result in renewal. Presented by their adherents as the antithesis of both orphanage and factory, the cottage asylum and the junior republic—and the old-fashioned individualism for which they were made to stand—held out the promise of curing some of the ill effects of modern mass society.

Placement as Fairy Tale, or Melodrama in Real Life

But as the previous chapter's examination of sentimental fiction argues, displaced children were themselves often proposed as the solution to such malaise. To be sure, one reason the orphan trains were targets for criticism during the early Progressive Era was that concerns about the presumed delinquency of the trains' young passengers continued. At the same time, however, one may also discern more and more anxiety of a precisely opposite kind, namely that precious children were being placed with inferior adults. This section explores the turn-of-the-century controversy over various kinds of "inappropriate" placements, a debate that indicates the extent to which fiction's use of the metaphor of displaced child as treasure had entered real life.

Anxiety about the possible delinquency of orphan-train riders was not new, of course. I have already noted complaints made in the 1870s that the New York Children's Aid Society—which at that time, Marilyn Holt observes, did sometimes recruit its youthful emigrants from prisons (121)—was exporting delinquents in an effort to purify New York City at the expense of the hinterlands. If anything, however, one might expect such concern to have diminished by the century's end. For one thing, the Society had moved away from its initial practice of scooping up street children and sending them westward at the earliest opportunity. Its habit was now to acquire the train riders from orphanages (Holt 65), which by the theories of the day would have discouraged delinquency either by sapping the child's energies or by giving him or her a crash course in "civilized" manners and morals. Moreover, the Society could point to impressive success stories among its graduates. As its fiftieth annual report noted in 1902, "one [alumnus] became Governor of a state, and one of a territory, two have been Members of Congress, two sheriffs, three district attorneys, three county commissioners, and several have been members of state legislatures." Others entered law, medicine, teaching, business, or the ministry, besides the predictable career of farming, while "over one thousand entered the army and navy" ("Half a Century" 553). The implication was that all were productive, honest, and patriotic citizens. Indeed, even the

Society's critics could not point to much delinquency on the part of former orphan-train riders, although in part the absence of statistics here may reflect the Society's notorious tendency to lose track of its erstwhile wards.

Nevertheless, various states, including Michigan, Minnesota, Indiana, Illinois, Kansas, Missouri, and Pennsylvania, enacted legislation designed to make the orphan-train project more difficult. Sometimes such laws were sweeping in their scope, such as Indiana's 1899 act prohibiting the importation of children by any association or person (the children's blood kin excepted) who had not received the written consent of the Board of State Charities and posted a bond of $10,000; the hefty price tag immediately ended out-of-state placements (Kelsey 91, 94). In other states they were more limited, as in the case of Kansas's 1903 regulation that "No probate court was to permit the adoption of any minor child sent into the state through the auspices of any association incorporated in any other state until all requirements governing adoption had been met"; these requirements included the furnishing of a "guarantee that the child was healthy in mind and body and not [of] 'vicious character'" (Holt 153). As few conventional orphanages of this era would have sought to place out a child (whether through the Children's Aid Society or through their own offices) known to be mentally or physically disabled, the character standard was the most meaningful requirement here. Depending on how it was applied, it would have barred the adoption (although not the indenture) of those whose records included even minor delinquencies. Kansas's strictures were typical; as of 1901, all laws of this kind mandated the removal of any imported child who became a "public charge," whether in a reformatory or an almshouse, after entering the state (Kelsey 90–91).

Such legislation reflected old-style perceptions of dependent children as expense rather than treasure. To be sure, turn-of-the-century sociologist Carl Kelsey argued that among the motivations for passing laws against "dumping" was concern for the child, not merely concern for the taxpayer: out-of-state agencies, he noted, found follow-up work difficult, so that children were vulnerable to abuse. Then too, many of the states that passed laws to discourage orphan-train placements had developed big cities of their own, with their concomitant population of needy children, so that legislators sought to establish that charity began at home. But even this sensibility suggests a feeling that dependent children represented a drain upon resources that prudent men should limit by all means possible. Certainly, those involved in the placement debate continued to expend time and energy calculating the relative costs of placing out and institutionalization. As we have seen in Chapter 2, the latter was deemed an evil not only because it seemed less natural than family placement, but also because it was expensive.

But at the same time, we may also discern the growth of an opposing sense that receiving an orphan was a privilege to be jealously guarded. Such was the concern about the placement of children in "improper" homes that the matter reached the United States Supreme Court. The case in question involved a group of urban Catholic children, mostly of Irish extraction, that was sent to Mexican-American families in an Arizona mining town in 1904 and subsequently "rescued" by an outraged mob of Anglo citizens who denied the right of the Catholic orphanage to privilege religion above ethnicity and social class in choosing foster parents for its charges.

Linda Gordon has christened this episode "the great Arizona orphan abduction." As Gordon details in her book of the same name, the orphanage under whose auspices the children went west—the same New York Foundling Asylum that had been praised by Jacob Riis and Anne O'Hagan—was then assuming responsibility for some 1,900 children a year, of whom about one-quarter became orphan-train riders. The Sisters of Charity, who ran the Foundling, worked with local priests across the country to find Catholic homes for the prospective emigrants before putting them on the trains, hoping both to minimize exploitation and to ensure that children handicapped by presumed illegitimacy and dubious heredity would get sound parental guidance. Yet a vigilante group protested this set of placements in Clifton and Morenci, moved not by fear that the forty waifs and orphans sent out from New York City represented urban delinquency or an undesirable public burden, but by the sense that the Mexican-American families who proposed to take them in were not good enough for the children, whose whiteness would be jeopardized by their new homes. Moreover, the vigilantes who appropriated the children— adopting nineteen of them into their own families, not as servants but as beloved sons and daughters—took their case to the Arizona Supreme Court and won. Since the Foundling's appeal to the United States Supreme Court was dismissed on the ground that the latter court lacked jurisdiction, the lower court's ruling stood.

Gordon's thorough treatment of the case and its racial and gender angles precludes extensive discussion here, but her findings may be placed in the context of several additional circumstances. First, as Elaine Tyler May observes, Progressive Era social workers' "more compassionate view of the poor" had led to a policy shift: increasingly, the trend was to oppose the idea of removing children from their original homes, except in the direst of circumstances (87). While many commentators still looked upon the birth families as the cradles of crime, some of the belief in the destitute child's essential innocence was spilling over into sympathy for that child's parents. This phenomenon is perhaps more pronounced in fiction; consider the care with which authors spotlight the virtues of the parents of protagonists such as Rebecca Randall, Fauntleroy, and Freckles, among others. But it appears in much nonfiction as well, such as Sherman C. Kingsley's 1904 advice to social workers, "We should not remove a child from his family because . . . some one can pay, or because we know an ideal family where a child is wanted. Above all, in the darkest hour of their lives, parents should not be asked to sign away their children" ("Child-Saving" 276). The result was what May (quoting Julie Berebitsky) terms "the first major 'baby shortage'" in American adoption history (87), one that would be further intensified in the 1910s and '20s when mothers' pensions became popular. The Arizona children's status as treasures reflects, in part, the workings of the law of supply and demand.

Second, it is worth noting that while the 1904 case had an unusually high profile, it was not unique. The following year, the Foundling was to make another controversial set of placements, sending another group of New York City children to North Dakota to live with German-Russian families who were subsequently described as living in "poor, dirty, or squalid homes." To be sure, investigation by New York State Board of Charities officials found the charges baseless. Presumed racially superior to their Mexican-American counterparts, the North Dakotans were (the officials stressed) German by blood despite a century's sojourn in Russia, and "had evidently retained their characteristic [German] love for neatness and comfort in their homes" ("New York Foundlings" 349). But, significantly, Alden Fearing's apparent reference to this case in 1914 remembers the situation rather differently. Note also how Fearing represents anti-dumping legislation as designed to protect the (valuable) child rather than the community:

> At one time, a large number of orphans were obtained from various sources by a community of Russian Jews in South Dakota [*sic*] who organized them to perform their agricultural labor. They lived in sod huts with dirt floors and had practically nothing to offer in the way of home life. Following a disclosure of these conditions, the legislature of South Dakota passed an act forbidding the placing-out of children in that state by societies except on giving a bond for $2,000 in every case. Compulsory inspection naturally followed. (195)

Fearing's recollection that the Dakota children were wanted as farm laborers appears to have been at fault. "We could discover nothing to warrant the belief that any of the children had been taken because of any desire to utilize their services," wrote the investigators at the time, "and the fact that they were uniformly under five years of age is of itself sufficient to dispel any such suspicion" ("New York Foundlings" 349). As Gordon observes, the Arizona children, who ranged in age from two to six, were also too young to be of much use in a mining town (119). But here too, the children's exact status was a matter for wild surmise. One element of the Arizona case that especially disturbed the vigilantes was the rumor that the Mexicans had paid the local priest for the children—or, as one New York journalist put it, that the children "had actually been sold at so much per head to irresponsible Mexicans" ("Both Sides" 7).[4] Treasures, it seems, should neither be put to base uses nor turned too obviously into commodities.

The misconceptions and assumptions about the Arizona placements are worth examining here because they suggest a tendency to view real-life situations in terms of the melodramatic paradigms of contemporaneous orphan fiction. Especially relevant is the fiction's tendency to depict orphans as crypto-aristocrats whose sojourn with unappreciative or brutal (here, racially "inferior") adults would end when the children made their way into the hearts of more perceptive individuals. Gordon's research suggests that the original adoptive parents, while by no means wealthy, were "better off than average . . . all probably legally married . . . an aristocracy among Mexican workers" by virtue of their literacy in two languages (71). As a group, they showed signs of upward mobility, and their desire to adopt additional children was probably at least partly an outgrowth of this relative prosperity. Coverage of the case in Anglo newspapers and in social-services journals such as *Charities,* however, represented these parents, "with possibly one or two exceptions," as members of "the lower class of halfbreed Mexican-Indians . . . impecunious, illiterate, unacquainted with the English language, vicious, and, in several instances, prostitutes and persons of notoriously bad character" ("Case" 449). In contrast to this image of squalor and sexual immorality (a point that seems calculated to evoke fears of miscegenation, never far from the surface in the era of Jim Crow), the children were described not as waifs of uncertain background, the offspring of parents who might in other circumstances have been characterized in terms very similar to those applied to the "half-breed Indian families," but as "children of unusual beauty and attractiveness," special and valuable ("Case" 449, 448). In other words, they were represented as identical to the newly desirable protagonists of turn-of-the-century orphan fiction, a circumstance that may indicate either the power of such fiction to shape perceptions of real life or the extent to which the fiction articulated ways of looking at dependent children that were already widespread within the larger society.

The comparative youth of these children also deserves more emphasis, since it is this factor that would have been the most important in identifying them as appropriate candidates for sentimental rather than utilitarian adoption. The Foundling, indeed, was consciously seeking the former disposition. As early as 1886, Josephine Shaw Lowell remarked that the more than two thousand children that this organization had placed out in recent years had gone to families "at so young an age, that there can be no suspicion that they have been taken from any motive but the desire to adopt them as the children of the homes which received them" (*Care* 204). Just as stories such as *Big Brother* and *Timothy's Quest* stress the distinction between the instantly lovable toddler and the older child who must expect to earn his or her keep, nonfiction writing from this era differentiated the "chubby, dimpled baby, at once 'Monarch of all he surveyed'" (as "The Orphans," an 1894 orphan-train article in the Columbus, Kansas *Star-Courier,* put it) from school-aged youngsters of eight or nine, looked over like "so many cattle" by prospective parents who gloated that they "will be able to do all the chores in a short time" ("Children Given Away," Burlington, Iowa *Gazette,* 1889). Not only were contemporaneous authorities aware that, as social worker Hastings Hart put it in 1902, "Applications for little children are much less likely to be selfish than for older children" ("Discussion," 1902 *Proceedings* 403), but requests for the very young were becoming much more frequent than had been the case as recently as 1880, when Anne Richardson lamented the difficulty of placing children "too young to be taken as helpers" (197).

But this is not to suggest that sentimental adoption had erased utilitarian placement. Rather, the two coexisted, despite novelists' critiques of the uneasiness of the juxtaposition. The journalist who produced "Children Given Away" was probably not striving to arouse indignation or pity in his or her audience; despite what today's readers might consider the inflammatory nature of the phrases I have quoted, the article's tone is variously jocular and matter-of-fact, not melodramatic. Its primary purpose seems to have been to encourage fostering orphan-train children on any terms. Thus while it recognizes that the toddler may attract love, its attitude toward older children is relentlessly practical: it assures readers that "as far as could be seen there was no viciousness in [the children's] natures" and that "there have been but few cases where the children [from the New York Juvenile Asylum, founded in 1851 to care for children under twelve and now known as the Children's Village] have failed to give satisfaction." Moreover, the writer adds, the conditions of such "adoptions" are not onerous for the adults, who need only promise to provide food, clothing, medical care, job training, four months of schooling annually, moral and religious education, and a stake of fifty dollars and a bible when the child turns eighteen.[5] The job-training requirement, of course, licensed the foster parent to set the child to any work that might prove convenient for the household. In other words, the article seems primarily designed to emphasize how adults would benefit in material ways from becoming foster parents; the children's good is not the issue, since it is taken for granted that they would be better off in private homes than in institutions or on the streets.

Thus the priority of many placement officers was simply to insert their charges into any respectable home; sentimental fiction's demand for a *loving* home was an unrealistic luxury. For John W. Douglass, in 1901 an agent for the Washington, D.C. Board of Children's Guardians, the real distinction was not that between children who were working as servants and those who might hope for sentimental adoption, but rather that between children who were in institutions or on their own and those who— in whatever capacity—"were in family homes, growing normally in the soul-reaching and uplifting influences which the environment of a good home exert[s] to counteract and destroy hereditary pernicious tendencies" (243). Similarly, the Children's Aid Society of Pennsylvania sometimes arranged adoptions, as the influential charity worker William Pryor Letchworth wrote in 1897, "but more generally [the children] are boarded until old enough to earn their living, when they are permanently placed, without compensation, with the family with which they have been boarded." That is, on reaching the age of usefulness, the child would take over from the Society the task of paying its foster family for its upkeep; as Letchworth comments, "The rearing of children in this way becomes a business," not a matter of sentiment (582). Even so, he considers it a "successful business," since whether or not it leads to adoption, it enables the formerly institutionalized child to find a home of sorts.

But other social-work professionals sound more like the writers of sentimental fiction in criticizing the placement system's callousness, and especially in couching their criticisms in terms of the children's vulnerability and worthiness of love, key qualities in the defining of the displaced child as treasure. The adjectives and adverbs used by S. J. Hathaway, speaking on "Children's Homes in Ohio" at the 1890 Charities and Correction conference, recall the emotions of the contemporaneous orphan tale:

> Some people want children . . . for cheap servants, some to be company for them in a vacant home, or while the head of the family is away at work. Not all, by any means, come because they love children. The majority of the children placed out under the old [i.e., inadequately supervised] system had a hard time of it. In fact, it was equivalent to the State taking their tender lives in charge for a time, and then ruthlessly throwing them away. (*Care* 210)

Similarly, at the 1899 conference, Robert W. Hebberd of New York warned of the "Dangers of Careless Methods," citing the case of a tubercular girl dying in an almshouse, a victim of poor placement: "at quite an early age [she] had been placed in a family home, evidently to become a household drudge, where she was exposed to such unfeeling treatment as seriously to undermine her health" (173). Indeed, the need for greater supervision of foster parents was a constant theme among social workers during this period. We may interpret this circumstance not only as recognition of the children's value but also, in part, as an outgrowth of the Progressive desire to push more and more families toward a particular model of enlightened child rearing.

To be sure, Hebberd's fellow speaker Edward A. Hall was more pragmatic than sentimental, even while he urged home placement for the children's sake:

> In the spring a farmer's fancy gently turns to thoughts of a good, strong, healthy boy of about fourteen years of age, who is not afraid to work for his board and clothes; and we usually have more applications for boys of this age than we can supply. At all seasons of the year the demand is good for girls from twelve to sixteen years of age, to "help take care of the children and work around the house." If the families are respectable, it is

always best to place boys and girls in such homes rather than keep them too long in institutions. . . . The beautiful, lovable homes that we read about, where people live who are lying awake nights, ready to take to their hearts the undesirable children of society for the dear children's sake, are few and far between. (183–84)

It is telling that Hall sees adoptable children as "the undesirable children of society." In his view, most displaced children have been "recruited from the ranks of the most degraded and degenerate specimens of humanity in our large cities"; such youngsters are the offspring of "generations of those whose mental and moral weakness was also the result of heredity" (178). They would seem, then, to have nothing in common with the strikingly attractive protagonists of contemporaneous orphan fiction. Nevertheless, despite his casual criticism of these children, despite his implication that they were bred to be bad and so were mentally and morally inferior from birth, even Hall is not oblivious to the sentimental power possessed by the youngest of them: "The best results in my experience of placing children in homes have been where children were placed in families to board, under three years of age. The innocence and helplessness of those infants so endeared many of them to the love and affection of the families that, when it became a question of separation, they asked to be allowed to adopt the child" (184).[6]

If sentimental adoption was more likely in fiction than in fact, then, it was nonetheless gaining ground even in real life. Capitalizing upon this perceived "innocence and helplessness" of the young, some organizations were finding it possible to abandon the concept of orphan-as-laborer altogether. The Chicago Orphan Asylum apparently arranged no indentures after 1880. It also changed the wording of the form it required adoptive parents to sign, so that the phrase "doth bind" (an echo of the apprenticeship system) became "instructed, reared, and treated in every way . . . as if . . . the natural child" (qtd. McCausland 64). Similarly, Daniel Hurley writes that the Children's Home of Cincinnati "denied that the children [it] placed in country homes were either 'bound out' or 'apprenticed'"; as early as 1879 it was announcing that on the contrary, "they are required to be received into the family" (51). The Foundling had always selected its younger wards for emigration; now, even the New York Children's Aid Society began to emphasize the placement of preschoolers and to play down the idea of the children's usefulness.[7] And when, in 1898, Byron C. Mathews spoke of possible motivations for seeking to add an unrelated child to the family, the child's potential as servant was not among them: "There are many lonely homes in which the only occupants are parents whose children have left them to make homes of their own or possibly have died. There are many others in which the only occupants are husband and wife, who have never had their homes brightened by the presence of children of their own. There are still other homes in which the only child is a girl, and a boy may be desired, or the reverse may be the case" (370). As in the Arizona case, the orphans' value here was clearly psychological and emotional, not pragmatic.

Gordon argues that the Arizona "orphan abduction" depended heavily on motherhood's turn-of-the-century cultural power. The abortive Mexican-American adoptions, the amassing of the mob, and the courtroom proceedings, she contends, were all dominated by women's emotional presence even in their physical absence (308, 159). Moreover, Progressivism too was often "maternalist," preaching "the primacy of motherhood to civilization" and the need for child-saving (Gordon 197). That political and social reformism embraced such subjects as housekeeping and nutrition, children's playgrounds and children's natures, certainly indicates that women were parlaying their private-sphere expertise into a public role, as does women's prominence at events such as the annual Charities and Correction conferences. Thus we may read the validation of home in the placing-out debates, like the prevalence of female authors within the genre of orphan fiction, as part of a larger (and generally successful) political endeavor on the part of women. Focusing their social criticisms on the plight of the displaced child enabled female reformers to combine an acceptance of traditional gender roles with an activist desire to change society in accordance with feminine ideals.

But it would be inaccurate to suggest that in contemplating the early Progressive Era, we may best regard dependent children as a kind of youth auxiliary to the feminist movement. They were that, but they were other things as well. If orphan fiction acknowledged the power of the home, it dwelt also on the moral and emotional flaws of the family, dysfunction that was to be healed not by women but by the young. Similarly, the controversy over displaced children in factories and orphanages, which permitted the airing of both hostility to and acceptance of society's increasing mechanization, was by no means exclusively female. And finally, as Chapter 5 will illustrate, displaced children were not simply the vehicle through which women critiqued society, but frequently also the vehicle through which society critiqued women. In short, displaced children were often used during this period—as at other times—as a way of discussing a wide array of subjects of importance to both sexes, subjects that bore upon both the place of the individual vis-à-vis the mass and the best way to solve the ills of the nation.

5

Adoption and Women, 1907–1918

In the early twentieth century, women's gender role was especially volatile. Comment on women's capacities, social function, and right to seek fulfillment in nontraditional ways was intense from 1870 onward, and the late Progressive Era saw major developments in this debate. As historians have often noted, in these years "sexuality emerged as a subject of widespread discussion" (Marsh and Ronner 120); the first graduates of women's colleges had reached positions of responsibility, exemplifying new possibilities for career women; and the suffragists' anticipated victory was expected to cause dramatic changes in American politics and policies. In such a climate, that both conservatives and radicals stressed motherhood, and that displaced children offered a forum for comment on maternity's (re)construction, seems inevitable.

This chapter will examine how five strands of the adoption debate between 1907 and 1918 were used to discuss the "woman question": the adoption campaign mounted by a popular women's magazine; the representation of nontraditional adoptions, especially by spinsters, in fiction and nonfiction; the emphasis within juvenile orphan fiction on how adoption might transform women; the conclusions about the mother's role reached at a prestigious conference on dependent children; and the conflicting stances on motherhood, both biological and adoptive, taken by American eugenists and their opponents in contemplating the constructed family. All these discourses interacted, sometimes positively and sometimes negatively. But in each case, the rhetoric of adoption occasioned both tributes to motherhood and examinations of feminine failings. Both sets of commentaries illuminate commentators' personal and cultural anxieties.

"The Home That Needs a Child": Adoption by Mail

In November 1907, the *Delineator,* a Butterick publication edited by Theodore Dreiser, began its "Child-Rescue Campaign." Every month, the magazine announced, it would introduce two or more children available for adoption, placing-out, or indenture; readers attracted by the winsome photographs or pathetic stories could request the children by writing to the relevant adoption agency or to the editors. Directed by James West, an orphanage alumnus who had been unplaceable because of a tubercular hip, the campaign drew the attention of social workers and politicians as well as the *Delineator's* natural audience. When in November 1910 Dreiser's successor discontinued the child-rescue page and West left to become secretary of the Boy Scouts, the magazine could boast impressive achievements. It claimed to have found loving homes for the 150-odd children advertised and for more than 1000 others as well. It had founded the National Child-Rescue League "to consolidate grass-roots support" for its efforts (Crenson 10). And capitalizing upon West's friendship with Theodore Roosevelt, it had inspired the 1909 White House Conference on the Care of Dependent Children, which led in turn to a series of similar domestic summit meetings and contributed to the 1912 establishment of a new government department, the U.S. Children's Bureau.

As Julie Berebitsky contends, the campaign was responding to America's "changing definition of motherhood" (52). One might also argue that it spoke to the changing definition of womanhood overall, as did its venue. A popular women's magazine founded (as *The Metropolitan*) in 1870, the *Delineator* originally existed to disseminate dress patterns, a focus that lingered even after the periodical began manifesting Progressive impulses in 1905. The dress patterns, notes Martha Banta, relied upon principles of efficiency and "uniformity" by establishing norms for the female body. Custom tailoring gave way to "mass-produced ready-mades" in a system that "followed the ideal [of pattern models] laid down by the small arms manufacturers in the 1850s" (Banta 282) and subsequently applied to Union soldiers by the inventor of clothing sizes, Brigadier General G. H. Crosman (Michaels 84). In their home sewing, then, readers were reminded of the extent to which their bodies conformed—and ought to conform—to the average; individuality in this context was undesirable.

But in counterbalance to this potentially dismaying reflection, the child-rescue campaign implied that the featured "orphans" were special. Although a reader whose application for a particular child was unsuccessful might be offered another in its stead, a circumstance implying that a child was a child was a child, the pictures and stories stressed their subjects' uniqueness. The children profiled were of different sexes, ages, personality types, and ethnic backgrounds, although all but one (a Japanese-American baby girl) were white. In other words, on one level the campaign reassured women that despite America's ongoing transformation into a mass society, individual humanity as represented by these children—and, by extension, the reader—could still flourish. Berebitsky finds that the *Delineator*'s editors ultimately felt reluctant to run the profiles, since they cared more about changing policy by ending institutionalization than about placing children one by one. Yet the profiles were rhetorically indispensable: readers insisted on "respond[ing] to the children as individuals" (68).

Moreover, while the children were theoretically available for indenture, the campaign was geared toward sentimental adoption, avowedly to help both the children and the adults, especially the women, who took them in. As the title of the first article noted, the campaign simultaneously addressed "The Child That Needs a Home" and "The Home That Needs a Child" ("Delineator" 716). Thus, early in the series, Lydia Kingsmill Commander, author of *The American Ideal: A Study of Race Suicide*, stressed the horrors of the childless home and of the "queer, selfish people, dead to natural instincts," who refused parenthood (722–23). Margaret Marsh and Wanda Ronner note that such criticisms had long circulated—they quote feminist Jane Cunningham Croly's 1869 remark that voluntary childlessness bespoke a woman of "deformed and misshapen heart and brain" (98)—but it was largely a Progressive Era innovation to see the decision not to reproduce as unpatriotic and antisocial as well as unnatural. The "crusade against children," Commander argued, hurt society still more than it did the young.

For the child's familial function was moral and emotional rather than practical. It is "children who do the saving," she wrote; "To be responsible for a child . . . whether he be your own by birth or by adoption, is the old, old way of purifying the dross out of human nature." The child's "hardest task" was to help its mother deal with the dross of *male* nature in particular, "To bind his restless, roving father to the home, and teach him the beauty of lifelong love between one man and one woman." She added that "where there are children, marriages are less lightly broken" (830). As Christopher Lasch observes, in 1920 the divorce rate was fifteen times what it had been in 1870 (8); Commander thus offered adoption as the answer to a major anxiety of the day. But while Commander identified the husband as the potential problem within a family and strongly advocated women's rights, she also implied that wives have little power to correct their men's domestic failings. The role of adopted children, evidently, is to supply the moral and cleansing influence that mothers lack.

On another familiar level, the campaign affiliated itself with muckrakers who sought to change society by purveying mingled outrage and pathos to the masses. Moreover, testimonials from prominent citizens and reformers, including Mrs. Robert La Follette, Mrs. William Jennings Bryan, Edith Rockefeller McCormick, Judge Ben Lindsey, and Homer Folks, provided both reformist and aristocratic imprimaturs. But their comments, too, stressed that adoption benefited mothers at least as much as children. "Who can say which is the more pitiful, a homeless child or a childless home?" asked Cleveland's Progressive mayor Tom L. Johnson; Jacob Riis added that "the birthright of every child is to have one pair of loving arms around its neck, and the happiness of every woman [is] to feel its baby heart throbbing against her own" ("What Others" 100). The longing to *become* a mother might trump even the longing to *have* a mother.

By emphasizing the childless woman's moral impotence and emotional neediness, the magazine celebrated motherhood as a primordial force separate from childbearing. Depictions of the maternal instinct as women's major sensual drive, surpassing sexuality in power and demonstrating the purity of (at least) middle-class femininity, were common from the 1850s through the 1920s. But as this chapter will argue of other late Progressive Era texts, the *Delineator* articles prescribed a solution both to unfulfilled maternal urges and to styles of femininity that might seem socially dangerous. By adopting children, women either could cease to be something *other* than mothers (career women, neurotics, participants in race suicide) or could redeem apparently antisocial activities by showing their compatibility with child rearing. As Berebitsky notes, the campaign painted adoptive motherhood as a "patriotic and civic duty" that would turn discarded and potentially criminal children into productive citizens, a goal congenial to Progressive philosophy (55). But from a conservative point of view, motherhood was a more suitable outlet for women's citizenly impulses than something more public. The redeemer was herself to be redeemed.

The civic-minded adoptive mother was pitted not against conservatism, but against that favorite Progressive Era whipping boy and symbol of an impersonal society, the orphanage. Most of the campaign's complaints about orphanages took an anti-industrial stance, privileging private, personal, and traditionally female approaches to domesticity. Thus Ernest Bicknell, superintendent of the Chicago Bureau of Charities, asked rhetorically in February 1908, "Are the children in our institutions being subjected to a round of mechanical routine which crushes rather than develops individuality and resourcefulness?" ("As Others" 252). A March 1908 piece entitled "Doesn't Anybody Want a Little Boy?" decried "the brand of the institution . . . the brand of the impersonal, the unindividual," the identically clothed orphanage children "all, all alike." An editorial on "Machine Charity as Found in the Orphan Asylum" added asylum officials to the list of victims of industrial philanthropy, decrying "work for others from which the inspiration has been banished, in which the individual touch is of the most perfunctory character" (781). And W. B. Sherrard of the Children's Home Society of South Dakota called for "another Carrie Nation, whose little hatchet would smash the doors of every orphan asylum in the land" ("Where" 121, 120). His remark foregrounded the gendering of the battle lines by casting prospective adoptive mothers as dauntless reformers pitted against an entrenched, and implicitly masculine, bureaucracy.[1]

That the *Delineator* youngsters deserved better was the constant refrain. The logo accompanying each month's adoption column came from the sign displayed by a foundling hospital of the Italian Renaissance; it showed a swaddled infant with outstretched arms, at once begging Christian mercy and projecting a Christlike quality of its own. The early columns, especially, stressed that the children profiled were not merely as good as but better than the average child. Thus seven-year-old Evelyn (of "American parentage") had "inherit[ed] from her mother . . . a personality of marked refinement that has survived the vicissitudes of a not always desirable environment" ("Delineator" November 1907, 717), while the four-year-old offered alongside her possessed not only "a rare smile that warms and tugs at one's heart" and "that wholesome, vigorous look that only perfect health gives," but also a brain "so unusually active that he is two years ahead of his age in his studies" (718). Tony, an Italian-American, was "a child of refinement and delicate sensibilities, with no apparent trace of a probable peasant heritage" ("Delineator" December 1907, 930). Toddler Marion had been abandoned by "a well-dressed, attractive woman," evidently of the same social class as the magazine's target audience, and Janet, the daughter of American citizens, had "manners [that] are all that the most fastidious parents could desire" ("Delineator" January 1908, 98).

Like such earlier fictions as *Timothy's Quest,* these descriptions reassured prospective parents that adopting these children might even be safer than bearing one's own. Moreover, while most orphanage inmates of the era had at least one living parent, the *Delineator* children often resembled the orphans of fiction by being "absolutely alone in the world, fatherless and motherless, and without a known relative" ("Delineator" April 1908, 608). In practical terms, this trait meant that they would be available for adoption, since many parents who checked their offspring into institutions intended to reclaim them and would not sign away their parental rights. But it also made the children more appealing to readers who might demur at the thought that blood kin might appear later to challenge the placement or simply to embarrass the new family.[2]

The early articles also tended to insist upon the virtues of the biological parents—or at least the mothers. Unmarried mothers were said to have been led astray ("Physically strong, simple, loyal and devoted, she deserved a better fate than that which befell her" ["Delineator" December 1907, 929]), deserted wives to have lacked the financial resources to bring up their young. Even wives who themselves played the deserter could be excused, as in the case of the mother who removed her two toddlers from the custody of their alcoholic father: "with the heroism of the true mother instinct, she surrendered her children" on finding that she could not support them ("Delineator" January 1909, 101).

Such rhetoric played to the growing eugenics movement, which stressed heredity; scientifically informed adoptive parents were more likely than ever to stipulate that their child-elect have a biological mother of good

character. Accordingly, desirable heredity was advertised (or manufactured; see Berebitsky 60) whenever possible, as in these descriptions from
February 1910: "He has inherited good blood and good health," and, of a
girl whose mother died after giving birth and whose father did not rear her,
"Her Presbyterian parents transmitted to her the right sort of moral fiber,
and even though she has been 'boarded around' for the ten years of her
life, she has not suffered from environment" (129). But evidently heredity
could overcome environment only when the former was good and the
latter bad. Thus Riis dismissed as a "bugbear" the theory of Cesare
Lombroso—himself a *Delineator* contributor—that "heredity was insurmountable" (Riis, "God's Children" 809). On the contrary, he claimed, "I
should not be afraid of taking a little child into my home, whatever its
ancestry . . . for I should know that I was doing God's work with His child,
and He would attend to the outcome" (810). Consistently, the magazine's
experts minimized heredity's power to harm.

Given the shortage of adoptable children that lay at the root of the
campaign's success, however, it was possible to offer children who represented a greater risk—although the profiles downplayed that risk.[3] When
children had problematic histories as the offspring of unmarried parents,
alcoholics, or destitute immigrants, the magazine worked around these
drawbacks. If Emily's unwed mother "does not want her own history repeated in the experience of her daughter, so the baby is offered for adoption where environment will obliterate all possibility of bad hereditary influence" ("Delineator" June 1909, 805), the stipulation made Emily all the
more desirable, since to win her was to have one's rectitude publicly certi-
fied. Similarly, Baby Dimples, "the pride and joy of the household in which
he is now boarding," was born into conditions liable to disturb adoptive
parents; when a placement officer "was asked as to his parentage, he
gravely replied: 'say nothing—the less said the better'" ("Delineator" June
1908, 1052). But in a shrewd piece of applied psychology, this description
appeared on the same page as the continuation of Lucy Huffaker's article
on "Waifs Who Have Become Famous: Some Geniuses Who Have Honored
Their Foster-Parents' Names." These "waifs" included Alexander Hamilton,
Edgar Allan Poe, Rosa Bonheur, and Moses; many, Huffaker noted, were
illegitimate, and most were born into poverty, yet their ability to "glorify
their adopted names" was beyond question (1052). *Delineator* readers, who
included many housewives, were invited to conclude that adoptive motherhood represented their best hope of public recognition. Indeed, the less
promising the human material with which they were working, the greater
the potential triumph.

Gender and age, too, could pose a problem. The same column that
offered the androgynously nicknamed Dimples noted, "The child-placing
agencies tell us that the majority of people want one child, a little fair-
haired, blue-eyed girl between two and four years old" ("Delineator"
June 1908, 1003). This comment, reiterated by adoption agencies and

journalists during this period and supported by letters from *Delineator* readers,[4] suggests not only a preference for children of Northern European ancestry but also the extent to which sentimental adoption was becoming dominant. As toddlers have little immediate practical use, it was surely the little girls' emotional value that adoptive parents were acknowledging: their conformity to societal ideals of childish attractiveness and their presumed capacity, both as infants and as girls, to give and excite love. Observing that boys are harder to place because "[they] are less tractable than girls; they are noisier; they are more trouble," the column added, "The *Delineator*'s personal experience in child-placing would seem to indicate that even boys are a pretty popular article. Three hundred applications were received for Bobby, almost as many for Fritz; indeed all our boys have found good homes" (1003). In presenting four boys and no girls as its June adoption possibilities, then, the magazine followed its usual strategy of simultaneously acknowledging and dismissing potential obstacles.

But the campaign's greatest challenge—and the one that it delayed taking up the longest—was to place the physically imperfect. As the experience of Gene Stratton-Porter's Freckles suggests, such children were often considered unadoptable.[5] Both within and beyond the *Delineator*'s pages, many child-placement experts proposed that long stays in orphanages be reserved for "those who are abnormal," as Ida Husted Harper wrote in January 1908 ("What Others" 103). Few were concerned about the warehousing of such children unless, like West, they had experienced it. Presumably the personal history of the man behind its orphan-placement project influenced the *Delineator*'s decision to buck standard practice and the influential eugenics movement by finding homes for the physically "unfit."

This phase of the campaign began when the magazine offered, in November 1908, an eleven-year-old girl who had suffered a badly burned hand as a toddler. The next step was to advertise readers' views. February 1909 saw the publication of letters from members of the National Child-Rescue League; one came from a "stone deaf" Massachusetts woman. It asked, "But what about the children who are *not* normal—who through no fault of their own, are blind, or deaf, or crippled, and whom, therefore, nobody wants to adopt? Don't *they* need love and home and appreciation just as much as, or even more than, the others?" ("National" 251). Since "love and home and appreciation" were usually defined at the time as not only what women existed to provide, but also what women most wanted, this comment suggests a natural alliance between the needy child and the magazine's readership.

And by August, readers could conclude that the issue even here was not children's needs but adults'. A roundup of letters from readers included one from the adoptive parents of five children, of whom two had had major health problems on their arrival and one had come to them blind (after treatment, he had later gained partial sight). The family was poor—so poor, indeed, that they had been forced to cancel their *Delineator* subscription—but nonetheless hoped to adopt again. The point was that whatever one's adult burdens (this couple reported the loss of their only biological child and their fortune), children could lighten them, not by offering practical help but, paradoxically, by requiring from their parents a still greater outlay of "anxious care and time." Thus "frail and puny" or disabled children were as well equipped as any to sustain adults emotionally. In fact, because they demanded unusual effort from their caregivers, they might prove unusually rewarding ("Good News" 134).

Having printed such comments from readers before it began offering children who might be deemed seriously damaged, the *Delineator* could be said to be responding to its constituents when it began advertising youngsters such as five-year-old Claude in September 1909. Claude, evidently a polio victim, was distinguished by his inferiority to the usual *Delineator* child:

> When one decides to adopt a child, it is natural to search for a boy or girl physically perfect. For that reason the children who are defective or lacking in comeliness have little chance of obtaining the loving care which they need more than the boys and girls without any handicap. Most of the children offered by *The Delineator* have been far above the average in beauty and intelligence—all strong, healthy and well developed. This month we ask a home for a little boy who is lame. ("Delineator" September 1909, 211)

The selling angle here was that Claude was a charity case, his unusual neediness fitting him to parents who wanted an outlet for virtue more than an outlet for thwarted parental drives. As an editorial of July 1910 put it, "Shouldn't the children with some of these minor physical defects make the greater appeal? Life is going to be more trying for them. How much greater the mercy which prevents it!" ("Concerning the Magazine" 3).

And by the following September, a month after the magazine identified West as the author of the child-placement column, the column was hinting that prospective parents' objections to seeming defects might be arbitrary. The seven children offered that month included fourteen-year-old Jim, one of whose legs was four inches shorter than the other; six-year-old Harold, whose speech was impaired; a four-year-old called "No-Chance Joe," who had a harelip and cleft palate—and nine-year-old Charley, whose "handicap" consisted of red hair and freckles. Reported Henry Thurston of the Illinois Children's Home and Aid Society, whose wards Charley and Joe were, "When [Charley] was sent to another foster home . . . the reception that he got from real kind-hearted and good people was as follows: 'I wrote for a nice-looking boy. Do you think that is a nice-looking boy with red hair and all the spots on his face? . . . I want a good boy, a nice, white-looking boy, with black or dark hair'" ("Delineator" September

1910, 208). Yet boys such as Charley and Joe might have "qualities far superior to those possessed by many a boy of attractive exterior." The comment served several functions, at once suggesting parity between Charley's complexion and the afflictions of Joe, Harold, and Jim; reprimanding the "kind-hearted and good" foster parents for privileging appearance above character; and reminding readers that unpromising children might bestow unsuspected emotional benefits upon their benefactors. Given the magazine's largely female audience, we may take such remarks as both implied criticisms of feminine superficiality (mother-love should go more than skin deep) and tributes to feminine insight (the best women will see the superiority of the apparently inferior).

Utilitarian adoption still existed, especially in rural areas. Placement officers continued to describe as current the practice of sending out older children as farm workers or servants, and did not always put it in a negative light (see, e.g., Reynolds 17, C. Williams 23). But the tide had turned, in that sentimental adoption as practiced by the urban middle class was now rhetorically dominant. And inexorably, adoption was being linked with privilege. Viviana Zelizer notes that a New York State Charities Aid Association study of foster fathers' occupations in 1898–1900 and 1920–21 shows a marked change in social class: nearly three men in four of the earlier group were farmers or laborers (skilled or unskilled), while most of the later fathers were white-collar workers (191–92). More and more writers were suggesting that adopting a child was a proof of status moral and financial. As Arno Dosch observed in 1910, "Foster-parents no longer preen themselves with conscious rectitude for having adopted a baby. . . . Now they cry, 'Look at the fine baby we have been allowed to make our heir'" (432). In women's magazines, the "fine baby"'s commodification as a luxury article turned adoption into conspicuous consumption.

Thus receiving a *Delineator* child was increasingly framed as winning a competition in which victory depended upon being recognized as the right kind of mother. Such encomiums could appear in legal rhetoric as well, as in a 1915 case in Washington State, *In re* Potter, in which the judge making out an order of adoption wrote that "the one who voluntarily assumes [the] privilege [of caring for a child] must have far deeper maternal instincts than one who is an unwilling mother" (qtd. Modell 31). At other times, however, adoptive parents might be seen as emotional invalids seeking a child by way of a cure. Thus Dr. Charles Gilmore Kerley wrote in 1916 that adoption is "a very effective prescription against premature old age" as well as "neurasthenia, despondency, and habitual grouch, particularly in men" (105), while an adoptive father told the *Woman's Home Companion* that his son's arrival had made a major emotional difference to himself and his wife: "Think what I was in our childless days; think what Grace [his wife] was . . . then ask yourself who the philanthropist is" ("Making" 5). By 1917, the superintendent of the Illinois Children's Home and Aid Society was warning that placement officers should investigate "whether or not a distracted wife is urging her request for a child in the vague hope of reforming an incapable husband," or whether a husband had an "intense desire . . . for a bond that [would] deter an unfaithful wife" (Reynolds 17).

This argument that without a multigenerational family life *adults* could not grow morally was essential to the orphan fiction of this period, which more than ever presented adoption as the key to the moral reclamation of the new mother. More specifically, as I have suggested above, adoption might be offered as the solution to the new century's version of the "woman question," holding out the prospect of satisfying and/or taming women's desire for achievement within and beyond the home. But nonfiction discussion of adoption and foster care incorporated other themes as well, some of them inimical to the support of (sentimental) adoption represented by the *Delineator* campaign. Between 1907 and 1918, we see increased efforts to keep children and birth parents together, both by providing subsidies so that poor but worthy parents could rear their own children and by working to eliminate causes of dependency, perhaps by encouraging wage-earners to take out insurance. We also see anxiety about the nuts and bolts of placement work: Were agencies keeping adequate records? Did they do follow-up work after placements? Did the state exercise enough control over private agencies? Such questions were prompted both by concern for the children and by a sense that adoption should not be too easy.

Adoption and the Nontraditional Family

One reason that adoption was both welcome and suspect was that it was an alternative route to maternity. Like the late nineteenth century, the early twentieth was obsessed with motherhood. Sometimes this obsession was used, as it had been from the 1870s onward, to dissuade women from seeking degrees or careers, on the ground that such achievements would unfit them for their "natural" function. Sometimes, conversely, it provided a national forum for what Carroll Smith-Rosenberg calls "public mothers" (263), politically minded women who specialized in children's issues.[6] Motherhood, announced the pundits, was the crowning achievement of a woman's life, the greatest gift she could give to society, the greatest happiness she could find for herself. Women who refused it were furthering race suicide; they were selfish or unfulfilled. Conversely, of course, women who bore illegitimate children were immoral. Motherhood required marriage.

Unless one mothered another woman's child. While the practice was unusual, adoption by single women or pairs of women was by no means unknown. Of fifty-eight children legally adopted under the auspices of Clara Spence and Charlotte Baker (founders of what is now the Spence-Chapin Agency) in New York City between 1910 and 1916, two went to single mothers (Kerley 107); Berebitsky lists various prominent professional women who adopted children outside of heterosexual marriage in the 1910s (104–107).[7] After all, adoption could be viewed as a way for spinsters to put their maternal instincts to use; it could save them from neurosis and their adopted children from the horrors of institutional life. In this light single-parent adoption looked socially conservative, an acknowledgment that motherhood was women's primary function and that women desired nothing so much as a family to serve. But adoption by spinsters could also appear radical, a way for women to be fulfilled without men. It could demonstrate an alarming independence, a simultaneous rejection of marriage's confinement and usurpation of marriage's rewards. In the latter case, it merited condemnation—but how was one to tell the traditionalist from the revolutionary?[8]

The situation was additionally complicated by America's ambivalent attitude toward female sexuality. One strand of Victorian morality, which continued influential at least through the end of the First World War, claimed that good women were above sex. If what women really wanted was motherhood, sex was not the only means to that end. But other Victorians, including some social-purity activists, both acknowledged and celebrated women's sexual pleasure within marriage (see, e.g., Gay 141). By the 1910s, as the backlash against "Victorianism" intensified and Freud's popularization made repression suspect, virginity in mature women increasingly looked pathological rather than virtuous.[9] Women who sought to adopt children as a way of avoiding the marriage bed were out of step with their culture. In addition, women's "passionate friendships" and "Boston marriages" were beginning to lose their erstwhile respectability.

Thus anxiety about spinsters' potential perversity sometimes barred nontraditional adoptions even before the 1920s. Some social-service professionals opposed placing children with unmarried women on the ground that such placements offered an undesirable environment. We see single-parent adoption condemned by rescue agencies such as the Guild of the Infant Savior, which held that "non-productive members of society [i.e., the unmarried] . . . 'are not fit persons to take care of a child'" (Patterson 410); the adjective "non-productive" connotes the abnormality of the dead end, hinting that failing to act on one's (hetero)sexuality is both immoral and perverse. Berebitsky adds that by 1916, the New York Children's Aid Society "had stopped placing children with single women" (115). In contrast, women's magazines, which addressed married and unmarried alike, tended to be sympathetic to the idea. Since such magazines typically assumed that adoption was motivated exclusively by love, they were not prepared to consider single-parent adoption a rejection of normalcy or a form of social protest—or at least they hid social protest behind sentimentality. Even so, stories and articles on the question permit contradictory readings, maximizing audience appeal by catering to multiple stances.

Consider a triumvirate of pieces featuring single-parent adoption, which appeared in *Harper's Bazar* and *Good Housekeeping* between September 1912 and February 1914. The last of these, a description by Texas journalist Judd Mortimer Lewis of his unpaid efforts to place homeless infants, remarked that "baby-bureau work" was "full of heartaches, of heart-breaks, and of happinesses. Always the men and women who undertake it find depths of suffering, examples of renunciation, and heights of happiness which they had not dreamed existed" (194). The article implicitly promised, in other words, to furnish the satisfactions of melodrama to its readers, and thus it contained anecdotes designed to wring the heartstrings. One such tale concerned a spinster teacher, near retirement age, who pleaded that Lewis send her "a baby to adopt, whether boy or girl, but a cripple or a helpless invalid; a child that would always need her love, and could never go away and leave her!" (197). As of the time of writing, Lewis had not been able to find a suitable child. Nevertheless, the article implied that the teacher had his sympathy.

The suggestion was that the physical incapacity of the wished-for child matched the emotional neediness of the spinster, whose work had provided only an unsatisfying "family" of youngsters who could always get free. Deprived of marriage and biological children, this career woman had become *plus maternelles que les mamans*. Readers could see the vignette as proving that the public sphere could not satisfy a woman's deepest cravings, a conservative stance. But they could also take it as a hint that adoption might not only remedy the sorrows resulting from having a job rather than a family, but also permit the kind of perfect match between mother and child that might not be available in nature, since, like the teacher's students, a biological son or daughter might have left her in adulthood. Hence adoptive single mothers could have it all: a career in youth, the child of their imaginings in late middle age.

The latter is the implication of a pair of stories by Elizabeth M. Gilmer published in the same magazine in 1913. The first, "When the Dream Fails," tells of a wealthy fifty-year-old artist who has lost hope. Her despair is rooted in her childhood experience as an orphan raised by a reluctant relative, when her fantasy that her parents would come back to life and reclaim her went unfulfilled. Ditto her adolescent dreams of marriage: men "proved to be little, and mean, and selfish, and tyrannical, with neither mind nor heart" (684). Finally, she has concluded that she will never be as great an artist as she had once hoped. In short, this apparently successful woman has experienced neither family life, nor romance, nor true career satisfaction. Any happily married reader, however obscure and untalented, can feel superior.

But all is not lost. In "The Dream Regained," the narrator returns to the artist's studio a year later, and finds

> her latest picture, which the critics had already acclaimed her masterpiece.
>
> It was . . . the picture of a little child, pushing open with rose leaf hands a great, grim, barred door that looked as if it might have resisted

the strength of a hundred giants. The face of the child was all soft, delicate, baby curves, but the eyes were mystic. In them was hope, and promise, and fulfillment—the eternal something that makes the struggle of life
worth while. (829)

She also finds the artist's inspiration: her newly adopted daughter, Mary.
Mary represents the era's ideal orphan, being "a pretty little thing, about
three years old, with a riot of golden curls, and big blue eyes, and a rose-
bud mouth" (830). Since her biological mother (herself an aspiring artist)
has died, she also has no relatives to complicate the placement.

For all Mary's charms, the artist originally has no intention of adopting
her. But orphans are potent. Mary begins her infant wiles by murmuring
on the first night, "I love you, booful lady" (830). She becomes what the
artist terms a "toy," accepting "a little blue velvet coat . . . and tiny patent
leather shoes, and a smocked gown in which I knew she would look like a
Kate Greenaway picture" (831). That is, she appeals both aesthetically (she
can look like the ideal commodified child) and psychologically, enabling
games of dress-up that address her patron's need to revisit and revise her
own deprived childhood.

This vision of maternal experience is a spinster's fantasy come to life:
Mary makes no demands of the artist, but rather provides what the latter
demands of her, down to the picturesque appearance. Small wonder that
faced with so conformable an infant, the artist doubts her own arguments
about "what a care a child would be, how much it would interfere with my
work, and with my personal liberty, and [how foolish I would be] to take
such a burden upon myself" (831). Having established that Mary would be
more likely to satisfy than to thwart her adoptive mother's needs, the artist
can take her on permanently; Mary's own needs come second. On resolv-
ing to adopt Mary, the new mother finds her "heart at peace as it had not
been for a long time before," and she regains her ability to daydream, not
about her own future but about her daughter's maturation, courtship, and
motherhood. What her "masterpiece" shows, she explains, is "A child's
hand opening the door to the House of Dreams for us, who have grown too
old to dream any more for ourselves" (831). The child's highest function,
then, is to permit the adult to live through her. Moreover, the story suggests, adoption offers both a substitute for public success (perhaps the artist
will prove a better mother than painter) and a way of reaching it (becoming a mother *makes* her a better painter).[10]

"The Dream Regained" reveals the incompleteness of the conservative
story that preceded it. No longer may the untalented but happy wife pity,
as unfulfilled, the woman "who has won an honorable place for herself in
her profession" (Gilmer, "Fails" 683). The dyad formed through adoption
permits the adult multiple satisfactions: as artist communing with her
muse, as bereaved child comforting herself with fantasies of maternal
plenitude, as mother and prospective grandmother loved by two generations of young people. That Mary can even offer vicarious romance to the

artist suggests the completeness with which adoption may replace marriage. This mother can have it both ways, retaining her independence as a single woman but reveling in the prospect of seeing Mary's sexual urges satisfied. At fifty, an age when women are presumed to be past the important part of the female experience, the artist has shown through single-parent adoption that she can seize the best that life has to offer.

Still more overtly radical is Olivia Howard Dunbar's September 1912 piece in *Harper's Bazar,* "Miss Hildreth: 'Mother of Ten.'" The article profiles a New Hampshire "suffragist" and "strong feminist" who "admits no drawbacks to the practice of adopting children, even when the guardian is an unmarried woman. . . . Without being a man-hater, she feels that man is a domestic feature easily dispensed with, and that a father's influence is by no means necessary in the training of children" (444). She believes in sending girls to college and in training boys to keep house, and her interest in adoption began when a "friend of her own age to whom she was deeply attached," and with whom she used to summer, "interrupt[ed] this companionship" by marrying and bearing a child, inspiring her to acquire a baby so that she and her friend could share the experience of motherhood in "ecstatic rivalry" (443). The overtones of gender-bending and passionate friendship would have been unmistakable, if respectable, at the time.

Moreover, Miss Hildreth's experience might suggest that the distractions of marriage impede the full expression of motherly energies. As Dunbar notes, her "maternal emotion . . . seems practically inexhaustible" (443). The ten children of the article title are merely the current crop; five others have already left the family via marriage, death, reunion with blood kin, or (in "the astonishing case of a dangerously imbecile boy . . . of whom [Miss Hildreth] took entire care for fourteen years") institutionalization (443). She has raised her brood—and attendant menagerie, including six ponies and a bronco stallion—without nannies, "and at one time took the entire care of four children who were all under three years of age" (444).

Reeling at this picture, the reader may not notice that Miss Hildreth not only has redefined the family to exclude fathers, but is also attacking certain popular beliefs about maternity. First, "It is her deep conviction, and one, of course, which would be promptly disputed by the average mother, that she could not love the children any more if they were her own. The physical experience of motherhood, she maintains, is by no means an indispensable preliminary to a grown person's supreme love for a child and ability to care for it" (443). This belief is predictable in an adoptive mother, but despite her inability "to pass within arm's-length of the younger children without seizing them for rapturous caresses" (443), Miss Hildreth also critiques and redefines maternal love. Her first son, who died in early childhood, was "'the only one,' she confessed, 'that I have ever loved in that selfish, exclusive way that women should try so hard to guard against. But I did not understand then . . . how wrong it is to love a child in a way that shuts out other love'" (443).

Moreover, while the children are luxuries rather than practical helps to the family—she has decided, reluctantly, not to adopt any more because of the cost of college educations—she prides herself on not sentimentalizing childhood. Hence she denies the dominant belief in childish innocence and purity, arguing "that children are born without any of the assortment of virtues usually held desirable and that all these have to be patiently inculcated" (444). Nor is she even a unilateral supporter of adoption; she believes in keeping biological families together through mothers' pensions and has consciously sought no child but the first. To be sure, she sees adoption as a cure for the "vaguely romantic lamentations" of "the confessedly lonely woman," a stance that may seem conservative in its impatience with feminine self-indulgence, wistful fantasy, and leisure. But both Miss Hildreth and her profiler consider adoption a satisfactory alternative to marriage: "What better arrangement could there be than for all the lonely women and left-over children in the world to pair off with each other?" (444). The sketch's reshaping of conventions of family and romance suggests that even in the real world, women use adoption as a means of rejecting what some might see as the fundamental rules of their existence.

Of course, nontraditional adoption could work in other ways as well, as both fiction and nonfiction illustrate. Sometimes it was the method through which siblings could be transformed into parents. Thus the *Delineator* reported in August 1908,

> Ralph's placement has been rather unique. The *Delineator* children, up to date, have been placed in families where there was a husband and wife. Sometimes the longing for children is implanted just as keenly in the hearts of those who have never married, and Ralph is now a beloved son in the home of two maiden sisters and a bachelor brother. . . . These good people who received Ralph are grateful to *The Delineator* for stirring up their hearts, and, with the boy, rejoice in their mutual good fortune. ("Delineator" 260)

Since this placement, like all the *Delineator*'s placements, was said to be motivated by sentiment rather than utility, assuaging a "longing for children" and "stirring up [the] hearts" of the adults involved, it invites interpretation as forging a sexless but incestuous marriage à trois. But adoption's great advantage was that it represented a kind of immaculate conception. The ostentatious innocence of the means by which children arrived in families of this sort, the adults' applications approved by philanthropists and bureaucrats, permitted radical reconfigurations of conventional domestic patterns to look staid.

The insistence that even "rather unique" placements such as Ralph's were unremarkable probably owed something to orphan fiction, in which child rearing by unmarried pairs had long been common. The pattern extends at least as far back as *The Wide, Wide World,* in which Ellen occupies no fewer than three such households. It embraces such examples as the

Widow Douglas and her sister in *Huckleberry Finn,* Dearest and the Earl in *Little Lord Fauntleroy,* Miss Avilda and her servant in *Timothy's Quest,* Marilla and her brother in *Anne of Green Gables,* and Rebecca's two aunts in *Rebecca of Sunnybrook Farm.* Most simply, such families may reflect real social trends; more than 10 percent of American women born between 1860 and 1879 never married (D. Smith 224),[11] and the Civil War dramatically increased the number of widows in the preceding generation. But we may also interpret these celibate but fertile unions as a radical expression of delight in female autonomy, or as a conservative acknowledgment that raising a child is a task in which a woman must perforce engage, even if the child is not biologically hers and the only co-parent available is her brother, father-in-law, hired man—or sister or maid.

Ralph's *Delineator* adoption also resembles its literary antecedents in that the orphans in tales aimed at female readers likewise "stir up hearts," bringing romance or reconciliation or other expressions of feeling in their wake. Such denouements often have sexual overtones, even while they simultaneously celebrate innocence and purity. Moreover, as we have seen, the emphasis on sentiment in adoption flowered more quickly and vigorously in fiction than in nonfiction. Thus one thing we notice about the *Delineator* campaign and contemporaneous adoption articles in other women's magazines is the extent to which their ideological underpinnings suggest a new conformity to patterns established in domestic fiction.

But fiction could also share the insights of nonfiction. Consider a 1910 *Delineator* story by Dorothy Canfield, "Out of the Wilderness," which reads like a dramatization of the common complaints about childless spinsters' tendency to neurasthenia, time-wasting, and self-absorption. Here Evelyn Willis, a wealthy aesthete who resembles the emotionally sterile Eugenia Mills of Canfield's 1919 *The Brimming Cup,* is suffering from nervous prostration, for which her doctor has prescribed a sojourn in rural Vermont. Her landlady's lumberman has just died; when his widow contracts pneumonia, the landlady must nurse the patient, so that there is no one but Evelyn to look after the widow's son. Evelyn accepts this task reluctantly. She is disgusted by the baby's wails and stinks; she considers it "indecent . . . that anything in the civilized world should be so incredibly, intolerably unrestrained" (224). An inexperienced caregiver, she keeps cutting herself, burning herself, and missing meals in satisfying the baby's needs. She resents these inconveniences and denies the sentimental pleasures that her culture associates with infants: "'And there are people who say they like babies!' she cried aloud. '*They lie!*'" (224).

But rebellion cannot last. While she complains, "It would be the cheapest, most obvious Dickensese if I should come to *like* the abominable little creature!" (225), she begins to delight both in the child and in looking after him. When she accidentally runs a needle into him, "there vanished the last shred of the veil which hid her from herself. She snatched the baby up, holding him close to her breast to still his cries; she kissed him frantically again and again, crying out foolish, broken words of endearment and call-ing herself by all cruel names. . . . The mischief was done" (226). Her old ways make a last stand before sophisticated self-absorption becomes im-possible: "Her lifelong habit of introspection coming to the front, she tried to analyze what had happened to her, and 'It is like so many other vicious tastes,' she reflected whimsically, 'like smoking, like absinthe-drinking, it fastens on you all the more firmly because it begins in utter distaste and—' But the baby was wailing for more dinner. She never could go back to finish that line of thought, she never could begin another" (226).

The lesson is plain both to the reader and to Evelyn. Her doctor, who had thought that she needed someone to take care of her, was wrong: rather, she needs to take care of someone else. As a wealthy single woman, she has had too much freedom, too few responsibilities and emotional at-tachments. In order to become healthy and happy, she must become a mother. When, after three weeks, the biological mother dies, Evelyn ea-gerly adopts the child. And it is clear that she, not the baby, is the real beneficiary of the arrangement.

Motherhood lifts Evelyn out of two dangerous categories: that of the New Woman, bohemian and liberated, and that of the neurasthenic. In the early twentieth century, both types were associated with the rejection of woman's "natural" role as domestic goddess, and often condemned accord-ingly. Smith-Rosenberg supplies a profile of the female hysteric of late-nineteenth-century medical literature, whose resemblance to Evelyn sug-gests that Canfield was offering both diagnosis and cure for a malaise often discussed in her day: "Doctors commonly described hysterical women as highly impressionable, suggestible, and narcissistic . . . [and] complained that the hysterical woman was egocentric in the extreme, her involvement with others consistently superficial and tangential. . . . She was, doctors cautioned, essentially asexual and not uncommonly frigid" (202). If Evelyn's doctor has prescribed a literal return to nature, sending his patient from Manhattan's artificiality to Vermont's backwoods, caring for a baby has uncovered in her a natural femininity that she has not hitherto mani-fested. In the words of the title, she has come "out of the wilderness," back to a domestic space in which the sleeplessness and anorexia caused by her emotional illness have turned into sleeplessness and missed meals endured for a baby's sake: the symptoms are identical, but they now betoken health.

And since Canfield, like the physicians anatomizing female hysteria, suggests that her subject is asexual and cold, adoption is the only mode of parenthood possible to Evelyn, the only path to salvation. This point ex-tends into a wide variety of fiction and nonfiction critiques of Progressive Era femininity. The "childless home," after all, generally betokened a woman's failure rather than a man's, since motherhood was a moral im-perative while fatherhood was not. Childless men were not told that they had missed the central experience of their lives, and it was women, not men, who were held responsible for "race suicide." The feminists, career women, and epicene aristocrats associated with representations of single-parent adoption in the early twentieth century may be interpreted, on one level, as women who sought to refute charges that they were in revolt against the self-abnegation that their culture required of them. They might reserve the right to be sexually cold, financially independent, and emotionally autonomous, but ultimately they could not resist the demand that they become mothers.

The Apotheosis of the Orphan
in Late Progressive Era Children's Fiction

The women's magazine was not the only forum to describe adoption's transformation of lonely, embittered, or neurotic spinsters into fulfilled mothers. Children's orphan fiction, too, focused on the psychological miracles that adopted girls and boys could work on adults. If children (rather than women, as in the magazine pieces) were the protagonists of such narratives, adults, and particularly women, were increasingly identified as the figures who experienced growth and renewal. By 1910, orphans were presented as irresistibly lovable and potent not merely for their new families, but within their larger social environments as well. At the same time, we see the growth of another type of orphan fiction, what might be termed the theoretical variety; while still participating in the sentimental discourse, such novels illustrated precepts of sociology or child psychology. Together, the two models of story sketched a world in which children were valuable beings deserving appreciative and informed care. Along the way, they critiqued unsatisfactory forms of femininity, suggesting ways in which the problem of the orphan might intersect with that of the unfulfilled woman.

An example of the theoretical orphan novel is Canfield's *Understood Betsy* (1917), whose protagonist takes part in not one but two nontraditional adoptions.[12] As an infant, Betsy becomes the ward of her fluttery Aunt Frances (really her first cousin once removed), living with Frances, Frances's widowed mother, and their servant; ten years later, after Frances's mother contracts tuberculosis, the child is sent to Vermont to another spinster, Ann Putney, and Ann's parents. In a didactic sense, the novel's major point is to contrast Frances's femininity and child-rearing methods—inflected by parenting manuals, Mothers' Club meetings, and "a correspondence course from a school in Chicago which teaches mother-craft by mail" (4)—with the Putneys' more down-to-earth approach. Frances's style of parenting, which reflects the latest fashions in child psychology, smacks more of book-learning than of instinct; it produces an artificial, neurotic child, overly introspective, dependent, and nervous. Ann's common sense and her parents' unstudied affection create something sturdier.

Frances is something of an emotional vampire. Ostensibly, she protects Betsy against a terrifying world, so that the girl has become a creature even more affectedly "sensitive" than the aunt. But in reality, she uses Betsy to assuage her boredom with her "empty life" (3)—a role for the adopted child that other fiction of the era, including Canfield's own "Out of the Wilderness," notes more approvingly. Betsy's role as psychological defense is underscored by the fact that on her departure, Frances replaces her with a fiancé on whom she can lean: "He's so big and strong, and he just loves to take care of people. He says that's why he's marrying me" (198). The engagement both eliminates the need for Betsy to return to her original caregiver and implies that marriage is the last refuge of the incompetent.

Ann, however, seems to have been content without a child; nor does she need a husband. Tall, strong, commanding, and not a little masculine, Ann is wholly self-sufficient, although she and Betsy develop a loving master/disciple relationship. And Canfield shows that despite—or because of—her sexlessness and androgyny, Ann is a better role model for Betsy than is Frances. Having consciously patterned herself on her Vermont cousin, Betsy can earn enough money to get herself and a younger child home from a fair when a mishap leaves them stranded; she also sees Frances as she is, loves her anyway, and shows herself willing to take responsibility for Frances's happiness, even at the price of her own. In other words, she has grown independent, strong, clear-sighted, and mature enough to make sacrifices for others, a traditionally female role that Frances, ironically, is too fluffy to manage. It is the spinsterish Ann rather than the clinging vine Frances who represents true womanhood and the "backward" Putney home that shows real understanding of the child mind.

Hence this novel, which may look feminist today because of its approval of the powerful single woman, has a strong admixture of traditionalism—a mixture often found within the New England regionalist genre to which it belongs. One way in which *Understood Betsy* manifests this sensibility is by rejecting the sentimental model that asks not what adults can do for children, but what children can do for adults; Ann's competence distinguishes her from those contemporaneous adoptive mothers, from Frances to the women imagined by the *Delineator* campaign, who see parenthood as the answer to their emotional problems. While the Putneys love Betsy, they do not need her, so that they recall a model of adoption as philanthropy, a model pooh-poohed as out of date or unseemly in the magazines of the 1910s (see, e.g., Dosch 432; "Making" 5). Another adoption in this novel, the wealthy Mr. and Mrs. Pond's rescue of 'Lias Brewster, is likewise not motivated by Mr. Pond's sight of 'Lias respectable in the clothes that Betsy and her schoolmates have given him to make him look more eligible. Rather, it results from Mr. Pond's discovery of the boy "crying and crying and crying, digging his fists into his eyes, his face all smeared with tears and dirt" because his stepfather has sold the gifts to buy liquor, leaving 'Lias only "his filthy, torn old overalls and ragged shirt" (156). While sentiment is a factor here, the notion of child as savior is not: Canfield expects adults to take charge.

Moreover, as is standard not only in regionalist writing but also in children's literature from the eighteenth century onward, she privileges the healthy countryside over the effete city, the good old ways over modern innovations. As a city girl, Betsy was "a pale child, with a thin neck and spindling legs half-hidden in the folds of Aunt Frances's skirts. But she didn't look even like the sister of this browned, muscular, upstanding child" who is Betsy after some months in Vermont (162–63). The one-room schoolhouse she now attends, "only a poor, rough, district school . . . that no city Superintendent of Schools would have looked at for a minute, except to sniff" (86), educates her better than the up-to-date and impersonal school of her early life.[13] Betsy's new life is more productive than the old, and while the city gave her no understanding even of the mundane details of contemporary urban life, Vermont connects her to her heritage. In this context, Ann does not look like a feminist icon, the New Woman defiant in her "man's coat" (110), but like a throwback to pioneer days, a tribute not to the progressive but to the retrograde. At the same time, of course, Ann *is* a figure of authority and strength, traits underscored by her successful parenting, so that Canfield's criticism of the female neurotic is balanced by her tribute to female self-sufficiency.

Understood Betsy is unusual for its time in identifying the child as the creation of an emotionally influential adult rather than vice versa. Yet it is typical in evincing anxiety about the barren anti-mother who suffers from neurosis or coldness or willfulness. Thus spinsters saved by motherhood may be reunited with their sexuality as well, a pattern already evident by the 1890s. While Samantha Ann in *Timothy's Quest* and Aunt Jane in *Rebecca of Sunnybrook Farm* do not become biological mothers, their foster children free them from inhibition, allowing marriage in Samantha Ann's case and the memorializing of a lost lover in Jane's. Rebecca is the only person besides Jane's fiancé, killed in the Civil War, to glimpse "the heart of a prim New England girl when it is ablaze with love and grief"; the narrator notes that Jane "had never breathed a word of it before [revealing her feelings to Rebecca] . . . for there was no one who would have understood" (Wiggin, *Rebecca* 31, 154). In other words, Progressive Era fiction—perhaps especially within New England regionalist writing, which focuses on women's psychology—may use single-parent adoption to discuss the (hetero)sexuality of the officially sexless middle-aged spinster.

Moreover, the love between parent and adopted child is allied to the sexual urge, since the former may be enabled by, or may enable, romance. This theme dominates another pair of New England tales, Eleanor H. Porter's 1913 *Pollyanna* and its 1915 sequel *Pollyanna Grows Up*. Both, Alice Mills notes, rely on love tangles mystified "to the point of obsessiveness" and on an "insistence on sexual partnering possibilities between parent and child" (97, 100). While Mills's discussion of Oedipal desire centers on Pollyanna's relationship with her mother's former suitor, a sexual element also exists in the relationship between the eleven-year-old orphan and her guardian/aunt, Polly Harrington. The latter initially accepts her charge grimly, so that Pollyanna must seduce her into a more joyful motherhood, and the first volume is primarily a courtship dance in which Pollyanna performs childish "gladness" (acknowledged by the narrative to be something of a fabrication, since it requires effort) until Polly succumbs. The final mark of Polly's capitulation is her marriage to a man from whom she has long been estranged, but the signals of her sexual awakening—the face "alight with excitement and surprise," the "pretty pink" cheeks, the red rose (symbol of passion) tucked behind one ear (144–45)—pass not between Polly and her future mate but between Polly and Pollyanna.

Mills proposes that we read Polly as Pollyanna's double (93). If this is the case, the aunt's belated acquiescence to marriage when she is forced to summon her erstwhile lover, a doctor, to tend the child may seem a manifestation of the prepubescent girl's fascination with romance: Polly must marry because Pollyanna, at eleven, cannot. Yet Porter's use of doubling itself suggests marriage, insofar as the inhospitable aunt has had to open her home and even her bed to her niece, changing her habits, personality, and heart to suit Pollyanna's desires. And since forty-year-old Polly is initially cold and masterful, a wealthy and too independent woman without nurturing instincts, domination by her niece/daughter turns her from a pseudo-male into a Real Woman who must hand over her troubles to her husband. The parodic marriage to Pollyanna, in short, prepares Polly for a more conventional union.

The traditionalism of *Pollyanna*'s ending, in which love makes Polly "wonderfully tremulous, wonderfully different" (265), might be read as an antifeminist celebration of Polly's loss of autonomy. But that both the doctor and Polly concede that "it's you [Pollyanna] that have done it all" (265) directs authority away from the masculine, or even the adult, need to dominate. Social, emotional, and sexual power is with the child. Common enough in the era's sentimental fiction, this formulation nonetheless constitutes an attack on the cultural norm insofar as it suggests that authority—even sexual authority—need not be the perquisite of adult males. Most authors of classic orphan fictions are female (sentimental literature overall is a heavily female form), so that a narrative's criticism of a central female character entails an attack on one brand of womanhood by the representative of another. Authors such as Porter, already an established professional by the time of *Pollyanna*'s phenomenal success,[14] might well have felt reluctant to advocate the subordination of independent women to male hegemony. Using the figure of the orphan (usually a female orphan at that) as a mechanism for correcting the errors of adult women allowed criticisms of femininity that did not betray the principles of sisterhood.

Adopted orphans such as Pollyanna and Betsy fit this purpose psychologically in that their status underscores their alienation from their foster mothers and thus enables comparisons unflattering to the older women.

Moreover, in an era that idealized motherhood, single adoptive mothers were one of the few types of middle-class maternity open to criticism. Conventional mothers had an aura of the sacred: "Nothing in the home could match the radiance and love of a mother, for there was something transcendent about her. . . . She alone served as the guide for righteous living," writes historian Joe L. Dubbert, summing up the dominant ethos (310). But women who had not borne children might be capable of selfishness or folly. Whether they were condemned for being too dependent, like Canfield's Frances, or for being too independent, like Porter's Polly, they could be pilloried and redeemed in a way that "real" mothers could not.

Of course, not all adults in the orphan fiction of the era are single, and not all are female, although women form the majority. If Pollyanna's main task is to make Aunt Polly more feminine by strengthening her social ties and reintroducing romance to her life, the child also transforms the outlooks of widows, bachelors, unhappily married wives, bereaved mothers, and men at odds with their careers. A similarly influential Porter orphan, the eponymous hero of *Just David* (1916), uses his musical genius not only to reconcile a pair of warring lovers who resemble Aunt Polly and Dr. Chilton (she is rich and unfulfilled, he poor and self-sacrificing), but also to bring joy into the lives of a blind boy, the village idiot, an old miser, and the elderly man and wife who have given him a home. He saves this couple, Simeon and Ellen Holly, both financially and emotionally, sacrificing his inheritance in order to prevent foreclosure of their mortgage; teaching them "to look at the world through [his] eyes" (253); and finally reuniting them with their estranged son, whose place he has symbolically taken. By novel's end, Simeon has capitulated to love; though "a strong man, [he] is shaken by an emotion that has mastered him" (323), and his discovery of unselfish fatherhood permits a long-delayed gratification of the "mother-love and longing in [Ellen's] pleading eyes and voice" (311).

Yet as this denouement implies, the emphasis on the orphan's emotional function persists whether that orphan is transforming women or men, and typically the child's task is to strengthen domestic ties by reuniting families, playing Cupid, or creating new parent-child dyads, as when Pollyanna persuades her mother's former suitor to adopt her friend Jimmy Bean. In other words, it is the problems of the private sphere, not the public, that the fictional orphan solves. As Perry Nodelman writes, these fictions are designed in part to tell the discontented adults who populate (and, potentially, read) them "that home is in fact utopia" (34). This message would appear to be aimed primarily at women; Nodelman, indeed, defines the traditional fictional orphan as female. Such orphans operate as substitutes for the ideal mother, whose role, like that of her Victorian counterpart, still included serving as the heart of the family, the source of tenderness and emotional fulfillment. And the effectiveness of the fiction that contains such children is suggested by the extent to which contemporaneous nonfiction commentary variously shares and points out this belief in the adopted child as domestic miracle-worker.

Mothercraft and Mothers' Pensions: The White House Conference of 1909

If the fiction of the period often functioned to expose adoptive parents' emotional limitations, suggesting that the weakness attributed to the American family came from within, the 1909 White House Conference on the Care of Dependent Children struck a different note. As Theodore Roosevelt, the conference's host, told Congress, "The keynote of the conference was expressed in these words: 'Home life is the highest and finest product of civilization. Children should not be deprived of it except for urgent and compelling reasons'" (*Proceedings* 5). In other words, the family, particularly the mother, was the nation's strength. Except in a very few cases, families were inherently healthy and moral—but were subject nonetheless to outside pressures that could cause the breakdown of the system. It was the conference's function to discuss ways of eliminating these pressures and facilitating the provision of substitute homes when circumstances necessitated this task.

The thirteen resolutions passed at the conference illustrate a two-pronged ideology of child-saving. While children were to receive an individualized upbringing, whether in private homes or in cottage institutions that mimicked the private home, child-saving was to become centralized and cooperative, with local agencies sharing resources, states overseeing local agencies, and the federal government overseeing all. In short, the value of private mothercraft (a favorite term of the era) was yoked with the power of public organization. The potential paradox was summed up in the conference's principal recommendation, that needy "worthy parents or deserving mothers" be subsidized with tax dollars so that homes, now effectively public rather than private, might remain intact (*Proceedings* 6).

Requested by an ecumenical group including Hastings Hart and John Glenn of the Russell Sage Foundation, Homer Folks, Thomas Mulry of the St. Vincent de Paul Society, Edward Devine of Columbia University and *Charities and The Commons,* Julian Mack of the National Conference of Jewish Charities, Charles Birtwell of the Boston Children's Aid Society, and Dreiser and West of the *Delineator,* the conference was a largely male affair, although the organizers took care to invite prominent women such as Jane Addams and Dr. Kate Waller Barrett, superintendent of the National Florence Crittenton Mission for unwed mothers. Indeed, Roosevelt's sponsorship seems partly a matter of male ties, namely his friendship with West—who had been invited to the White House in October 1908 for a conversation that led to the conference's convening the following January—and his recollections of his own father's involvement with the endeavors of Charles Loring Brace. (Roosevelt senior, quondam vice president of the New York State Charities Aid Association, actively supported the orphan trains and had referred to the Children's Aid Society one of its greatest success stories, a boy who would grow up to become governor of Alaska.) But the reformers at the conference nevertheless agreed that parenting was essentially a female activity.

Thus in the case of half-orphans, the conferees' assumption, even their wish, was that the surviving parent would be the mother. Widowed by disease or industrial accident, she might lack the means to care for her offspring; alternatively, she might have been deserted by a scoundrel who refused to support his children. The problem before the meeting, then, was whether poverty should force the separation of mother and child. Overwhelmingly, the consensus was no. "The mother that devotes herself to her child and household renders social service of inestimable value," opined Charles Henderson of the National Children's Home Society; "It is her right to expect compensation at the hand of [the] society that ultimately and often immediately is the gainer by her maternal devotion" (*Proceedings* 90). Speaker after speaker endorsed mothers' pensions, sometimes as the one exception to a general stricture against "outdoor relief" (56). Others sought to reduce the need for such subsidies by creating standards for workplace safety; passing liability laws to help the families of men injured or killed on the job; eliminating tuberculosis, a major cause of death for adults in their thirties and forties; mandating pension plans and encouraging insurance; and criminalizing men's desertion of their families, stipulating that the proceeds of the men's labor while in prison would be paid to their wives and children.

All this rhetoric assumed that the roles of mother and father were distinct. Adolph Lewisohn, president of the Hebrew Sheltering Guardian Society of New York City, argued that children belonged "with their own mothers, who can give them the parental love and the parental attention . . . which can not be obtained in any other way" (*Proceedings* 145). That "any other way" included the home headed by a single father became explicit in the next paragraph of Lewisohn's memorandum, which spoke of "the sheer inability on the part of the [widowed] father to give his children the home attention which they require" (145–46). The father's job was to provide for his family, a duty that the state could compel him to fulfill should he be irresponsible, or arrogate to itself or demand from his insurers or erstwhile employers should he die. In contrast, the mother's job was to ensure "the safety and importance of the home" by bestowing "the affection and love which emanates from the mother to the child," observed Simon Wolf, founder of Atlanta's Hebrew Orphan's Home (149). Maternity's emotional dimension put it beyond the ability of the state, the private charity, or the institution to perform, or perhaps even to express. As Rudolph R. Reeder, superintendent of the model orphanage at Hastings-on-Hudson, New York, said of the concept of the family home (inextricably bound up with that of the mother, he noted), it "is that of which poets sing, statesmen dream, and travelers write. We can not describe it—it is beyond description—but deep down in our race instincts we feel and know what it is" (140).

The very fact that the institution could perform the father's role successfully, feeding, clothing, housing, and educating its charges, underscored its emotional inadequacy. Although some of the speakers at the conference were orphanage superintendents, there was general agreement that while institutions run on the cottage plan were acceptable, old-fashioned congregate care could never hope to substitute for the family home. Expostulated Frank D. Loomis, general secretary of the Children's Bureau of Newark, New Jersey, "What! Shut a woman in a room with 50 noisy children and expect her to know and love each one as a mother knows and loves her little flock! In the close atmosphere of an institution! Confined there day and night! Good heavens!" (*Proceedings* 139). Reeder called for the orphanage "to be born again or go out of business. The life of the child in most of these institutions is so dreary, soul shriveling, and void of happy interests, the daily routine of marching and eating and singing and of lining up for whatever is to be done so stupefying, as to inhibit the child's normal development" (141).

Many speakers revealed their belief that displaced children should not have to work. Mrs. William Einstein, president of the Federation of Sisterhoods, complained of "institutions in which, under the guise of teaching industry, there is labor," a practice she wanted suppressed (157). Thomas Hynes of the St. Vincent de Paul Society linked child labor to delinquency and immorality, "as the children are compelled to go to work at a very early age and before they are either mentally or physically equipped for the struggle of life, and naturally they fall by the wayside" (74). And Martha Falconer, superintendent of the Girls' House of Refuge in Philadelphia, denigrated "young married people who come and want a strong, healthy girl to adopt. They want to take that child into their own family and treat her as their own. That sounds on the surface very beautiful. What does it usually mean? It usually means they want cheap labor. They want to adopt her so that no [social worker] may come to visit" (130).

Such sentiments represented a rejection of procedures that had been the norm in adoption and foster care for most of America's history and were still widely followed. Yet the conference participants apparently considered sentimental adoption's value so obvious that they saw no need to pass resolutions on the topic. There was disagreement on minor points relating to placement, to be sure, such as the laws in certain Western and Midwestern states against the exportation of orphans by Eastern placement societies; while a New York City placement worker, Charles McKenna of the Catholic Home Bureau, felt that "there should be and can be no argument in the negative" (188), South Dakotan Sherrard, Nebraskan Joseph Ruesing, and Indianan Amos Butler all complained of the practice, warning, in Sherrard's words, that "you eastern people must not expect to use the West as a dumping ground" (189).[15] But the idea so central to fiction and to the *Delineator* campaign from which the conference emerged, namely the emotional importance of the adopted child within its new family, received no discussion at all. Its very absence suggests the strength of the consensus: adoption was to be a valorizing of the personal, the emotional, and the domestic—indeed, of the feminine. Any other approach, such as defining the child as undesirable or as a worker, would potentially cause grave social problems.

While some historians see the 1909 conference as a watershed in the history of child welfare in America, others, such as Timothy Hacsi (39) and Crenson, assign it a more modest importance. As Crenson observes, "The White House Conference started nothing and settled nothing. But it did indicate the direction in which expert opinion was moving" (17). Thus the resolutions passed at the conference endorsed ideas that either already represented mainstream opinion within child-saving circles (such as the criticism of congregate orphanages) or were about to be translated into reality. Forty states had instituted the mothers' pension by 1920—commonly justifying the innovation by noting the conference's support for it, Crenson points out (17)—but the idea had been bruited about for a number of years before 1909. Similarly, the bill to create a federal children's bureau had been introduced in Congress in 1905, four years before the conference took place, so that the resolution calling for such an agency supported an existing political endeavor rather than inspiring a new one.[16]

But if the White House Conference may have had little practical impact in that it did not originate the principles it endorsed, its rhetorical impact was substantial. The meeting's venue, and its role as the first in a series (the second was held in 1919 and the third in 1930, although neither focused exclusively on dependent children), identified displaced children as a matter of national importance. Frequently cited in the years immediately after 1909, the White House Conference represented the apotheosis of Progressive Era political thought on adoption and foster care. Since the preservation of the original mother-child bond was the top priority, such placement efforts were presented as simultaneously desirable and regrettable.

Angels or Insects? Adoption and the Biological Mother

The rhetorical rehabilitation of the potential adoptee's biological mother, who had once been perceived as an obstacle to the child's advancement, owed much to the tendency of some reformers to see the destitute as victims rather than criminals. If adults, like children, were at the mercy of their environments, sinned against instead of sinning, perhaps *all* women were potential Angels in the House—even if they were too poor to have a house. The idealizing of maternity percolated through the economic layers, until many child-placement workers became convinced that separating children from their mothers was wrong even when the children might be adopted into a loving and affluent home. Thus Rabbi Emil Hirsch, president of the National Conference of Jewish Charities, could tell the White House conference that "the cause of unmarried mothers and illegitimate children is as yet too cruelly ignored. Even these children and mothers are worth saving [through mothers' pensions], and their cause is not in essentials different from that of other helpless mothers and children" (*Proceedings* 90).

But attitudes were in flux at this time, and representations of unmarried mothers are a case in point. Regina Kunzel notes that evangelical rescue workers such as Barrett, who herself argued at the 1910 Charities and Corrections meeting that illegitimacy should not separate child from biological mother, framed their twentieth-century understanding of unwed motherhood in terms of nineteenth-century melodramas of male vice and female naiveté (20–21). Caring for a child could both redeem a fallen woman and keep her from falling again, an idea that animated social-problem novels as early as the 1850s. Newly professionalized social workers, in contrast, tended "to see unmarried mothers not as endangered but as dangerous" (51). For Kunzel, the differences between these two stances "reveal the ways in which gender figured powerfully in the process by which a coalition of male and female reformers claimed to free themselves from gendered meanings" (3). In part, such differences also suggest ways in which a liberal vision of the effects of environment was coming into conflict with a determinist vision of heredity.

In his classic *Social Darwinism in American Thought,* Richard Hofstadter examines a similar divide in Progressive Era sociology. Many social scientists were increasingly interested in psychology, repudiating Herbert Spencer's attempts to apply Darwinian biological theory to human interaction. Spencer's identification of instinct as the key to the workings of society still had adherents, but the theories of men such as John Dewey, who insisted upon the importance of social and intellectual environment in shaping individual responses to the world, represented the cutting edge (156–59). Simultaneously, however, the 1900 rediscovery of Gregor Mendel's work caused excitement as the scientific community became aware of the fundamentals of genetics. The revelation of the mechanism of heredity caused some theorists to see heredity as all-powerful. The eugenics movement, imported from Britain, "grew with such great rapidity that by 1915 it had reached the dimensions of a fad" (161).

Eugenics had mixed implications for women. The eugenists' emphasis on biological determinism downplayed the power of the wife and mother to uplift her family through her moral influence and her position as the heart of the household. (As both fiction and the White House Conference suggest, mothers, presumed to be the primary caregivers, played a far more significant role in conceptions of children's home environment than did fathers.) Rhetorically, however, eugenics had much in common with the social purity movement, over which women exercised considerable leadership and which devoted substantial effort to critiquing masculine mores. If purity reformers sought to impose a single (female) standard of sexual conduct so as to eliminate venereal disease and prostitution, eugenists, too, warned against indiscriminate passion and male sexual eclecticism. It was no accident that the inferior line of Kallikak descendants sprang from the sexual error of a middle-class male. Martin Kallikak's liaison with a barmaid was anathema to purity reformers, eugenists, and virtuous women alike. Eugenics was, of course, intimately concerned with motherhood and thus seemed an appropriate area for women's involvement; in the United States as in Britain, women took active roles not only in popularizing eugenic ideas, but also in developing eugenics' scientific and technical side. Hence we cannot classify the environmentalist strand of the debate as predominantly female and the hereditarian strand as predominantly male, just as Kunzel cannot classify her evangelicals as female and her professional social workers as male. Rather, each position offered the sexes different sorts of power, apportioned in somewhat different ways.

We can, however, argue that the environmentalist stance was considerably friendlier to adoption, despite the belief of many environmentalists that the best way to save children might be to give their mothers enough money to keep the family together. The new popularity of eugenics had potentially negative consequences for adoption, since strict hereditarians held that, however good the home that the adopted child might find, there was no making a silk purse from a sow's ear. If the *Delineator* rhetoric suggested that only good heredity counted and that the right kind of adoptive mother could easily correct any inborn defects in the child, many eugenists believed not only that biology was destiny, but also that the biological influence of the bad mother was probably the most potent factor determining the child's future. Thus psychiatrist William Healy, founder of the Juvenile Psychopathic Institute of Chicago, which specialized in treating delinquents, fair-mindedly advised those considering adoption (a practice he clearly considered too risky to be practical) that not *all* mentally subnormal mothers would produce subnormal children (173). Healy's omission of subnormal fathers from this pronouncement suggests a feeling that they were not worth mentioning, whether because the mother's genetic contribution would outweigh theirs or because while no normal woman would mate with a moron, normal men might be less discriminating.

Other psychologists, too, argued for a correlation between illegitimacy and subnormal intelligence, again because illegitimate children were often assumed to be the offspring of a feebleminded mother and a normal—if unscrupulous—father (Carp 18, 66). And again, it was the mother who would pass her intellect on to her child, with disastrous social consequences; Goddard's Kallikak study, which traced the feebleminded strain in the family not to the profligate Martin but to his barmaid partner, had "concluded that feeble-mindedness [was] 'largely responsible' for paupers as well as criminals, prostitutes, and drunkards" (Hofstadter, *Darwinism*

164). As Kunzel points out, from about 1910 onward giving birth to an illegitimate baby was frequently regarded as de facto evidence of subnormal intelligence (52). Since foundlings were presumed to be illegitimate, eugenically minded adults might be forced to rule them out as prospective family members, even though as healthy infants unencumbered by blood relatives, foundlings would otherwise be prime candidates for sentimental adoption.

The children of the foreign-born similarly disturbed hereditarians. Stephen Jay Gould notes that in the United States eugenics quickly became a tool for "proving" the immigrant's intellectual inferiority (166). Since, like foundlings, the children of the immigrant poor were still disproportionately inhabitants of orphanages (Hacsi 121), the "discovery" of their genetic inferiority would again have worked to discourage their adoption. Not coincidentally, it was during this period that child-savers began to advocate that court records of adoptions be confidential, thus protecting children and their new parents from what had become the potential social embarrassment of having their status known (Carp 39). In this context, orphan fiction's emphasis on the astonishingly potent virtue of the adopted child (and sometimes on his or her extraordinary talent, as in the case of Porter's *Just David* and Jean Webster's *Daddy-Long-Legs*) looks embattled, a response to scientific developments that might threaten adoption's very foundations. We may also gain further understanding of the motivations of the *Delineator* campaign in stressing the "American" qualities of the children profiled and the worthiness of their mothers. Indeed, that both this campaign and the orphan fiction retained a focus on older children that consorts oddly with the new dominance of sentimental adoption may suggest a connection with what Kunzel characterizes as a widespread cultural horror over the threat posed by feeblemindedness (54): some hereditary mental problems, as Healy warned, would not become evident until the child was comparatively well grown.

The popularity of eugenics was in large part a response to the same conditions that were producing many of the children available for adoption. The arrival of immigrants "hard to assimilate because of rustic habits and language barriers," and so presumed mentally subnormal, together with the growth of slums in America's expanding cities and the economic downturn of the turn of the century, created social problems that looked to many like "the beginning of a national decline" (Hofstadter, *Darwinism* 162–63). Progressive Era environmentalist rhetoric proposed one cure for these woes, namely converting marginalized working-class children (orphans, waifs, slum-dwellers) to middle-class mores through missionary activities that included both adoption and the reclamation of disadvantaged mothers; hereditarianism proposed quite another. Eugenics promised to halt America's downward slide, but only via the increased propagation of the fit. Insinuating genetically inferior stock into the elite breeding pool through adoption was no way to solve the problem of race suicide.

Pace the *Delineator's* West, one effect of such rhetoric was to strengthen social workers' tendency to assert that "mentally, or acutely physically defective children" should be kept in institutions rather than offered for adoption (Reynolds 14). Moreover, the 1910s witnessed a strong feeling, visible also at the 1909 White House Conference, that family medical histories should be obtained for each potential adoptee; many institutions refused to place the offspring of the feeble-minded or insane (see, e.g., Hurley 82). Such documentation could function like a brand name, certifying the displaced child as adoption-worthy, the carefully inspected result of a sanitary production process. The need for vetting smacks of the desire for the modern and scientific, but also of a sense that there are limits to what the upright and civic-minded adoptive mother can hope to accomplish. It may be no accident that the adopted children who appear in the fiction discussed in this chapter are disproportionately the biological offspring of adults already known to, and in some cases related to, the adoptive parents. Such arrangements are not only true to life (historically, many adoptions have indeed involved nieces or nephews, neighbors or grandchildren); they also suggest the confidence that accompanies the known quantity.

Conversely, rural placement workers at the 1913 meeting of the Massachusetts Conference of State Charities expressed what Fearing characterized as "serious opposition" to the idea of accepting displaced children from Boston into their communities. They claimed that such children, inadequately vetted by "physiological and psychological examination," would bring "disease or degeneracy into a group of children that previously were morally and physically clean" (195). The influence of the foster child, in other words, was likely to trump that of the worthy mothers of the foster child's non-displaced peers, a comment that again implies a certain weakness on the part of the conventional family. The fear was a form of the xenophobia and distrust of the urban waif that had existed in America for many decades, but the rhetoric that clothed it had taken on a newly scientific guise.

Of course, even during the height of the eugenics fad, it remained rhetorically possible to assert the importance of environment over that of heredity; some commentators even invoked hereditarian texts to prove their point. Dosch, for one, brought into play in his 1910 article "Not Enough Babies to Go Around" the hoary example of "Margaret, mother of criminals":

> Twenty years ago there came under the supervision of the Children's Aid Society of New York a boy whose natural instincts were so weak and debased that his family history was secured in an effort to understand his case. At the beginning was Margaret. . . . As she grew older she corrupted her two younger sisters, and among them they started this evil family. Of 709 descendants, ninety-one were illegitimate, 129 were prostitutes,

eighteen owned establishments of bad repute, and sixty-nine died of disease. During the hundred years there had hardly been one decent member in the entire family. (437–38)

The list of the crimes of Margaret's progeny continued for another half-paragraph. Yet here is Dosch's punch line: "Naturally [the boy in question] was not told these things, and under careful rearing he has developed into a colorless man. There was nothing essentially bad about Margaret; she merely lacked care" (438).

Dosch's conclusions here are identical to those of Elisha Harris, Margaret's first publicist (to be sure, the boy's transformation into a "colorless man" is hardly inspirational), but they fly in the face of eugenist dogma of the 1910s such as Goddard's Kallikak study. Moreover, the captions to the photographs illustrating Dosch's article took a still stronger antihereditarian stance, suggesting that environment could bring about rapid, even instantaneous, changes. Sometimes these changes were purely cosmetic; a caption headed "The Transformation—in One Day—of an Orphan" read: "In the morning he was a waif; at night he was a somebody to be considered. The first photograph shows him in his accustomed garb. At the 'institution' he was first stripped of his shawl and then given an outfit with 'pants.' By night he had been adopted, dressed as became a son of well-to-do parents, and taken to his new home" (433). But others had to do with character and intelligence, hinting that feeblemindedness might be a product of environment: "Fresh from a 'Home'; the face is dull and has the 'institution look.' The photograph below shows the same child three months later" (434); "A typical institution boy and the same boy a year later. The growth in character is decidedly apparent" (435); "The imprint of a Chicago 'poorhouse' is in the dull face of this child. A month with a foster-mother produced the bright boy shown below" (435).[17] Like the *Delineator* rhetoric urging the adoption of the products of unspeakable environments, the latter caption emphasizes feminine redemptive power. For Dosch as for the *Delineator,* there was no such thing as bad genetic material as long as there were good adoptive mothers.

As the next chapter will detail, the struggle between environmentalists and hereditarians continued during the 1920s. But although eugenics remained an important factor, contributing heavily to the "scientific" cast of adoption rhetoric at this time, environmentalism eventually triumphed. Some of its resurgence may be attributable to its acknowledgment of domesticity's power to make a difference, an idea that meshed with the immense outpouring of writings on the American home in the 1910s and '20s. Many of these texts expressed anxiety about what was happening to the American family and to marriage, child rearing, and traditional values in an era in which women were gaining power and authority within the public sphere. If individuals' fates were written in their genes, their parents' divorce or their mothers' exercise of the franchise could matter little, so that commentators who took a conservative stance on gender roles found it essential to support the concept of the mother's ongoing moral influence over her children. Indeed, this concept was so firmly rooted that even some hereditarians found themselves paying tribute to it. Even in eugenics, some parents were more equal than others.

6

Adoption Up to Date

The Rhetoric of Mass Individuality, 1919–1929

A February 1923 report by the U.S. Census Bureau entitled *Children under Institutional Care* found that the nation contained 1,558 orphanages housing 140,312 children.[1] Of these children, fewer than 10 percent had lost both parents. According to C. C. Carstens, executive director of the newly founded Child Welfare League of America, "It is not surprising that the number of full orphans is small, because if they have any reasonable measure of attractiveness in physical or mental qualities they are eagerly sought by childless families" (134). Young children, he added, were especially easy to place; although "the number of children placed for adoption after they have reached the age of four seems to be materially reduced," the adoption of "infants and children under four is probably more extensively carried on than previously" (132).

The census report and Carstens's comments on it touch upon several factors important to understanding adoption rhetoric in the 1920s. First is the large number of orphanages; more such institutions existed in the United States during this decade than ever before or since (Hacsi 35). While the number of children inhabiting any one asylum was usually lower than had been the case in 1910, the total asylum population had nearly tripled since 1890. To be sure, orphanages were more likely to be run on the cottage plan than formerly, and the nation's population—which had more than doubled between 1870 and 1910—continued to grow, with a concomitant rise in the number of youngsters needing public assistance. Moreover, the First World War (which killed some 115,000 Americans) and the influenza pandemic of 1918–20 (which accounted for more than half a million) swelled the numbers of half- and full orphans; many more children lost parents than entered asylums. But even taking such factors into account, it is plain that the long and vituperative campaign against congre-

gate care had not yet succeeded. Numerically speaking, the mass production of children in institutions was more common than ever.

As Carstens also noted, the tide was nonetheless against the orphanage.
For one thing, professional and public feeling increasingly favored social
intervention, including but not limited to mothers' pensions, to shore up
the biological family. The New York Foundling Hospital abandoned orphan
trains in 1927, the New York Children's Aid Society in 1929; both moves
were inspired not only by the existence of adequate local foster care but
also by the existence of new services for the children of the urban poor. In
some cases these services, which included summer camps, playgrounds,
day care, and kindergartens, were sponsored by the placement societies
themselves (Holt 164). Such sponsorship signaled, among other things, a
rejection of the earlier hostility toward birth parents, partly because observers increasingly doubted that orphanages or foster homes could do better for children than the original families could. In this post-Mendelian
moment, even if heredity was not all-important, blood ties mattered.

But Carstens's comments also reflect a demand for children who were
considered likely objects for sentimental adoption. In an intensification of
earlier trends, older children looked less suitable than babies and toddlers,
although as recently as the *Delineator* campaign it had been possible to
present preteens as desirable. Timothy Hacsi estimates that in the 1920s,
orphanage inmates' average age was ten, up from seven or eight in the
1860s (119); a study done in Massachusetts and Pennsylvania at the start
of the decade found that "approximately 85% of the 2770 minors of
known age . . . were less than eleven years old at adoption and that the
largest proportion was between one and five years" (Parker 17). What we
might hyperbolically term the graying of the asylum is one confirmation
that perceptions of orphans' use value had been inverted. With the decline
of utilitarian "placing-out," children once thought undesirable because
they were too young to work were now more easily placed than their seniors, on the theory that they would more readily bond with their new
parents. In a day that saw both continued pressure on the middle class to
reproduce and a sharp decline in the birth rate—18 percent of married
women in the 1920s bore no children, and for about two thirds of these
women infertility was not volitional (Marsh and Ronner 143)—adoptable
infants were often at a premium.

Conversely, as laws governing child labor and school attendance became more potent, children who were not adopted remained longer in
institutions before entering the workforce (Hacsi 130). Here again, sentiment was a factor. As Katharine Hewins of Boston's Church Home Society
remarked in 1924, many orphanage workers "fought honestly for the re-
tention of the institution . . . placing in their minds being synonymous
with exploitation" (101). Although utilitarian placements existed well after the Second World War,[2] opposition to the idea of the utilitarian child
continued to mount. Thus, in an essay printed alongside Hewins's article,

Edmond J. Butler of New York's Catholic Home Bureau for Dependent Children asserted that "the most successful results occur in the cases of children placed when below the age of 5 years." He recommended against placing out boys over fourteen or girls over ten, as "under these circumstances flagrant exploitation of child labor and neglect of schooling are apt to occur." One example of this "exploitation" was that teenage girls might have to provide care for other children or for infirm adults (36)—a fate that would have seemed reasonable to placement officers even forty years earlier. Similarly, in his essay "Safeguarding the Dependent Child's Physical and Mental Health," Dr. Horace H. Jenks warned that "A boy of 12 must not get up at 4 or 4.30, clean the stable, water the stock, milk the cows, and then get a hurried breakfast and go to school, and return in time for the same stable chores in the afternoon" (120). Again, farm chores appear in a more positive light in nineteenth-century orphan fiction or the early rhetoric of the New York Children's Aid Society. Indeed, to identify the foster parent as a farmer was rather outmoded; by the 1920s, children were more likely to be placed in urban or small-town settings.

Moreover, whereas a modified (and informal) system of indenture had once been the backbone of orphan-train placement, a 1927 Children's Bureau study of indenture in Wisconsin unequivocally condemned the practice, by then allowed in only twelve states. To work children "virtually as unpaid servants in households and on farms" was now seen as child abuse, whether or not these children were also "deprived of schooling and . . . cruelly treated" (qtd. Holt 179). But that the dependent child would—and should—be put to emotional use was taken for granted, as in the *Literary Digest*'s 1923 assertion that "Foster-parentage averts the divorce evil, prevents solitude, and satisfies the maternal instinct not otherwise requited, and it seems to be not an entirely unselfish attitude, tho [*sic*] just as beneficial to the child as if it were, that prompts some people to give the comforts and rewards of home life to some orphaned child" ("Cradles" 35).

The concepts here look familiar; we have seen them advanced repeatedly in the adoption rhetoric of the Progressive Era. But increasingly, 1920s commentators used self-consciously new diction in recommending adoption.[3] One writer of 1922, pediatrician Henry Dwight Chapin, president of the Children's Welfare Federation of New York and husband of the founder of the Alice Chapin Adoption Nursery, makes the classic sentimental argument that "children give more than they take. They are the great civilizers and humanizers of the race" and can turn any woman into "a Madonna" (162, 160); adopted children "have brought life and brightness into drab homes" (202). But even as he embraces this emotional and quasi-religious stance, Chapin touts adoption as a "very satisfactory 'sublimation,'" a way to cure "neurasthenia and hysteria" in wealthy spinsters, à la Dorothy Canfield's "Out of the Wilderness." He adds that it can produce hybrid vigor: "some of our older families [would benefit from] engrafting children who, although having a poor social inheritance, may yet be the possessors of a healthy organic inheritance" (195–96). The emphasis on what children could do emotionally for their adoptive parents is hardly new; we have seen it in the fiction of the 1890s and even earlier. But the psychological and biological terms in which Chapin frames his endorsement of adoption do indeed represent something fresh.

Similarly, a paper presented at the 1923 National Conference of Social Work by Robert Kelso of Boston's Council of Social Agencies, predicting that "The congregate institution is to disappear, leaving behind it the temporary shelter" (208), was correct without being surprisingly prescient. After all, it followed two decades' worth of scathing remarks about orphanages from novelists and social-service professionals. But its title, "Passing of the Stone Age in Care and Custody," deserves attention for its emphasis on modernity, its suggestion that a commitment to congregate care signals primitivism. In contrast, Kelso's reference to the Stone Age implicitly establishes him and other members of the anti-orphanage coalition as scientific and up to date.

In this context, we might return momentarily to Carstens in order to contemplate the innovations suggested by his affiliation. The Child Welfare League of America was a private organization founded in 1921. By the late 1920s it offered advanced training for people already employed as social workers; published a bulletin that printed articles by authorities such as pediatrician and child psychologist Arnold Gesell; hosted professional conferences; and performed consulting work in an effort to improve existing orphan asylums. It quickly became "the most important private national agency for child welfare," working with the federal Children's Bureau to reform adoption policy and educate both adoption workers and the public (Carp 25). In other words, it was a sophisticated operation, committed to raising standards within the field of social work by bringing the latest social-scientific insights to practitioners and institutions. If the child-welfare organizations that had been the first major players on a national or quasi-national level, such as the New York Children's Aid Society, had originated in an atmosphere of energetic amateurism, the Child Welfare League was earnestly professional.

This investment in professionalism was hardly surprising, given the new maturity of social work as a field (a transition, points out Regina Kunzel, that involved the embrace of "objective, rational, and scientific language" [2]) and the climate of the 1920s as an era in which the expert was king. The bureaucracy associated with adoption mushroomed during this decade. By 1929 every existing state had an adoption law; many also had laws governing placement procedures, record keeping, and the licensing of adoption agencies. This plethora of rules reflects the belief that children were precious resources to be protected, as well as the opposite and lingering conviction that children available for adoption needed supervision if the nation was to be protected from their presumed bad heredity or incipient delinquency. It also reflects, of course, the increasing bureaucratization of American life overall. The "children of the state" shared with adults a tendency to be licensed, tabulated, and viewed in terms of statistics—even while, as Clare McCausland notes, "'Individualize' was the watchword" of cutting-edge theory and practice in the care of dependent children in the 1920s (116). More than ever, the adoptable child appeared to stand at the intersection of individuality and the mass.

This liminality led to a characteristic way of representing orphans on the part of pro-adoption forces: such children were described as being, in a positive sense, part of the crowd, the possessors of abilities that would permit them to succeed through strategies of cooperation and assimilation rather than through their difference from others. They were to be deemed individual and special, but not alarmingly so; the social threat posed by the nonconformity of a Huck Finn or the disconcerting maturity of a Sara Crewe had been neutralized, especially by the authority of popular science. For although by 1929 many principles that would govern adoption throughout the century were firmly in place, the date marks neither the end of ambivalence nor the beginning of a golden age. While sentimental adoption had become dominant, proponents still had to combat the suspicion that adopted children were inferior. In the hands of earlier child-savers such as Charles Loring Brace, adoption had ostensibly been the means of rectifying an inequality caused by the immorality, poverty, degeneracy, and/or immigrant status of one's birth parents. But to many in the 1920s (and later), adoption itself constituted a bend sinister, so that intervention might mean taking extraordinary steps to keep the child with its original parent(s), however immoral, poor, degenerate, or foreign they might be.

Consequently, adoption's advocates in both the fiction and the nonfiction of the 1920s tended to normalize it by suggesting that the constructed family could be made predictable by adhering to certain carefully worked out standards. Sentimentality was now the dominant mode, in that the emotional bond between adoptive parent and child was to be the principal motivation for adoption. But the language of sentiment was going out of style. For the spiritual melodrama of sentimental fiction was not only a relic of a Victorianism from which the postwar world sought to distance itself; it also represented the orphan as extraordinary, turning adoption into an epiphany of the sort that a complacent adult might think unnecessarily drastic. (Foster parents in such narratives, as we have seen, often find the emotional metamorphosis forced upon them by their wards uncomfortable.) And while newspapers trumpeted adoption stories at the extremes of the social scale, from lurid accounts of baby-farming to heartwarming tales of movie stars and millionaires whose chief ambition was parenthood, by the 1920s adoption was a bourgeois affair.

Thus writers urging adoption invoked child psychology, statistics, social workers' newly "scientific" expertise, and historical precedent to demonstrate its safety; tempered melodrama with a matter-of-fact approach; and stressed the ordinariness of the resulting family. While they still touted the attractiveness of the adoptable child, the virtues they imputed to such children—"personality," industry, competence, and loyalty—were more down to earth than those of the jewel-like orphan of Progressive Era fiction. And because this promise of competence extended beyond the child to embrace also the social-service profession and the adoptive parents, adoption donned a guise appropriate to the postwar world. In a "nerve-shattered" era, as Chapin put it, it was necessary to make use of modern scientific advances in order to rear better, stronger children (7). Chapin's *Heredity and Child Culture,* for one, bristles with quotations from scientific, academic, and medical authorities as well as with insights drawn from the author's experience as the husband of the proprietor of an adoption agency, all designed to show that heredity is "under the control, to some extent, of society and the individual" (21).

Chapin's invocation of concepts such as "control," "correct[ing] a faulty social heredity" (58), and the "constructive and permanent work" that caregivers may do on the characters of young children (4) provides a useful illustration of another way in which adoption rhetoric intersected with more general modes of expression of the day. In the 1920s, "mastery" was an indispensable watchword, both a concept embracing specific skills and a coveted personality trait that itself represented a skill—and a commodity—because it could be learned. Commentators thus offered adoption as an important venue for the exercise of domestic mastery. In a reversal of earlier sentimental fiction, such mastery was no longer to belong exclusively to the Pollyannas and Tom Sawyers, but to the adults once represented as subject to manipulation by their juniors. Prospective parents were promised that if they embraced a newly scientific selection process and intelligent techniques of child rearing, they would construct an adoptive family remarkable for its reliability and cohesiveness; moreover, they could discover within themselves a new capacity for mastery. What Walter Benn Michaels terms "the technological fantasies of (self-)control embodied in the Progressive cult of the scientific manager" (94) were to be made available to the middle-class household through modern adoption. This chapter will explore how the adoption rhetoric of the 1920s played to these fantasies not only in professional texts within the field of social work but also in the mass-circulation periodical and juvenile series fiction.

The Un/Sentimental Orphan in Mass-Market Texts

In the increasingly matter-of-fact atmosphere of the 1920s, children's fiction and popular magazines, the venues that had traditionally been most likely to depict the parentless child in a sentimental light, often played down or denigrated emotion—while still allowing it to form a quiet continuo in the background. In writings of this kind, both the loss of the original parents and the acquisition of new ones might receive little attention. Narratives focused rather upon the details of enlightened child rearing within the new environment and assumed that adopted children existed to be cherished. This emphasis upon an intellectual understanding of child psychology (as opposed to late-nineteenth-century empathy) spoke to the preoccupations of a generation that was embracing a scientifically informed modernity and replacing a feeling-laden mode of expression with a prose that privileged the sparse and economical. Yet the new, ostensibly anti-sentimental narratives asked readers to take for granted certain principles on which sentimental adoption was based, such as the primacy of environment over heredity and the parity (at least) of the adopted child with his "natural-born" counterpart. In their aggressively matter-of-fact approach, these modernist accounts upheld the very ideas that they affected to scorn.

Consider, in this connection, Honoré Willsie's autobiographical account "The Adopted Mother," published in the *Century Magazine* in September 1922. A *Delineator* contributor at the time of that periodical's child-placement campaign, Willsie was a former editor of *The Woman's Magazine;* in the latter capacity she had been required to provide her readers with "information as to the where and how of child adoption" (658). This task had given her the expertise, and the scientific and technical mindset, necessary to persuade her husband (who had earlier held that adopting a child was "looking for trouble" [657]) that modern adoption had few risks because

> child adoption as handled by a scientific organization had reduced the gambling element to about fifty-fifty with the own-child hazard. You ordinarily know far less about the eugenic history of your husband's family than you do about the ancestry of the child you have adopted under proper circumstances! I wanted the boss [Willsie's husband] to get this, and I wanted him to feel that while he suspected that I was actuated by deeply sentimental reasons, I was actually going about the matter dispassionately, that I was learning with my mind and not with my heart. (660)

In keeping with her strategy in these domestic negotiations, Willsie consistently suggests that "stupidity and sentimentality" are allied, that in handling the dependent child "nothing is so terrible as ignorant sentimentality may be, nothing so tender as the ruthlessly scientific system is" (657, 658). She warns people contemplating adoption to ask the right eugenic questions: "Was the physical stock of the family below par, so that there was no surviving relative of either parent to take the child? What were the family traits that brought about the dependence of the child? Were these traits the result of environment and external pressure or of inherent and heritable traits?" (663). Attention to science will enable one to avoid many pitfalls.

Similarly, in describing her handling of her son and daughter, she details her analytical approach to child rearing and the care she takes to extirpate bad habits. Her status as adoptive parent, she claims, gives her the advantage of objectivity: "I am undoubtedly stricter with my children than any own mother I know, because I see my children more clearly than own mothers do. I doubt very much if I love them now any less than the others, but I certainly started unhandicapped by the blind love that makes them see dimly" (666). Both as adoptees and as denizens of a postwar world crying out for productive adults, her children bear a weight of future responsibility that develops in Willsie a fierce "determination to help them conquer the weakness that would mar their success as human beings." Here, mastery is crucial to motherhood. No sentimentality, no excessive maternal "tenderness," can be tolerated given the gravity of the context within which she is rearing her young. One adoptee is the ambassador for all, since "The whole structure of child-placing rests on the success of the children who are placed," and failure in good citizenship jeopardizes "that long procession of little bloody feet moving up from the children's hell" of exploitation and drudgery (666).

Yet while Willsie's comments and tone are often so clinical as to chill today's readers, her point about the "children's hell," among others, hints at an idealization of childhood, a desire to see orphans leading the idyllic existence that forms the happy ending in sentimental orphan fiction. And indeed, Willsie's explanation of her own motives in adopting partakes of all the emotionalism of any turn-of-the-century orphan tale. Her memoir begins with an account of the central trauma of her childhood, the loss of her beloved baby sister. Willsie's "little child," the infant who "was to [her] what the rainbow must have been to the lonely and bewildered voyagers stranded on Mount Ararat" (655, 654), died of diphtheria at age three in 1891, when the older girl was eleven. The death, she remarks, inspired her to become a writer in adulthood, in an effort to re-create her sister imaginatively, and to adopt children to fill the void. In a nice bit of neo-Victorian spiritual melodrama, we also learn that the ineffectuality of little Honoré's prayers for her sister's recovery turned her into an atheist, a state that lasts until the son and daughter who have replaced the baby ask her about death and receive a "halting" but sincere religious explanation. Willsie ends on this note: "I had wandered far. But two pairs of trusting tiny hands had set me back upon the 'slope which leads through darkness up to God'" (668). The moment would not be out of place in *Timothy's Quest* or *Little Lord Fauntleroy.*

Nor are late-nineteenth-century attitudes to be found only at the beginning and end of the article. Throughout, Willsie ratifies domestic ideals as well as debunking them. If, as a salaried employee herself, she notes that because the war has "upset the economic equilibrium of the world," even wealthy married women have a duty to work, she simultaneously upholds the Victorian principle that "the individual home [is] the nucleus of the nation. . . . On the sanctity of its women and the integrity of its homes rests the ultimate virility of the nation" (667). Similarly, despite the tributes that she pays to the scientific selection of prospective adopted offspring and despite her assertion that associating with child-placement experts has "educat[ed]" her into choosing good specimens (663), the love-at-first-sight choice of little "Gray-Eyes" and his sister "Blue-Eyes" is clearly to be understood as sentimental. Of the latter adoption, Willsie remarks that "the hand of fate was on me the moment I saw her, and I had to bring her home. . . . The boss had by this time developed a certain quality of resignation that I have observed is common to most fathers. And, anyhow, answer me this: What man ever held out more than fifteen minutes against a tiny blue-eyed, yellow-haired female, with the beguiling manner inseparable from the perfect blond? Scientific? Businesslike? Hah!" (663). The world of science and secularism is shown as both defeated by and cooperating with that of sentimentality.

But the up-to-date scientific strain in Willsie's piece has an important rhetorical function. As Julie Berebitsky notes, Willsie is using "the modern ideals of science and choice . . . to cast adoptive families' difference from blood families in a positive light" (86). We learn that the best "child-placing organizations . . . [take] full advantage of . . . advances in science" and do "all that science could do for the right handling of a child's body, mind, and soul" (Willsie 658). We learn that they assure the public "that bad habits are not heritable" (659). And we learn that after testing "frowsy, uncouth, foul-mouthed children of ignorant and disgusting parents" and certifying them normal, the agencies turn them "into pleasant-mannered youngsters purified of body and mind" (670). By all these methods, modern child-savers (and Willsie, their self-appointed mouthpiece) persuade the childless that adoption can be safe. It is because of the imprimatur of science that sentimental adoption is possible in the world of the 1920s. Trusting in the brand name of a reputable orphanage, educated middle-class adults accept the children, prepared like Willsie to bring them up intelligently and systematically—and find, perhaps, that as in the old sentimental pattern, it is the children who accomplish the greatest reforms.

Accounts by male authors of the 1920s could display the same tendencies as Willsie's article. In "Our Adopted Son: An Experience in Bringing Up Two Boys Who Are Not Blood Brothers," published in *Ladies' Home Journal* in 1924, a father describes his and his wife's adoption of a boy named Joe, brought into the family to provide companionship for their biological son, Bill.[4] Again we find science invoked, both in references to the "unconscious" and "subconscious" minds ("Our Adopted" 35) and in remarks about genetics: "In spite of the almost irresistible force exerted by all the minute daily pressures of the home environment, there is such a thing as heredity." The latter force, the writer comments, may doom even a child from a "respectable" background, since "queer hereditary traits [may] combine with unaccountable vigor in one member of a generation. Such a person is a biological sport" (166). Parents therefore need both skill and luck to rear any child, but the adopted child most of all: "If their best energy isn't continually going into this business of supplying mental and spiritual air for the little ones to breathe, into studying . . . their complex little natures and helping mold them into the best development of which each is individually capable, why, probably they'd better keep out of the adopting business" (166). Raising a child does not come naturally; success in parenting should be understood not as a matter of instinct or affection, but rather, as in Willsie's formulation, as a question of mastery, the product of intense thought, "study" or "education," and careful attention to child psychology. Like child-saving, it requires credentials.[5]

But while the account is cast in a modern idiom, it too nonetheless contains an old-fashioned message. Joe's virtues have the effect, common in the sentimental fiction of an earlier day, of uplifting the entire household, although they are presented as secular qualities appropriate to a society of go-getters; the child, too, exhibits mastery. We learn that he is

> contributing to our family life qualities of industry and sturdy, uncompromising logic in all matters of practical, everyday living that would not have been there in anything like the same degree if he had never come. We owe that to him. And we shall owe more.
>
> Already I can see that he is going to check a tendency toward careless extravagance that runs through the rest of us. And his unquenchable determination to do well everything he does is a dynamic force in the household. (168)

We hear also of the boy's conscientiousness, loyalty, and sense of responsibility. The author takes no credit for these traits, explaining that Bill, reared in the same environment, manifests them only in imitation of his brother and not because his parents have instilled them in him. Rather, they may be part of Joe's genetic inheritance. Although the family knows little of his background, "He seems to have deep in his nature a feeling—certainly it lies deeper than his conscious thoughts—that education is a privilege to be earned with hard work and even with a sense of gratitude. That, I fear, is not the commonest American attitude. I don't know where he gets it. There is something old-worldly about it" (35). The ethnic otherness long associated with the displaced child, in other words, here appears to have produced a boy steeped in the Puritan work ethic, enabling Joe to serve as a secular missionary to his adoptive family.

And although emotion has to some extent gone underground in this article, it is nonetheless present. Thus we hear that when Joe is put to bed, "he will suddenly throw his arms up, draw his adopted parent down by his face with a tight squeeze, and whisper an impulsive expression of gratitude that comes clear from the bottom of his warm little heart. It is hard at such moments to keep the eyes dry" (168). Similarly, despite his remark that "this paper was not designed to be a sermon," the author has a preachment to make: "Basically, all this business of raising children comes down, I think, to the attitude of service. There isn't much satisfaction in the self-life" (168). If the article ends on an unemotional note by presenting adoption as a civic duty ("The parents of today are molding, for better or for worse, the citizenship of tomorrow. . . . We all, I believe, should be undertaking to train one or more children, our own or somebody's, as the opportunity may arise" [168]), the rewards promised are less patriotic than sentimental: the grateful child's hug, the gratification of forming a bond "for better or for worse" (35).

Orphan fiction during this period likewise partook simultaneously of the sentimental and of a down-to-earth rejection of emotional excess. Both strategies were used, as Berebitsky notes of nonfiction accounts, to "normalize adoption" (83)—and still more, adoptees. While exceptions certainly exist, the typical 1920s orphan plot shows the outsider becoming an insider, seamlessly stitched into the surrounding society until his or her membership in that society is unassailable and even unobtrusive. And indeed, as if in tacit capitulation to this ideal of the invisible adoptee, the 1920s saw a considerable falling-off in the number of orphan stories produced. Much of what exists from this decade is historical fiction, some of it designed to inculcate patriotic ideas about America as the land of opportunity for those whose native countries had no place for them (the subtitle of one 1924 novel, Cornelia Meigs's *The New Moon: The Story of Dick Martin's Courage, His Silver Sixpence and His Friends in the New World*, suggests the general thrust of this type) and all tending implicitly to identify the homeless child as a denizen of a bygone age.

Caroline Dale Snedeker's *Downright Dencey* (1927) is typical in hinting that the orphan problem is a relic of the past, best solved by applying modern energy and "personality." The title character of this tale of Nantucket in the 1810s and '20s is not an orphan, but a hoyden who can run as fast as any boy and throw overhand with accuracy and force. Her feistiness and readiness to break rules make her a misfit in her own conformity-loving society, so that she serves as a precursor of the androgynous girl valorized by 1920s fashions. Thus when she teaches a boy of unknown parentage to read, attracts his love, and socializes him into respectability, readers may sense that the spirit of modernity is reaching back into the past to rescue children ignored by a more callous time. Through his bond with Dencey much more than through his later ties to the adults—who are more closely identified with their era—Jetsam gains an identity, a home, and a place within the Society of Friends. The "terrible, intimate responsibility" that she feels for him (314) is shared by no one else in the narrative. (The adults, and Dencey's peers, initially assume that a boy of unknown parentage, starved emotionally and intellectually for his first twelve years, cannot be salvaged in adolescence by being granted a rudimentary education, some secondhand clothes, and food pilfered from the family pantry—but they are wrong.) Her concern for this displaced child is a major component in Dencey's own alienation from her family and peers; by implication, it also differentiates the 1920s from the 1820s. Human "jetsam," the reader may well conclude, no longer exists in the modern era.

But historical fiction may be an unnecessarily complex indicator of the cultural milieu that produced it because it attempts to chronicle at the same time the concerns of an earlier day. By way of a 1920s orphan saga with a contemporary setting, we might contemplate at greater length Josephine Lawrence's six-volume Linda Lane series, published between 1925 and 1929, which exemplifies the efforts of the fiction of the day to show the adoptee's gradual integration into society.[6] We first meet Linda when she is thirteen, a three-year orphanage veteran who has been rejected by seven sets of foster parents because of her insufficiently meek attitude. The unrepentant Linda's explanation that the foster parents "thought [she] was a doormat" (*Linda* 11) strikes the keynote of her character: she wants to be treated like any other girl. As the orphanage matron sniffs, "She thinks she is important and the people who take her to board must consult her tastes and wishes" (18). The saga thus begins by noting a disjunction between the treatment of children with parents and those without, in that the culture decrees that the former deserve respect, consideration, and consumer goods (allowances, pretty clothes, and attractively decorated bedrooms loom large here) while the latter exist to make themselves useful. The identification of this distinction as unnecessary and unfair is the main point of the first volume.

For Linda quickly finds a home with a dressmaker named Carol Gilly, herself described as "a born doormat" by a more assertive neighbor (134). Miss Gilly's difference from her peers is manifested by her wish to "take a little girl and try to make her happy," as opposed to lightening her own burden by getting help with the housework (39). Her instinct that orphans deserve as much happiness as anyone else and operate according to the same psychological rules distinguishes her from the other adults in the story. Thus Linda's new teacher is surprised to find her "'just like any other girl,'" believing "that there should be something to set her apart—a girl without parents and a home of her own, couldn't be like the girls who had these blessings and took them for granted" (59). Similarly, Linda's new neighbor and another woman leap to the conclusion that the child has stolen a squirrel scarf, although had Linda had "a father and mother and a regular family, [the women] would never have suspected [her] of such a thing as stealing" (118). Only Miss Gilly sees from the beginning that Linda is indeed "just like any other girl."

Miss Gilly's insight into Linda comes from instinct rather than from the education and conscious thought touted by the magazine articles cited above, but it is both shrewd and effective. Those used to dealing with displaced children—experienced foster mothers, orphanage personnel—have found Linda unmanageable, evidently because they believe that such children are inherently different from others, serving a different social function and manifesting a unitary and unchildlike personality. But Miss Gilly, a neophyte in child rearing, consults her memories of her own childhood and her sense of what is appropriate in a hostess/guest relationship. With these guides, she instantly perceives what Linda will respond to: a locking chest in which the child can keep her treasures private, dried lavender in the bureau drawers, and attractive clothes (35, 36, 40). Reassured by these signs that her new caregiver will grant her respect and the right to individuality, Linda is happy to feed chickens and help in the kitchen, although she has objected to being of service in her earlier foster homes and in the orphanage. To be sure, it is also important that the chores she does for Miss Gilly are her own idea and not the reason for her presence in Miss Gilly's home, but the seamstress's knowledge of the child mind is presented as the first sign of the mastery that the timid woman has lacked.

Linda's intractability, it turns out, has arisen from her subordination. In her new home, it becomes evident that she is a born manager, full of energy, executive ability, and independence. As such, society needs her—and vice versa. In the second volume, *Linda Lane Helps Out* (1925), she even bestows the name Independence on a stray dog she adopts, "because that is the quality I admire above all others: I think independence is the finest thing and the most precious thing, in all the world" (89). That her interlocutor challenges this opinion, remarking, "Independence isn't everything," invites the reader to think of important things that might require interdependence—a loving family among them. Normalcy demands that the child not stand out to the point of being unable to interact with others, and that Linda's special talent is for management requires, of course, that she be part of a group rather than a brilliant loner. As Michaels points out, Frederick Winslow Taylor "redescribed independence as 'isolation'" (84); for Linda as for the scientifically managed worker, the truest independence is cooperation.

Unlike earlier orphan heroines such as Sara Crewe, Anne Shirley, and Rebecca Randall, then, Linda is not notable for imagination or poetic talent. That is, she is not the kind of romantic figure who is at once constructed by and a contributor to the literature of sentiment. Rather, she is a down-to-earth, capable type, an "androcentric or androgynous" girl (Johnson 66) who requires only freedom of action to exert mastery and become a productive modern woman. The sensible Miss Gilly, whose own competence is revealed through her association with the child, allows Linda the scope for development that 1920s child-rearing experts recommended and that Linda's early life (in which her status as orphan trumped her status as child) denied her.

In other words, the narrative simultaneously asserts Linda's essential similarity to "any other girl" (even the young Carol Gilly, now her opposite and complement) and her right to be treated as an individual. We see the same pattern throughout the series; even the narrative's status as series fiction encapsulates the tension between mass-production and uniqueness. That Linda exhibits all the loyalty, competence, industry, and responsibility that the anonymous author of "Our Adopted Son" claims for his boy Joe suggests that she may represent a new model of ideal orphan, a type updated for the 1920s. At the same time, observers insist that she is unusual: "She had personality—that was it. Linda's personality was vivid, distinct.

She would always be somebody" (*Linda* 32). Invoking "personality" was a favorite device of the period, used to sell products from correspondence-school courses to perfume, all touted as making the buyer stand out from the herd (see, e.g., Morey). But it also serves to differentiate Linda from the old vision of the orphanage child homogenized into a characterless lump, inferior to the child raised within a normal family. In standing out from the herd, in fact, orphans are "just like any other girl." Discussing middle-class identity formation, Michaels writes that in the 1920s (and earlier), understandings of individuality were changing under the pressures of mechanization, with the result that sometimes "an individual . . . [could] be an individual only by belonging to some class" (83). Substitute "group" for "class," and Linda comes to represent not only the orphan seeking ratification by "normal" society, but also any other denizen of the 1920s who might have experienced social self-doubt.

Moreover, if the family formed in the first book attracts unflattering attention because the constellation of shabby middle-aged spinster and thirteen-year-old state-subsidized foster child is both unusual and déclassé, the rest of the series smooths out these domestic abnormalities. The third installment, *Linda Lane's Plan* (1926), rescues Linda from her uncertain status as ward of the state; when Miss Gilly's cousin leaves her fortune to the dressmaker, the latter is enabled to adopt Linda as her legal daughter. No longer will the child be the recipient of charity. Indeed, the astute reader will have predicted this plot twist, since even in the first volume, Linda is evincing a desire to be on the other side of the handouts. She takes an immediate interest in five-year-old David, an orphan who lives with a curmudgeonly grandfather. David initially functions to establish that there are people lower on the charitable totem pole than Linda herself, since he causes Linda to muse, "I feel so sorry for that little boy. . . . I wish I could do something to help him." Miss Gilly's reply, "Well, some day perhaps you can. . . . I guess there will always be children who need helping and the thing to do is not to forget or to be too busy" (126), both points a moral (even people as poor as Linda or Miss Gilly have a duty to their neighbor) and suggests Linda's own rise in status: she is now one of the helpers rather than one of the helped.

But after his grandfather's death David, too, begins to rise, first attracting the attention of a rich woman who believes she wants to adopt him (but who backs off when David's presence in her home shows her the difficulties of parenthood) and subsequently joining the Gilly ménage as Linda's little brother. For just as Lawrence rejects the oddity of wealth for David and later for another of Linda's adoptive siblings, baby Joy, asserting that it is better to belong to the more down-to-earth and altruistic middle classes,[7] Linda rejects the oddity of being an only child, preferring membership in a group. Her ambition is to be part of a sizable family, one containing not just a mother but also siblings and grandparents. The narrator remarks, "And what more natural, from Miss Gilly's rather individual viewpoint, than for the dressmaker to use her inheritance in making Linda's plan come true?" The older woman sees multiple adoption as a way to make up for years of loneliness and to assuage her craving for "young life around [her]"; she offers "a real home with love and training and a chance for a practical education," a proposal that combines a sentimental motive with the kind of instruction in good citizenship emphasized in the autobiographical magazine articles discussed above (*Experiments* 34–35). Soon the house contains a comparatively standard family of four children (Linda, David, Joy, and Patty, a girl about David's age), their mother Miss Gilly, and "Grandma Poore," a hard-up widow of sixty or so who is "heaps of fun and . . . look[s] like a story-book grandmother" (*Plan* 158).[8]

This family, none of whose members are related by blood, bears a striking resemblance to one assembled by an earlier orphan, the title character of Carolyn Wells's 1899 *St. Nicholas* serial *The Story of Betty*. But while both groupings include, besides the protagonist, a destitute old woman for grandmother, a brother, and a two-year-old girl, there is a significant difference in that Betty, an heiress who acts on her own to "buy" a family, finds her long-lost mother at story's end. Their reunion reveals the inadequacy of the family she has purchased, as the narrator remarks that "she was happy now, truly happy; and she realized that all her life she had been starving for true human affection. This, she now understood, was the longing that had kept her hungry heart unsatisfied. . . . At last mother-love had made for Betty a home" (1024). For Wells's heroine, mothers cannot be bought or adopted; only the birth mother is the genuine article. Twenty-five years later, however, Linda finds Miss Gilly and the other members of the family wholly satisfactory and proclaims that it feels "nice!" to be adopted (*Experiments* 16). The adjective's very blandness suggests the normalizing project under way.

Indeed, the series suggests that the biological family is at least as likely as the constructed family to be abnormal, or at least dysfunctional, precisely because it lacks the professionalism and mastery that the 1920s associated with adoption. Thus Linda's widowed neighbor Mrs. Hampton tacitly acknowledges her inability to cope with her undisciplined brood whenever she sends them over to play (uninvited) at Miss Gilly's house. Wealthy Mr. and Mrs. Pine find that when they leave their children to the care of the servants, who lack the authority to mete out punishment, chaos ensues. Although Mr. Pine is a potential inspiration for Linda because he is a former orphanage inmate who has made good, he concedes that his offspring are spoiled and that he has been an ineffectual father ("They have their own way too much—I must see what I can do" [*Linda* 240]). And Mary Rice, oldest child of a widowed invalid, has been soured by having had to serve as primary caregiver for her many siblings—for whom, as for her mother, she has little affection—and to do all the work of the household because it contains no functioning adult. Mary's existence involves exactly the kind of involuntary drudgery, expended without emotional recompense, that was the lot of countless nineteenth-century orphans and that Linda has rejected in her earlier foster homes. Lawrence's point would appear to be that having a family is no guarantee of happiness or privilege. The abnormal and character-destroying existence that outsiders such as Linda's teacher or Mrs. Hampton take to be the orphan's inevitable lot may equally well be associated with life in the bosom of one's birth family.

Thus a conscious irony of the series is that Linda, first shipped from one reluctant relative to another and then relegated to the orphanage and to multiple foster homes, is more competent in family matters than anyone else, with the possible exception of the equally familyless Miss Gilly. She provides better care for the little Hamptons than their mother does, while also requiring Mrs. Hampton to shoulder more of the responsibility for overseeing them. The Pines invite her to spend a summer as "one of the family—you will be waited on—you'll have no household drudgery of any kind" (*Linda* 245), if she will help to manage the children while their parents are in Europe. Here too she makes a success of her endeavor; the narrator comments that "the household seemed to turn naturally to her, young as she was" (*Helps Out* 67), and when all the servants quit because (as Linda herself has been in the past) they are unappreciated, starved of leisure, and falsely accused of misdeeds, the thirteen-year-old runs the house. In taking a firm line with the Pine children, Linda considers that she is doing more for them than their parents do: "I don't think they have a fair chance at all—no one tells them what is right or wrong or cares what they do, as long as they are not annoying any one" (*Helps Out* 247–48). In this context, that Linda's career plans involve "hav[ing] a large orphan asylum, and bring[ing] up the children the way I wasn't brought up" (*Sister* 228) is both an indictment of the usual treatment of orphanage inmates and an assurance that those in Linda's care, at least, will be in the hands of an expert.

As for Mary, her situation has a lengthier resolution. *Linda Lane's Problems* (1928) establishes that Linda can live Mary's life better than Mary can. The two girls briefly trade places, Mary getting a week of the beach vacation that should have been Linda's, Linda standing in for the older girl on the hardscrabble farm. Although the situation is unpromising, since the weather is stifling, the work unending, and the grocery budget tiny, Linda inspires in the younger Rice children more affection than they feel for their sister. She elicits their willing help around the house, stages picnic suppers, and redecorates Mary's room in her free time. The room's transformation (which costs almost nothing) underscores that the transformation of the family is equally possible—or would be if Mary had a tenth of Linda's domestic and emotional mastery.

Conversely, the final two volumes show that when Mary has the chance to share Linda's life (she joins the household as a long-term guest so that she can attend school), she has difficulty integrating herself into this more pleasant existence. Newly endowed by Miss Gilly, like Linda herself in

Linda Lane, with a pretty bedroom and attractive clothes, Mary differs from Linda in being unable to express her gratitude. The chance of an education only depresses her, since she has no desire for the teaching career for which she is fitting herself and finds it hard to get along with her classmates. While another figure in the series, teenage orphan Corey Wood, instantly displays energy and *joie de vivre* in the new life Linda finds for him, Mary is gloomy until Linda interests her in an alternative profession—interior decorating, a choice inspired by Linda's transformation of Mary's farm-house bedroom. When Mary wins a wallpaper-designing contest and gains entree into a prestigious decorating firm, her own newfound sense of mastery makes her less prickly. But it is Linda, predictably, who has impelled Mary to enter the contest, Linda who has served as Mary's inspiration (the wallpaper designs are named for her)—Linda, in short, who is the bridge to social integration and personal fulfillment for her non-orphaned peer.

Deidre Johnson accurately observes that Lawrence eschews "turn-of-the-century feminine sentimentality [for] a more contemporary perspective" (70). Nevertheless, the series provides an update rather than an about-face; as Johnson also remarks, Linda has much in common with the orphan of pre–First World War fiction, who is notable for changing her environment to suit her own personality. Linda merely performs this central task of the protagonist of sentimental fiction in an unsentimental way. The emphasis on a brisk rather than a heart-tugging mastery reflects the dominant strategy of the pro-adoption discourse of the 1920s, namely the effort to play down the perceived risks of raising someone else's child by suggesting that even the exceptional orphan should be accepted as normal. Thus if Linda's genius for management causes her to try to revise Miss Gilly's approach to life (she hopes to break her benefactor of her "doormat" tendencies), Linda is susceptible to Miss Gilly's equally valid efforts to manage her. The orphan is at once remarkable and the same as everyone else; the series highlights her spiritual kinship to a number of disparate figures, from Mr. Pine to Corey Wood to Miss Gilly and even Mary Rice. This revelation of the ordinariness of the extraordinary individual holds out to adoptive parents the prospect of satisfaction in two (contradictory) kinds: they may take pleasure in the spectacle of their off-spring excelling even while they bask in the knowledge that adopted or not, their son or daughter is "just like any other child."

"How Foster Children Turn Out": A Study in Normalcy

In 1924, under the direction of Sophie Van Senden Theis, the New York State Charities Aid Association produced a groundbreaking study whose findings had much in common with the precepts of the Linda Lane series—so much so, indeed, that we may see it as the series' nonfiction counterpart. Assisted by a statistician, sixteen field workers, an "advisory committee" of social-work luminaries, and sundry additional helpers, Theis investigated the lives of the 910 children placed by the Association since August 1898 who had turned eighteen by 1 January 1922. The overall tone of the study is strongly pro-adoption and optimistic that most foster children will make good; indeed, even of the 182 individuals judged to have turned out poorly, nearly half are described as "harmless," being weak or intellectually lacking rather than vicious.

Mingling science and sentiment in a fashion familiar from the magazine articles examined above, the study bristles both with facts and tables and with dramatic personal histories. Yet like the Linda Lane series, it distances itself from sentimental writings on adoption not only through its insistence on the scientific accuracy of its findings, but also through its emphasis on the attractive normalcy of the typical adoptee. Consider the saga of Mary, who was taken at age ten from her "extremely bad" family after the clan was found living, half-starved and poorly clad, in a boxcar (Theis, *Children* 30). Despite an almost total lack of education and disciplinary training, she has become a veritable poster child for adoption. Environment has been all-important; in her "unusually good [foster] home with people of intelligence, culture and means," she grew into an "attractive, charming and well-mannered" young woman who "has adopted many of her foster mother's aristocratic ways and has apparently assimilated as much of the foster background . . . as if she had been born into the home" (31). But Theis does not present the girl as remarkable within her new social milieu. "Active and wholesome," notable (like Lawrence's heroine) for her "good sense" and executive abilities rather than for her intellect, Mary has dropped out of high school to manage her widowed foster mother's business affairs and household, occupying herself with upscale group activities such as tennis and golf (31).

The wholesomeness and family loyalty prominent in Theis's description of Mary are keynotes also in descriptions of other foster children identified as successes; indeed, these traits seem to define success for adoptees, for Theis as for Lawrence. To win the researcher's approval, an individual must manifest not talent but contentment and an ability to get along with others. The American heritage of most of the sample notwithstanding, the goal is assimilation; the children are judged, at least in part, on their readiness to identify their well-being with that of their foster families or to accept community values. Theis's emphasis on what she repeatedly describes as the "refinement" displayed by some girls within her sample hints that an adherence to upper-middle-class gender norms is also a plus. If many of the original parents were violent, alcoholic, mentally ill, or sexually loose, children who show the ability to internalize the social rules flouted by their biological mothers and fathers merit special praise.

Thus mastery wins points, but so do loyalty and responsibility; all three traits, of course, are crucial to Linda Lane's success also. Christine, whose biological mother repeatedly tried to kill her, "is a devoted daughter" to her foster parents, "often giving up her own pleasures" for their sake. Like

Theis's Mary, she has abandoned her education after her foster father's death, the better to care for her mother, and her sacrifice proves that "had Christine been an own child, the feeling of loyalty and devotion could not have been stronger" (30). Another child, once "dangerously cruel and intractable," was placed with "people who apparently had an unusual understanding of a boy's mind"; his "moral disabilities" have vanished, and he is now "wholly honest, reliable and responsible," traits shown by his lodge membership, the respect that his neighbors have for him, and his "devot[ion] to his foster parents" (34). And Olive, daughter of a feeble-minded slattern and an unknown father, occupied six foster homes and was "boisterous, stubborn and hard to control" until, at age twelve, she entered a foster home in which she soon had to assume "the entire responsibility of running the house and caring for her foster mother, by this time an invalid" (34). As an adult, "she is well known for her generosity and kindness to the sick people in her neighborhood," "has for years been secretary or superintendent of the Sunday School," and is a loving and sensible mother (35).

With these individuals as with Linda Lane, success seems synonymous with fitting into one's community (particularly one's foster family) and exhibiting niceness and normalcy rather than talent of a kind that might set one apart; as Kunzel notes of 1920s social work in general, "maladjustment" was increasingly identified as a source of trouble (Kunzel 44). Conversely, failure for Theis means an unwillingness to accept conventional standards and to develop emotional ties to others. Although "intelligent [and] attractive," "pretty and well mannered," and "a competent girl and not lazy," Anna "is defiant of public opinion and continues with determination along the immoral ways that she has selected for herself." Having given birth to an illegitimate baby, "She had no affection for this child and gave it away" (Theis, *Children* 43). Oliver, a "bright" African American teen, "has low standards of living and is proud of it. . . . He can perfectly well earn good wages, but prefers to loaf most of the time," supporting himself by gambling and by forging checks (43). And after seven years in an orphanage and five in an unsatisfactory foster home, Cora is "a dull, sullen girl" who refuses to allow social workers "to get on friendly terms with her. . . . She has a grudge against the world." While she has been a good mother to her baby (conceived out of wedlock), her marriage to its father quickly collapsed, and "She does not have the respect of the community" (44). Lone wolves, rebels, and nonconformists are judged unworthy even if they have native ability; people active in clubs or churches, or enjoying warm relationships with their foster parents, are to be considered successful, whether or not they are productive in other ways.

But despite the title of her study, Theis's greatest concern is not cataloguing "how foster children turn out," but rather suggesting why they turn out as they do. The question's complexity receives due acknowledgment. As influential social worker Homer Folks points out in his foreword to the volume, "It is not a study of environment versus heredity," but a battle "between inheritance plus early environment on the one hand and later environment, personal and community, on the other" (Theis, *Children* 5). Nor could it be assumed that the foster homes were inevitably superior to the children's birth homes. While about 4 percent of the children whose family histories are known are considered to have unimpeachable heredity, 20 percent of the foster parents have provided "poor care." Thus a child identified as having a good background might well have been placed in an environment that eroded his or her inherited advantages.

As Mary Ross noted in summarizing Theis's findings, "poor care"—defined as "the failure to understand [the child] and his needs, the setting of a bad example to him, unreasonable demands upon him, or harsh treatment"—does not necessarily correlate with low income. "Material advantages," Ross observed, "were not the determining factors in selecting or rejecting a foster home"; rather, placement officers set a premium upon normalcy, seeking to insert their charges into "the homes of self-respecting kindly families, such as make up the large part of any social group." Moreover, as in both Lawrence's novels and the magazine accounts discussed above, "'Excellent care' meant a sympathetic understanding of the child's nature which encourages the utmost development of his aptitudes and possibilities" (Ross 384)—a form of empathy that need not depend upon social class. Success as an adoptive parent is potentially available to all, because it requires expertise rather than money.

Predictably, the children who received "excellent care" often turned out better than those whose foster homes "aroused in the children antagonism and a spirit of rebellion," as Theis put it in presenting her findings at a 1924 conference ("Children" 124). Heredity, however, was found to be of little account, since youngsters of predominantly bad family background— about 80 percent of the group—were as likely to turn out well as their counterparts born of virtuous parents or of "mixed" marriages between one good and one bad parent ("Children" 121–22).[9] But the single most important factor, Theis argued, was age at the time of placement. Those sent to foster parents before their fifth birthdays "showed a marked superiority in development over the group older at placement. A large proportion of the younger group have proved to be competent, well-adapted, happy individuals. They are in a larger proportion law-abiding and steady" ("Children" 123); again, note the value assigned to traits suggesting responsibility and contentment, as opposed to a potentially erratic brilliance or nonconformity.

Some of these rosier results presumably stemmed from the greater adaptability associated with extreme youth; commentators in the 1920s, like their counterparts today, assumed that going to a foster home in infancy was less traumatic than going as an older child, after one had put down roots elsewhere. But Theis suggested also that the caregivers were more likely to respond warmly to a younger child and that this response was crucial to the child's development: children placed at earlier ages "were given a better education and had the advantage of more sympathetic and understanding care from their foster parents," while in such instances it was also more likely that the bond between parent and child would "be a complete substitution for the natural parent-child relationship" ("Children" 123, 124). This finding suggests why Linda Lane, placed at the advanced age of thirteen, can nonetheless be represented as a success within a 1920s text that strives to be up to date: Theis's study's title told only half the story. The question was not how foster children turn out, but how foster families turn out. No less than the child, the adult was under scrutiny, and since heredity was judged irrelevant, the environment furnished by the foster parents—especially in terms of those parents' warmth and child-rearing talent, both qualities that Lawrence's Miss Gilly has in abundance—was crucial. Any abnormality in the child in later life reflected adversely upon the caregivers.

Finally, for both Lawrence and Theis, one measure of adult warmth was the readiness to turn foster care into legal adoption. In part this criterion reflects the bureaucratic approach of the 1920s, as the informal adoptions so common in other decades were increasingly frowned upon. Nevertheless, while an earlier commentator might have emphasized the money that this procedure saved the taxpayer, or the institutional space freed up for another needy child, Theis focuses on emotion. She writes, "Of all foster relationships the closest is usually that existing between foster parents and children who have been legally adopted. It most nearly resembles the natural tie between parents and children in understanding and affection; indeed it often seems a complete substitute for it. It is the foster relationship raised to the nth degree of closeness" (*Children* 119). We may discern a hint that adoption is less emotionally beneficial than belonging to a "natural" family, as it may or may not pinch-hit adequately for the "natural tie." Similarly, the adoption of older children is slightly less good than that of younger ones; according to Theis, "It may exist with *almost* as complete an adaptation between parents and children over five at placement as with children placed younger" (119, my italics). Nevertheless, legal adoption is an important tool in ensuring that foster children "turn out well."

But if the study should be considered in the context of a move toward sentimental adoption that had been at work for several generations, it also displays traits characteristic of the 1920s. Among the latter we may identify a preoccupation with mastery, in that Theis offers her audience confidence in their ability to manipulate matters so that foster care may end happily. The study does not overtly claim to be assembling a list of rules for increasing the chances that foster children would succeed, but covertly, it invites the reader to do just that. Thus potential adoptive parents are assured that heredity and early environment are comparatively insignificant. If a child is placed before age five with parents who display decency, affection for their charge, and insight into child psychology, he or she will probably do well. What Ross's summary terms "the power of intelligent foster care" is supreme (383)—but this power is within the reach of any normal adult. Good fostering does not demand unusual force of character, large cash reserves, or specialized training on the adult's part (although the social classes usually associated with mastery, those composed of business leaders and professional men and their wives, now get the lion's share of fostering opportunities). As Lawrence's Miss Gilly demonstrates, one needs only common sense, a good heart, and an understanding of the child's individual talents.

These precepts are remarkable primarily for their straightforwardness; we might compare them to other attempts in the 1920s to reduce to a manageable simplicity complex procedures such as piano playing or effective public speaking. The reader who is not scientifically minded will be impressed by the authority of Theis's statistical tables but need not feel compelled to pore over them; similarly, such a reader will be relieved to learn that concepts such as genetics or the subconscious appear to be irrelevant. If the psychoanalysts of the day might have made hay with the effects of such early traumas as a homicidal mother or a nomad existence passed in boxcars, Theis turns the question into one more readily grasped, namely age at placement. And if we can indeed assume that this factor overshadows all others, then matters are looking up. For of the 2,453 children formerly in the charge of the New York State Charities Aid Association who had not yet turned eighteen by the end of 1921, Theis reports, nearly twice as many were placed before age five as were placed later in life. (Characteristically, she attributes the difference to mastery: the number of effective agencies for social work has grown.) As a consequence, she predicts "that the great majority of [the children] will find in their foster homes a permanent and satisfactory relationship" (*Children* 165). Conducted under modern conditions and guaranteed by the authority of the social-work profession, adoption and foster care have been repackaged as safe, sanitary, and understandable. Like Lawrence's series, Theis's study chronicles, above all, the triumph of normalcy for both displaced child and foster parent.

Mastering Adoption: Other Social Work Findings

Theis's study was widely reported and widely cited. In part it pleased its audience because it suggested ways of giving social work the status of a science (see, e.g., Kunzel 40); the mountain of data newly being collected on dependent children could be used not only to assist in individual placement questions, but also as fodder for impressive statistical projects. Even so, its appeal relied as much on its familiar conclusions as on its innovative approach. Social workers had long argued that younger children were the best prospects for placement, a contention ratified by the demand for two-year-olds from the turn of the century onward. Nor would readers have been surprised at the "discovery" that children reared in sensible, upright, and loving homes often turn out better than children who are abused. In examining other commentary by adoption workers of the period, we thus find some texts that are directly influenced by Theis's book and others that arrive at similar conclusions independently. Threaded throughout these writings, we also discover the themes of mastery and normalcy, assimilation into the mass and the possibility of standing out from the herd. Like Lawrence's series and Theis's study, the pronouncements of adoption experts in the 1920s have as much to say about the era's approach to authority and individuality as they do about the displaced child.

One work that acknowledged its debt to Theis was Ida R. Parker's *"Fit and Proper"? A Study of Legal Adoption in Massachusetts* (1927). Parker's volume straddles the gap between the secular-scientific and the religious-eleemosynary. The title page identifies her as "Associate Director Research Bureau on Social Case Work," a credential that affiliates her with what readers will understand to be a large and technical operation. At the same time, the book is "Distributed by the Church Home Society for the care of children of the Protestant Episcopal Church," a line that conjures up older and less intimidating visions. The inquiry itself, Parker notes, is similarly double-barreled, as it "is an attempt (1) to discover the extent and nature of adoption practice in Massachusetts; and (2) to learn how a certain group of adopted children turned out" (5). The study's first part, which "gives some indication of the size of the [adoption] problem in Massachusetts, throws some light on who the candidate for adoption is [and] by whom he is adopted, and tells something of court procedure," is modeled on a 1925 report by a Pennsylvania commission charged with examining state laws relating to children; the second part is modeled on Theis's work, although Parker conducts her investigation on a smaller scale.

Parker's first major point is that since the adoption "problem" is widespread, it requires modern bureaucratic methods for its control. She estimates that 60 percent of legal adoptions in the state involve parties unrelated by blood. Most adoptions are effected without the help of adoption agencies; many more involve deceit and the falsification of records, usually in order to conceal illegitimacy. As a result of the amateurism and ignorance surrounding such proceedings, she claims, children are being placed in families ill equipped to deal with them. Some adoptive parents "now regre[t] allowing the placement without proper investigation"; others have gone so far as to "retur[n] the child, which bears their name and for which they are now responsible, to its natural mother" (33). With such stories in mind, Parker calls for standardizing placement procedures—paradoxically, so as to give each case personal consideration. Detailed in a case record compiled by an experienced social worker and examined over a lengthy trial period, the displaced child is to become a specimen in a social-scientific taxonomy in order that he or she may be viewed as an individual and assigned to an appropriate home.

Parker's call for such methods is the more urgent because she perceives most displaced children as inherently inferior. Because such children are, in her view, disproportionately the biological heirs of social misfits and mockers of morality, extreme measures will be required before they can be established as normal members of respectable mainstream society:

> Frequently adoptive parents, aware that adoption involves certain risks, begin the search for a child fully determined to choose one of good inheritance, and are surprised to discover that normal families of good stock seldom give away their children even in the face of poverty, death, or other adversity. . . . The residue available is likely to include many children from the less responsible sort of families. (26)

And to clarify what she means by "less responsible," Parker provides twenty-five case histories of children available for adoption. While Theis's thumbnail sketches are generally upbeat tales of children whose disastrous beginnings are erased by good experiences after placement, Parker's focus primarily on the children's descent from adults marked by a tendency to alcohol abuse, unrestrained or illicit sexuality, chronic unemployment, and general "peculiar[ity]" of temperament (24); by implication, the children are likely to embrace the same fates in later life.

Thus Parker's book is inclined to emphasize the need to protect adoptive parents above the need to protect adopted children. Thorough scrutiny by seasoned professionals is necessary if naive adults, eager to become parents and insufficiently concerned about provenance, are to be prevented from inadvertently accepting abnormality and degeneracy into their families. Even so, Parker ends the first section of her treatise with a brief discussion of "unsuitable adoptive homes" (that is, adoptions by abusive, immoral, near-destitute, or chronically ill parents), and concludes the whole on an uncharacteristically sentimental note, asking in impassioned tones, "How much longer must helpless children of Massachusetts wait for their State to extend that measure of protection against unsuitable adoption which they so sorely need?" (60–65, 130). This rhetorical move reasserts her kinship to more optimistic writers such as Ross, who ends her summary of Theis on a similar emotional plane, averring, "Here were a thousand children, only a score of whom had what one could fairly call a good background and origin. They were put in the care of plain, simple, understanding folk. They made good. Is [foster care] pouring water into a sieve? These thousand children answer no" (433).

Despite what might initially seem the pessimism of Parker's book, then, her ultimate point resembles that of Willsie's article and Theis's study: if the participating adults have enough background in the subject, adoption can be safe for all parties. The second part of the work traces the outcomes of a hundred adoptions completed (or nearly completed) between 1900 and 1921. Fifty-eight of the children were known to be illegitimate; almost all came of parents judged intemperant, criminal, insane, and/or promiscuous; and most were under ten years old at the time of adoption. Parker divides the children into two groups. The fifteen in Group A were "adopted independently of social agencies" (80), while the eighty-five in Group B were professionally placed. For Parker, this question of professional involvement—far more than factors such as heredity or age at placement—is the crucial one: "It is significant that the group of children adopted through agencies shows a much larger proportion of persons who have already become or give promise of developing into 'capable' adults than the group adopted independently of organizations" (129).

Hence while one of the children in Group A is said to have found a satisfactory home and a handful have formed adequate ties to their new families, most of the descriptions are selected for their hair-raising qualities.[10] Several of the children have been sexually abused by their adoptive parents. Two children adopted by unbalanced couples are themselves edging toward mental illness, one "constructing an imaginary world of her own in an attempt to escape from unpleasant reality" and the other "suffering from a mental conflict due partly to the conditions under which he had lived in the adoptive home" (89). And one woman, said to be a promiscuous drug addict and ex-convict, "seemed to have a mania for taking children but did not give them even intelligent care"; she has fostered or adopted at least three children. Two of them have been removed from her control, partly because she has neglected them and partly because "fraud had been practiced on the court at the time of adoption in that the woman did not say that her husband . . . was colored" (87).[11] In the twilight zone of extra-bureaucratic placement, adoptive parents are as likely as birth parents to exhibit a pathological deviation from the norm.

The adoptions of the Group B children have been noticeably more successful. Whereas fully two thirds of the individuals in Group A have unsatisfactory relationships with their adoptive parents, characterized by "slight affection[,] indifference or even antagonism," not quite one quarter of the Group B families are experiencing this kind of emotional strain (125). Even the adoptions by relatives have proven "much more suitable than were three of the four adoptions by relatives which were put through without agency assistance" (97).[12] The adoptive parents range from unskilled workers to professionals and executives, but in no cases do they manifest the abusive or "peculiar" tendencies identified in the Group A parents. In part, Parker suggests, this greater stability may result from better understanding of the children's capacities, gained from agency screening procedures. Given thorough medical and psychological evaluations of the young candidates (although, she notes sadly, agencies do not always make use of intelligence testing), prospective parents can become aware of traits that they might not be willing to accept in their child, and halt the adoption before it takes place.

Although Parker implies that adopted children are more likely than others to suffer from mental deficiencies or psychological disorders, she concedes that "Properly safe-guarded adoption may be a social asset as well as a social expedient" (130). Many of the families in the study derive great happiness from their adopted children, and Parker concludes that about 80 percent of her sample (half of the Group A children and 85 percent of those in Group B) consists of individuals who "may be regarded as assets to society" (127). But the proportion of failures is too high for her liking, so that on page after page she urges the use of what one cited authority, Charlotte Towne of the Children's Aid Society of Pennsylvania, calls "methods that possess the discriminative technique of science blended with the creative spirit of art" (qtd. 128). Or again, quoting Gesell's "Psychoclinical Guidance in Child Adoption," she describes adoption as a procedure so complex, a "problem of such importance[,] that it 'cannot be entrusted altogether to good will or to intuitive impulse or even to unaided common sense'" (129–30). This emphasis on science rather than sentiment, mastery rather than chance, is for Parker the way to maximize an adoptee's chances of successful assimilation into a family and into society. The expertise of the placement officer will ensure the ultimate normalcy of the constructed family.

To some extent the presence of adoption horror stories in accounts such as Parker's seems to have been a response to the Progressive Era's establishment of sentimentality as the dominant rhetorical mode in discussing child placement. Invoking the dispassionate authority of science was the obvious tactic in such cases, as we see exemplified in the 1924 comments by A. H. Stoneman of the Michigan Children's Aid Society:

> Innumerable stories have been written and printed telling of the happy results of the adoption of a child, in many cases the lucky outcome of a reckless adoption. It is time the public should hear about some of the unhappy developments of just such placements, and why. Especially is it desirable that stories be told of the exceedingly happy results which are coming from the more scientific procedure of the best adoption agencies which base their procedure upon thorough knowledge of the child and of the home where it is placed.
>
> The child-placing agencies of this Conference should, in an organized way through farm journals, trade papers, Sunday supplements, and the popular magazines, send out stories which will reach the hearts of the American public and so eventually rectify the present misguided sentiment in regard to the adoption of children. (145)

Note, however, that what Stoneman is proposing is not the abolition of sentiment, but rather the yoking of sentiment to science. The sentimental adoption unsupported by "scientific procedure" is to be debunked, certainly, but only in order that it may be replaced with the scientific sentimental adoption, which like its predecessor is to be enshrined in "the hearts of the American public" through the lowbrow media.

Stoneman and Parker were only two of many commentators of the period who called for ever more authority to be vested in the social-work bureaucracy. Non-agency adoptions were to be discouraged; Stoneman, for one, called for legislation to restrict "advertising or publicly offering through the press a child for adoption or indenture" (147), a move that would inhibit not only baby-farming but also phenomena such as the *Delineator* campaign. Conversely, the agency's role was to be expanded. Proposed mechanisms for its growth included investigations of the heredity of adoptive parents and a one-year trial period between placement and adoption, during which a social worker would visit at least once a quarter (Stoneman 147–48). And Hewins of the Boston Church Home Society remarked that even "the well-to-do and intelligent couple" required supervision by trained personnel during the adjustment process (110).

As Kunzel's discussion of unwed mothers illuminates (see, e.g., 64), calls for mastery on the part of the adoption worker owed much to the drive to establish social work as an exacting profession, a perception that would raise salaries and confer status upon practitioners. In Theis's words, "Expert work comes high but it is safe to say that it pays and that superficial and inferior work does not pay" ("Qualifications" 124). These sentiments influenced the production of manuals for the placement worker, which might begin, like W. H. Slingerland's 1919 *Child-Placing in Families,* with a rundown on the history of adoption from ancient Babylon onward—thus establishing the respectability of adoption's own heritage. Manuals both helped standardize social-work practice and identified adoption as a procedure to be restricted to the expert, so that in his introduction to *Child-Placing in Families,* Hastings Hart congratulated Slingerland on having "show[n] conclusively that child-placing is a most technical and responsible work, to be properly done only by people of a high degree of judgment, conscience, and training. He wisely opposes the employment of inexperienced or sentimental people" (Slingerland 21). Clergymen and other amateurs were to keep their distance or suffer legal penalties (45).

Such commentaries pushed for a new hierarchy in which the individuals recognized as morally and intellectually outstanding were neither the children (as in fiction) nor the adoptive parents (as in some women's-magazine articles), but rather the social workers. In Slingerland's words, adoption caseworkers "are to influence hundreds of immature lives. Their words and actions are to guide and control many impressionable young spirits. Upon their wisdom and judgment will depend the future welfare of the children, especially those whom they place in private homes, and of the families in which they are located. Only workers of a high type are fit for such service" (47). In other words, although all sorts of adoption texts during this period share certain traits, such as a ratification of modernity and a desire to disavow sentimentality, we may discern a significant rupture in terms of the location of individual authority. If the tendency of sentimental rhetoric had been to assert the emotional power of the private, domestic, and apparently powerless, often as embodied in children or housewives, professional rhetoric asserted instead the power of the public realm and the corporate body. Yet the power at issue remained what it had been in the more openly sentimental late nineteenth century: the ability to transform society through the uplifting of individual families, who would be brought to a higher standard of morality. And even if social workers were now to pull the strings, orphans remained the mechanism through which this transformation was to be accomplished.

Conclusion

We began this study with a glimpse of two girls known as "Little Orphan Annie," James Whitcomb Riley's nineteenth-century prototype and Harold Gray's 1920s model. Thus it seems fitting that we return to Gray's comic strip at the end. For his Annie, too, illustrates questions of individuality and mass culture, sentiment and anti-sentiment, authority and powerlessness, and the use of the displaced child to embody important social issues and criticize the domestic status quo. The long popularity of this mass-market adoptee not only marks her as perhaps the most successfully commodified orphan discussed in the present study, but also reveals her as an iconic figure. The fervor of Annie's fans suggests that Gray had his finger upon the pulse of the era.

Newspapers were full participants in the periodicals boom noted in Chapter 3. Founded in droves to take advantage of the newly increased reading public, they competed fiercely for that readership. Comic strips such as *Annie*—which debuted in the New York *News* on 5 August 1924—were circulation-boosting devices designed to appeal to a lowbrow audience. That Annie's instant success was more than superficial was demonstrated fourteen months along, when the commissioning editor, Joseph Medill Patterson, objected to Mrs. Warbucks's demand that Sandy be shot and pulled the strip from the Chicago *Tribune*. The volume and intensity of readerly outrage, which included a bomb threat, were such that *Annie* was instantly restored, and Patterson ran an editorial on the front page apologizing for his action; for some days thereafter, the paper printed letters from subscribers testifying to their devotion (B. Smith 17). In its heyday, the strip drew an audience of 16 million, appeared in 500 newspapers, and inspired both a successful radio serial and a long-running Hearst imitation featuring orphan Little Annie Rooney and her dog Zero (Simpson 238, 241; B. Smith 21).

According to Eileen Simpson, Annie's appeal stems from both her pathos and her indestructibility (243). But in the context of the 1920s, we might find additional reasons for the strip's success. For one thing, Annie combined the toughness of the tomboy, a figure often valorized in the 1920s, with the sweetness and self-sacrifice of the ideal nineteenth-century child. If an early installment shows Annie punching a prospective brother for mocking her raggedness, she tends to behave in a more Victorian way with Daddy Warbucks, both bringing out his softer side and, on one occasion, running away so that he will not have to choose between her and his wife (B. Smith 10, 19). Like Horatio Alger's Tattered Tom, she both undermined and affirmed cultural stereotypes of femininity and childhood, appealing to a wide range of readers while suggesting that the battle between traditionalism and modernity could have attractive results.

Then too, Annie's ambivalent relationship to authority recalls the representation of other adoptees and foster children of the period. Like Linda Lane, she starts life in an orphanage, where she is set to work scrubbing floors and constantly reminded of her status as charity child; again like Linda, she resents her subordination and longs to escape the system. But just as Linda cooperates upon entering Miss Gilly's home, Annie bonds easily with Daddy Warbucks, although not with his wife. If Warbucks, as a *nouveau riche* representative of Big Business (which Gray found a "maligned" group [qtd. B. Smith 12]), is both an outsider and a man with social clout, Annie too manages to occupy both the fringes and the center of power, and both do so in part by critiquing adult femininity. The oddly assorted and predominantly male group that eventually constitutes Annie's family—Annie, Warbucks, Sandy, Punjab, and the Asp—consists of individuals who can bond with each other precisely because they all normally find assimilation difficult. Their authority depends, in part, on the disapproval with which more conventional authority regards them, so that they simultaneously question the validity of the corporate mentality and reassure us that however peculiar we may be, kindred spirits lurk nearby. In an era that sought to advance what we might term "mass individuality," Annie managed to stand out from her herd by being the most conventional person in it.

In this regard, it seems significant that Annie's identity is perennially under siege. Her uncertain family status and past, her blank eyes, suggest a void that makes her rootless and vulnerable. She oscillates between rags and riches and bounces from family to family; in the strip's first few months, Annie's long-stay residences included Miss Asthma's orphanage, the Warbucks mansion, a foster home headed by the exploitative Mrs. Bottle and her husband "Pop," and the pleasant farmhouse of Mr. and Mrs. Silo. Annie's protean circumstances, combined with her stubborn assertion of personality whatever her milieu, made her an ideal heroine for the 1920s—an era in which, as Michaels observes, individuality was undergoing a radical redefinition fueled by social pressures that included the mechanization and standardization enacted within both the orphanage and factories such as the one run by Warbucks. In a rapidly changing world in which individual "personality" was both touted and eradicated, adoption might seem at once terrifying and tempting, a unique way to escape one's past or to help others escape theirs.

To be sure, as we have seen, by the 1920s adoption increasingly involved not only a change of environment as a child moved from one home to another or from institution to private domesticity, but also submission to a growing bureaucracy whose goals included the compilation of ever more elaborate dossiers on clients' backgrounds, capacities, and experiences. This compulsive record keeping may be viewed as the social-welfare analogue to industrial standardization efforts such as the establishment of clothing sizes. The dossiers, too, were designed to ensure a satisfactory "fit" between parent and child—or between consumer and commodity, a metaphor made appropriate by the advertising of orphans as remedies for frustration or rocky marriages. Michaels remarks that the development of standard sizing depended on the creation of "a whole new set of individualizing and intimate facts about the wearers of those clothes," so that shoppers were "singled out" by being identified as members of a group unified by a common sleeve length. Paradoxically, then, "individuality [was] an effect of standardization" (84). The same point might be made about the orphans and adoptive families who came under the scrutiny of the "scientific" placement agency of the 1920s; even as they became part of larger classes unified by the degree of emotional attachment achieved or by the extent to which early handicaps might be corrected, they were anatomized as unique specimens.

So, for that matter, were the adoption workers. Moved toward standardization by the introduction of textbooks, degree programs, and certification requirements, they were simultaneously differentiated from the uncredentialed ladies' committees and clergymen who had once dominated the field. Frederick Winslow Taylor, notes Michaels, "had imagined that the mechanization of the worker would encourage . . . 'individual character, energy, skill, and reliability'" (89). These are virtues ascribed at once to "successful" foster children within Theis's study, to exemplary mass-market adoptees such as Annie and Linda Lane and the subject of "Our Adopted Son"—and to the highly trained caseworkers held up for our admiration by Slingerland and others. In the 1920s, mastery required some submission to external authority, if only that one might be advantageously shaped, appropriately trained, and fitted into the social context best suited to the exercise of one's talents. The rhetoric surrounding displaced children thus offered a primer for success that applied precepts far more widely current.

To be sure, 1920s rhetoric employed emphases, precepts, and stylistic fillips not characteristic of that of earlier eras. Even while we may discern a strong family likeness over time, the representations traced within the present work are marked by significant change; if Ellen Montgomery of *The Wide, Wide World* shares important traits with the upright and conformable adoptees of Theis's study, Riley's Orphant Annie is nevertheless not Gray's Orphan Annie. Each generation—including our own, of course—constructs its vision of the displaced child according to its own principles and needs. As Slingerland wrote in 1919, it is essential "that a propaganda be instituted and continued to educate the people as to the aims, plans, spirit, and character of organized child-placing. It must be fresh and vigorous every year. The propaganda of five years ago is almost as useless as a last year's bird's nest" (214).

Useless as "propaganda," perhaps, but invaluable as part of the historical record. As this study has sought to demonstrate, American writers and commentators have long used perceptions of the displaced child both to engage in major efforts at social engineering and to express deeply felt anxieties on issues central to our lives, including ethnicity, social class, work, gender, and family. Sometimes their rhetoric may seem to approximate children's lived experience; sometimes it has relied upon child-figures whose idealized virtue, plasticity, or lack of personality may appear more imaginary than real. Yet if we cannot conclude that nonfiction speaks more truly than fiction (especially since both forms rely upon the same rhetorical devices), neither can we conclude that the texts that stray the farthest from probability have less to contribute to our understanding than those that adhere most closely to fact. The importance of child-placing extends beyond the individual.

Notes

Introduction

1. See, e.g., Silverman and Feigelman 187; Cole and Donley 276. To be sure, toddlers were considered desirable acquisitions by the turn of the century; part of the objection to adopting infants had to do with their fragility. In the mid-nineteenth century, many infants admitted to orphanages and foundling hospitals died within weeks, victims of overcrowded and understaffed institutions that could provide little individual care. The advent of formula feeding in the early twentieth century eliminated the need for wet nurses and made adopting babies more practical.

2. See Askeland 487. I have preferred "displaced child" to "orphan" in this study, as a term embracing all children available for adoption or fostering. "Adoption" is itself a potentially confusing noun during the period I am discussing, as it might or might not refer to legal proceedings. Throughout, I use "adoption" to refer to a move that seems intended to make a child a permanent member of a given family, whether or not the arrangement has been ratified by a court of law; "fostering" designates a more temporary situation, usually one in which the foster parent receives practical benefits such as a salary ("boarding out") or the child's labors as domestic servant ("binding out").

3. Almshouses or poorhouses, designed to contain the unemployable of any age, had once been the designated repositories for the destitute young. By the 1850s, housing dependent children with adult delinquents and lunatics seemed undesirable, and many orphanages owed their founding to the desire to segregate the inmates by age. Susan Whitelaw Downs and Michael W. Sherraden provide figures that illustrate the rate at which orphanages took over the function of the almshouse vis-à-vis the dependent child: in 1790 almshouses held roughly 1,000 children, orphanages 200; in 1820 the figures had changed to 3,000 in almshouses and 1,500 in orphanages; and 1850 saw 17,000 in almshouses and 7,700 in orphanages. By 1880, however, orphanages had taken the lead, with 60,000 inmates as compared to 11,500 in almshouses, and in 1910 a mere 3,600 children lived in almshouses while 123,000 lived in orphanages (273). In New York State, the orphanage population tripled between 1870 and 1890 (Dulberger 8).

4. To be sure, a reader of children's fiction might become a social worker or lawyer in later life, just as *Huckleberry Finn*'s original audience could have included members of these professions. I speak rather of what reader-response critics term a text's "ideal" or "imagined" reader: the fictions that this book surveys do not assume specialized knowledge in their audience.

1. The 1850s and Their Echoes

1. Inheritance rights for the adopted were not uniform even after most states had passed adoption laws. Many authorities held that adoptees should not share

equally with legitimate biological children in the estate of an intestate parent. This concern lingered for years as a marker of doubts about whether adoption established the same emotional bond between parent and child that blood kin are assumed to have. For an overview of legal disputes, see Grossberg 276–78.

2. Warner expressed dislike for at least two of Sedgwick's tales (S. Williams 571), while Sedgwick, in turn, expressed dislike for Warner's father (Leverenz 189). But despite the authors' evident antipathy, the heroines and their taskmistresses have much in common.

3. Among the many examples of such rhetoric is Lydia Sigourney's *Letters to Mothers* (1839), which sees the mother as "a tutelary seraph . . . spreading perpetually the wings of purity and peace over its beloved shrine, and keeping guard for God" (qtd. Brodhead 20).

4. David Leverenz suggests rather that orphanhood sums up for Warner the condition of women, whose "essential aloneness shows in the title: not just 'the wide world' but 'the wide, wide world,' awesomely vast" (184).

5. An 1858 investigation found some 1,200 children languishing in Massachusetts almshouses alongside adults, "packed like sardines in double cradles and . . . cared for by pauper inmates" whom the investigators described as "a motley collection of broken-backed, lame-legged, sore-eyed, helpless, and infirm human beings" (Fearing 192). The image relies on, and intensifies, middle-class fears of the poor "family" as simultaneously fecund and degenerate.

6. It trailed Pennsylvania and Indiana (1855), Georgia (1855–56), Wisconsin (1858), Ohio (1859), Michigan (1861), New Hampshire (1862), Oregon and Connecticut (1864), Illinois (1867), Kansas (1868), California (1870), Maine (1871), Rhode Island (1872), and North Carolina (1872–73).

7. The accuracy of this figure, apparently derived from an 1849 report issued by New York City chief of police George Matsell (see Ashby, *Children* 38), is by no means assured, since such populations exist beyond the reach of the census. Other child-saving organizations made significantly lower guesses, such as the 1850 estimate by the founders of the New York Juvenile Asylum, which put the population of street children at 3,000 (Crenson 62).

8. For instance, the year that he founded the New York Children's Aid Society, Brace opened a school in which middle-class women filled in for inadequate working-class mothers by teaching girls domestic skills. Graduates could earn their livings as servants, but might also serve as missionaries by exercising their new abilities at home (Clement 199–200). The idea that the slum child might be used to redeem its parents survived in phenomena such as the New York schools of the late 1870s that trained girls as young as four to wash dishes, set tables, and launder clothes. According to *St. Nicholas* writer Olive Thorne, pupils may be too young to become housemaids, but "the mothers cannot be thankful enough; they have been taught better ways of doing common things by their little daughters." The program, she finds, "helps the girls themselves to better lives, does good to all with whom they live and associate, influences the parents and homes, and will, in the end, affect the big city itself" (410). And for a discussion of the similar mindset animating Jane Addams's Hull House nursery school around 1900, see Youcha 146.

9. Indeed, not until late in the century, Marilyn Irvin Holt observes, was adoption even a possibility under the Society's guidelines. This change came about when the Society shifted the locus of its recruitment efforts: "No longer were most

children being taken directly from city streets. Rather, the society removed children from private orphanages and had the approval of the New York City government to take children from public institutions for placement" (65).

10. Such advertisements were by no means unique to the Society. Broadsheets distributed by the New York Juvenile Asylum in 1888 promised to provide, at no charge, "desirable" indentured children "mostly of respectable parentage" and "worthy of good homes" (qtd. Holt 90).

11. *The Orphan Trains* quotes an 1865 letter from one foster mother, Mrs. Sallie Highland (I have modernized spelling and punctuation): "If he were our own son, we could not love him more than we do. We have given him our name—we call him Charley Highland. He thinks we are his parents, and we want him to. He is a good child; I believe it would kill him to part with us. I love him so much that it would break my heart to part with him."

12. Many farmers nonetheless continued to prefer older teenagers for their usefulness even after child-placers began to push younger children as more easily integrated into the family (Holt 139).

13. Geraldine Youcha notes that Darwin's "gemmule" theory was held by a number of reformers (195).

14. Ironically, Brace's efforts to use the orphan trains to "save" children from Catholicism as well as from squalor eventually spurred some Catholic institutions, such as the New York Foundling Hospital, to run trains of their own in order to supply children to Catholic couples. Would-be guardians were required to place their orders ahead of time, as the Hospital was unwilling to send out children in the blind hope that worthy Catholics would appear to take care of them.

15. As Peter Holloran has noted, Brace's organization resembled the Boston Children's Mission in that it avoided placing African American children in white families and rarely recruited foster families of color; the adoption of black children tended rather to be an informal matter arranged within the extended family (143–44), in part because few facilities within the dominant white society would accept them. According to Timothy Hacsi, in 1890 the United States contained a mere twenty-seven orphanages specifically for African Americans, while orphanages that were officially multiracial often housed only a tiny number of nonwhites: "Louisiana, Kentucky, Mississippi, and Tennessee each had one mixed asylum . . . holding a total of just five black children," while "only one of California's 'mixed' asylums held more than two black children"—and even it was 95 percent white (35–36).

16. Writing in the *New York Times* in 1998, Barbara Stewart anticipates that 3,000 children will attend summer camp on Fund scholarships and 7,000 will visit rural families, so that the Fund's annual clientele had thus only doubled since 1883. But if the operation's size has not changed much, the rhetoric has. Stewart emphasizes the feelings of the host families over those of the young guests: "Most families who invite a child into their homes enjoy the experience and want to repeat it. . . . [Jonathan's Fresh Air parents] feel close enough to Jonathan to keep in touch through the year, inviting him to the circus and to baseball games at Yankee Stadium."

17. For other *St. Nicholas* features on fresh-air efforts, see Gannon 264–65.

18. That Ford's article appears in a magazine aimed at children, and to a lesser extent their parents, may predispose it to take an optimistic approach. While writers of the 1880s did not shrink from describing to children hard truths of life (such

as the child abuse, overcrowding, and filth with which Ford's article begins), they typically implied that such situations might be remedied.

2. Money Talks

1. Relatively few admitted African American children, although black soldiers were almost twice as likely as white ones to die of disease, the major killer in this war. Moreover, while legitimate survivors of black Union soldiers were eligible for pensions, many children did not claim benefits because their parents had not been legally married (a privilege denied to slaves) or because, illiterate and unsure of their rights, they did not file applications (Clement 27–29).

2. Thus William H. Whitmore argued in 1876 that since "the subjects of adoption are so largely taken from the waifs of society, foundlings or children whose parents are depraved and worthless," to permit the adopted child an automatic right of inheritance worked against the public good. He proposed instead "some form of temporary adoption [that would] extend only to the period of the minority of the child, with a stipulation for a reasonable provision for it on attaining its majority, if the adoption be not then ratified" (74); such a move would help to keep property out of reach of the inferior.

3. Of course, Huck is at least as dubious about "sivilization" as it is about him; even in *Tom Sawyer,* Twain makes clear that the boy is happier as an outcast.

4. Social class could work differently in earlier orphan narratives. Consider Lydia Maria Child's "The Cottage Girl" (*Juvenile Miscellany* September 1828), which describes the adoption of working-class twins into two families, one headed by a wealthy couple and the other by a poor laundress. When brother and sister meet years later, their class differences cause constraint and anxiety; the boy's parents expect (wrongly, as it turns out) to find the girl low and unrefined, while the girl worries about her clothing and deportment. As Carolyn Karcher puts it, "everyone is relieved when she elects to show her gratitude to the washerwoman by remaining with her, rather than to accept the rich family's offer of adoption" (71). Although the boy's adoptive parents give his sister an education and a wardrobe befitting a respectable girl of modest means, it is too late for her to become his equal. Fifty years later, authors would more typically have argued that neither sibling could readily be inserted into an upper-class family.

5. The ethnic tensions, represented by the animosity between Ben and the Squire's Irish man-of-all-work, Pat, play a comparatively small part. When Ben gets a job as the Squire's chore boy, he runs afoul of the older employee, who sees him as both a rival for the Squire's esteem and a social inferior who may legitimately be dominated. Ben himself resents these efforts at domination, even though we later hear that "Ben had been taught instant obedience to those older than himself" (Alcott, *Lilacs* 130). He hates Pat from the latter's first utterance, "Come out o' this, b'y, till I show ye the bastes [beasts]," a speech whose offensiveness seems to lie primarily in Pat's brogue (56).

6. Alcott approves of characters who form emotional attachments to their horses or dogs, as opposed to valuing them only for their utility. Orphans, arguably, come in for less sentiment.

7. Thorny's possessiveness toward his sister mirrors Jo March's toward Meg in *Little Women;* as Jo famously announces at the time of her older sister's engagement to John Brooke, she would like to "marry Meg [her]self, and keep her safe in the family" (190).

8. Somewhat similarly, the wealthy orphan Rose Campbell "adopts" an inmate of a baby farm in *Rose in Bloom*. She intends the act as charity and expects the placement to be permanent, but since such efforts have earlier been described as "excellent training for the time when [young women have] little darlings of their own" (109–10), and since we are told that her guardian "permitted Rose to keep it for a time at least" (267), we may conclude that the toddler's role is to enhance her patroness's resemblance to "some of Correggio's young Madonnas" (263) and to acculturate her to a future maternity. This informal placement will, one presumes, be brief.

9. Susan Gannon describes a *St. Nicholas* story of 1875, Olive Thorne Miller's "May's Christmas Tree," that tweaks this formula: a penniless orphan goes to her uncle's "'little grinding prairie home,' a veritable 'temple of work,'" and, by introducing Christmas customs and the concept of play, becomes "the cultural missionary they need to make their lives complete" (276). The rescued becomes the rescuer, a paradigm that would become more popular after 1885. (Miller appears elsewhere in the present book as Olive Thorne; she wrote under both names, as well as under her legal name, Harriet Mann Miller.)

10. Alcott's *Jo's Boys* (1886) implies that flight may sometimes be preferable to domesticity. This novel traces the fortunes of two former street urchins, weak, effeminate Nat and "firebrand" Dan. While Nat is grudgingly allowed into the extended March family when he wins the hand of Jo's niece Daisy, Dan is an ineligible mate for Daisy's wealthier cousin, "Princess" Bess, and goes West to die violently, his love undeclared. But the implication is not that he is too bad to join the March-Laurence clan, but that it is inadequate for him. Dan has always been Jo's secret favorite among her "boys," and his experiences in maturity explain why: he embodies her own anarchic and anti-domestic impulses. More masculine than anyone else in the sequence, Dan distills the revulsion against the constraints of femininity that Jo's society does not permit her to express. That *Jo's Boys* ends with the anti-domestic image of the orphaned wanderer dying romantically because the family cannot accommodate him interrogates the series' ostensible ideals.

11. Somewhat similarly, that Mrs. Moss's proposal in *Under the Lilacs* to "take [Ben] right home, and wash and feed and put [him] in a good bed" does not entail making him a full-fledged member of the family is instantly clear to the boy himself, who responds, "You're very kind, ma'am. I'll be glad to work for you" (33).

12. Kenneth Kidd observes that in emphasizing the "cultivation" of young men, "*Farming for Boys* is one of the earliest American texts to insist upon the need for professional boy supervision," presaging later movements such as scouting (148–49). Here as elsewhere, the literary orphan functions as a predictor of cultural trends.

13. Nor does O'Connor ask for references, although the two men have never met before. Alger earlier has him claim, doubtless to counter criticisms of the Children's Aid Society's placement methods, "We are in constant correspondence with [the children]. We feel ourselves under an obligation to look after them still, and to show them that we keep up an interest in them. . . . They are ashamed to misconduct themselves, knowing that it will come to our ears" (31). But while Julius eventually sends in a progress report, Alger does not show the Society initiating follow-up.

14. See Moon for commentary on the homoeroticism of the foster-brother tie in Alger's works.

15. The brevity of my discussion here precludes an adequate rehearsal of the huge critical literature on Twain's boy books; a search of the MLA online bibliography at the time of writing turned up 590 articles on *Huckleberry Finn* alone. While the recent debate has focused particularly on race, see Segal, Knoper, Altschuler, Griswold, Shulman, and Marshall for thought-provoking arguments on *Huckleberry Finn* and family.

16. Thus the soi-disant king and duke, who like Huck are without known family and must live by their wits, likewise play many parts, from titled exiles to minister and deaf-mute to master of ceremonies and nude dancer.

17. The judge who first rules on the custody question "didn't know the old man; so he said courts mustn't interfere and separate families if they could help it" (Twain, *Finn* 35). That this view—which would become more common by the turn of the century—is based more on sentiment than on sense becomes clear in the next few paragraphs, which detail first Pap's drunken celebration and then the judge's naive attempt to "make a man of him" by taking him into his own house and offering sympathy and moral guidance. This mock-adoption of a "child" of almost fifty fails, indirectly endorsing the views of social reformers such as Brace that only the young are malleable enough to save, and then only if they are separated from their dissolute elders. Significantly, before Pap returns to claim him, Huck reports becoming acclimatized to the widow's genteel regime.

18. To be sure, he briefly passes himself off as one William Thompson of Hicksville, Ohio, but he does so only to better sustain the part of Sid, and quickly reveals his true identity.

19. Another, headed by Leslie Fiedler, sees the relationship as approximating a marriage.

20. This sum, 5 percent of Jim's market value, is also what Tom pays Jim for having endured an imprisonment that Tom could have spared him had he divulged Jim's status as freedman. In effect, Tom is at once acknowledging Jim's ownership of himself by paying the forty dollars to him rather than to some white "master," and turning him into chattel once more by ignoring his right to agree to the transaction.

21. As Altschuler remarks, his nomination of Miss Watson as this hostage expresses his animosity toward mother figures (33). But even this example suggests a hostility complicated by longing, since the Widow Douglas, not Miss Watson, is his primary guardian at this point, and Huck does not propose sacrificing her.

22. To be sure, such contracts sometimes disguised sentimental adoptions, since when adoption was not possible under existing state law or because birth parents had not permanently signed away custody, indenture gave the adult some legal right to the child. Even so, some states that had already passed adoption laws, notably Massachusetts, retained indenture decades after enacting such legislation; the idea that the displaced child should earn its way died hard.

23. By 1890, Marilyn Holt observes, the Home had intensified its rhetoric in this line, "making it clear to all concerned that its placed out were to be 'treated as *sons and daughters*' (emphasis in original), and that legal adoption was highly encouraged" (105).

24. Goddard's point, however, was that society should not permit the "feeble-minded" to reproduce, not (as Harris and Dugdale held) that they might be reformed and made respectable.

25. Paid foster care in America may have originated in Albany as early as the 1840s (Crenson 93). But it was not approved by a state legislature until 1882,

when Massachusetts instituted it after sixteen years of lobbying by the Board of State Charities and two years of experimentation on a small scale (188). By 1895, "boarding out," as the practice was then known, had enabled the end of state-supported institutionalization in Massachusetts.

26. Similar accusations were made outside the conference venue. Crenson cites the superintendent of the Albany Orphan Asylum, Albert Fuller, who complained in 1880 that most applicants for children were "too mean & penurious to pay for the help they need & want a child to fill a man or womans [*sic*] place without wages & with the intention of giving only what they are forced to in the shape of clothing & schooling" (qtd. Crenson 215).

27. Lasch identifies four sources for this anxiety: the increased number of divorces after 1870, the dwindling birthrate among the soi-disant "desirable" members of society, women's exodus from the home, and the "new morality" that sought to legitimize sexuality and problematize romantic love (8–12). As we will see later in this study, discussions of adoption (particularly in the periodical press) intersect with all of these phenomena.

28. This circumstance may reflect birth parents' belief that girls would be easier to raise, as most of these children (843) had two surviving parents and another 647 children had one. Crenson adds that girls were also easier to place because they were thought less "troublesome"; thus "boys usually outnumbered girls in orphanages" (76). (Even today, more boys than girls are available for placement in the United States.) Conversely, Peter Holloran finds that delinquent girls "were considered much more difficult to reform than boys" (51).

29. Of the remaining children, 209 returned to their native counties (possibly reclaimed by their relatives), 68 attained their majority and passed out of the system, 58 died, and 14 (presumably girls) married, thus gaining a legal protector other than the state.

3. Melodrama and the Displaced Child, 1886–1906

1. As Jerry Griswold notes, many of the bestsellers of the years 1865 to 1914 were orphan novels, including *Ragged Dick, Little Men, Tom Sawyer, Huckleberry Finn, Little Lord Fauntleroy, Rebecca of Sunnybrook Farm, Anne of Green Gables, Pollyanna,* and *Tarzan*. Thus, he concludes, "these works must also have been unusually popular among adults" (viii). Indeed, some—*Pollyanna* is one—were not initially aimed at children.

2. Riis, too, praises the Foundling Asylum, an institution run by the Sisters of Charity. And he too approvingly notes the nuns' custom of pressing into service as wet nurses mothers who have come to give up their babies, a practice that insists upon a display of maternal capacity even from women who reject their own motherhood. But permanent homes must await the orphan trains: Riis reports in *How the Other Half Lives*, "The sisters carefully encourage the home-feeling in the child as their strongest ally in seeking its mental and moral elevation, and the toddlers depart happy to join their 'papas and mammas' in the far-away, unknown home" (146).

3. For a thorough discussion of the rise of secrecy in adoption proceedings, see Carp.

4. See, for example, Susan Curtis Redfield's *St. Nicholas* story "Jack's Cure" (1890).

5. Money in itself, however, is no substitute for domesticity. L. M. Rutherford describes another Burnett tale, "Two Days in the Life of Piccino" (1892), in which a bored aristocrat, a childless widow, "buy[s]" herself an Italian peasant child. Rutherford writes that "Piccino is humiliated and unhappy in his rich surroundings. He is lonely for his family, scandalized by the frequent washings he must undergo, and mortified by the way in which he is treated as a pet by the heartless and whimsical woman and her monied friends. After two dreadful days of luxurious suffering, he runs back to his poor, grubby, yet loved existence with his family" (70). Here again, Burnett seems to be rebutting the attitudes of child-savers such as Brace, who saw nothing appealing in the dirt and fecundity stereotypically associated with despised Catholic minorities.

6. This practice was associated with Roman Catholic placement societies, which sought to secure Catholic homes for their wards; even so, this story contains no indication that Steven and Robin are anything but "American," a designation implying Protestantism to most readers of 1893.

7. During this shopping trip, Steven's attractiveness (despite his age) is underscored by an elderly banker's gift to him of fifty cents. The class distinction between the banker, who can appreciate him, and the Dearborns, who, despite their kindliness, define him as a worker, is no accident.

8. To be sure, the orphanage superintendent and Flossy the baby-farmer appear to have been unaffected by their contact with Timothy and Gay. Presumably Flossy is too hard a nut for even Timothy to crack, and the superintendent lacks the time to get to know her charges as individuals. Yet the amateurism that characterizes the parenting of Miss Avilda and Samantha also seems to make them more susceptible to the children's unconscious efforts at reform.

4. Metaphor and the Displaced Child, 1886–1906

1. In a typical article of 1889, *Good Housekeeping* exhorted readers that "Nothing can take the place of neatness and order. These depend much upon good management" (qtd. Youcha 121). Both *Good Housekeeping* and the *Ladies' Home Journal* were still pushing the "household efficient" in the 1910s (Tichi 79).

2. To be sure, we should not ignore variations from state to state; Massachusetts, for example, had by 1895 closed its public orphanages. Writing in 1901, Amos Butler of the Indiana Board of State Charities categorized states and territories according to which of four plans they favored: subsidized foster care, county orphan asylums, state schools (which, like county asylums, placed children through adoption or indenture), or tax levies to underwrite housing children in private institutions. More rarely, displaced children might still be sent to reform schools along with delinquents (211). Oklahoma and Alaska gave no public support at all, New Mexico very little; twenty-nine states and territories made no effort to find family homes for children, while other locations devoted considerable resources to doing so (214–15). Overall, the network of social services available to displaced children nationwide had expanded significantly since the 1850s.

3. Her complaint resembles Hoover's remark that "the vast, repetitive processes [of Taylorist production methods] are dulling the human mind" (qtd. Tichi 79). The future President, of course, was himself not only a humanitarian but also an engineer.

4. The image of child as chattel might have proved less horrific a generation or two earlier, as we see from the comparisons of displaced children to slaves

mentioned in Chapter 1. The journalist's awareness of the shock value to be exploited here is one indication of change, although the idea of nonwhites purchasing Anglos would always have raised hackles.

5. These conditions, based on traditional apprenticeship documents, were reasonably standard.

6. Henderson, too, wavered between seeing displaced children as undesirable and seeing them as compellingly attractive, writing in "The Relief and Care of Dependent Children" (1901): "The difficulty [in recruiting foster parents] increases when the child is a foundling of unknown and suspicious origin, sickly and motherless, or unattractive in appearance and wayward in habits. Placing out is promoted by the offer of at least part payment for the care of such children. . . . Frequently a natural attachment grows up between the waif and those with whom it is boarded, and then the foster parents are willing to accept legal responsibility and maintain the child" (*Care* 112).

7. To be sure, as Holt points out, "using them for farm labor was still a common reason for taking in these children, and admonitions to the contrary were often ignored" (139). She theorizes that one reason that the Children's Aid Society began recruiting younger children was the desire to minimize runaways; for one thing, adolescence was now newly perceived as a time of behavioral problems (138, 140). At the same time, however, sentimental adoption was clearly overtaking utilitarian adoption, and younger children were perceived to be of greater emotional value, since their capacity for bonding with their new parents was assumed to be superior.

5. Adoption and Women, 1907–1918

1. This mindset extended beyond the *Delineator*. Take the remarks of Mrs. J. H. Evans, secretary of the Children's Aid Society of Western Pennsylvania, at the 1910 Charities and Correction meeting. Urging the use of female volunteers to conduct home studies, she asserted, "Surely mothers[,] with their sympathetic hearts and innate intuition, can get at the facts in the various cases better than all the men in the universe, and we feel the service has been done for the love of humanity, not in the perfunctory way of paid workers along similar lines" (133).

2. Hence we see comments such as the one made in May 1909 of Baby Louise: "Her mother has surrendered all claim upon her. Thus she may be adopted without fear that some time her foster-parents will be disturbed by relatives who claim her" ("Latest Applicants" 695). Then as now, custody disputes between birth parents and adoptive parents were not unknown.

3. The *Delineator* reported dozens, sometimes hundreds, of applications for each child profiled. The situation was less extreme in the world of adoption overall; in 1909 the National Children's Home Society received some 10,000 applications for 6,297 children (Dosch 432–33). But even this ratio seems to have created a seller's market. So tight was supply, claimed Arno Dosch in *Cosmopolitan*, that "A Boston lawyer with a large income . . . applied in New York over a year ago for a baby girl with blue eyes, fair hair, and unimpeachable parentage. The other day he adopted a dark-eyed, black-haired little girl whose father died of drink and whose mother was in the madhouse. It was the best he could get" (435).

4. Take the missive from "L.B.G." published in January 1909: "As soon as I became convinced from reading the articles in your magazine that it was my duty and pleasure, too, to adopt a child, I began trying to find one. I have applied to

every Protestant Home in Mississippi, and none of them will let out a child of the kind I want. I want a little girl not more than three nor less than one and a half years old. She must be fair and blue eyed" ("Letters" 103, 133). Presumably "duty" prompted the adoption, "pleasure" the aesthetic guidelines.

5. To be sure, parents could sometimes be found for such children even before the *Delineator* began its campaign, and received special praise for their action. In 1902, Hastings Hart noted that "When we find people willing to take a child with a club foot or a child with one eye, and take that child into their home and lavish upon it love and devotion, we think the greatest work is being done" ("Discussion" 403–404). And a 1908 letter from Sherrard, printed before the magazine had otherwise raised this issue, remarked that the more virtuous the parents, the more difficult the task that they were prepared to undertake, "so that we are enabled to place blind, deaf and dumb, crippled and deformed children in the best homes in the land" ("Letters" 429).

6. Thus Linda Gordon credits maternalism with helping to establish the U.S. Children's Bureau (160). This agency, created to "investigate and report . . . upon all matters pertaining to the welfare of children and child life" (qtd. Carp 22), was the first federal bureau to be headed by a woman, Hull House veteran Julia Lathrop.

7. I have found no references to single-parent adoption by men, a circumstance that may reflect fatherhood's ongoing marginalization; see, e.g., Rotundo, "Body" 23, 30, and *Manhood* 287.

8. Berebitsky argues that adoption by unmarried women looked conservative, even "reassuring," until about 1920, at which time "Victorian constructions of sexuality, marriage, and parenthood had been replaced by a more modern sensibility" (113, 114). For further discussion of the multiple meanings available in mass-market texts about such adoptions between 1890 and 1918, see my June 2001 article "Nontraditional Adoption in Progressive-Era Orphan Narratives." Similarities of argument and subject matter between my work and Berebitsky's are coincidental, since her valuable insights (published in January 2001) were unavailable to me until some time after my article had been accepted for publication.

9. *Good Housekeeping* warned during this decade that the sex drive "will never be stopped except with satisfactions" (qtd. Faderman 62).

10. A rare male version of this plot occurs in François Coppée's "Adoption," reprinted in *The Chautauquan* in 1909. Here a hack writer takes in an impoverished woman and her grandson to save the baby from institutionalization. In part he acts out of a sense that he "has no talent, never has had," so that rescuing the destitute child serves as a substitute "for the book [he] ought to write" (254). But the adoption gives to "his [most recent] story, 'The Orphan of Belleville,' a certain something not to be found in the others," and "the foremost novelist of his time" compliments him on the "touches about children that are extremely fine, sincere, affecting." The writer explains his success by noting that "now . . . I am working from nature" (255).

11. The number was much higher among female college graduates; from 1870 through 1929, some 40 to 60 percent of this group remained single (Smith-Rosenberg 253). Disproportionately likely to embark upon careers, such women were the major target of masculine diatribes against race suicide. They also constituted the group to which single adoptive mothers tended to belong.

12. Another is Jean Webster's orphanage novel *Dear Enemy* (1915), which I have discussed elsewhere; see Nelson, "Days."

13. The text again has things both ways in its discussion of education. Canfield was a disciple of Maria Montessori, some of whose ideas, such as the tutoring of younger children by older ones, are illustrated in the Vermont school—yet this adherence to "advanced" principles, the narrative makes clear, is serendipitous. It is not the result of an unexpected theoretical sophistication on the part of Betsy's new teacher, but rather the survival of all that was good about the old-fashioned school system.

14. For an account of this success, see Griswold 215–21. Griswold sees Pollyanna as "one of the most cunning tricksters" since Tom Sawyer, since her manipulations serve to get the child her own way (218). But Pollyanna's way is also that of the dominant culture, in which Aunt Polly's emotionally and financially independent spinsterhood is dismaying.

15. Even so, the conference ultimately adopted a resolution against "undesirable legislation," conceding "the right of each State to protect itself from vicious, diseased, or defective children from other States," but observing that "the reception of healthy normal children is not only an act of philanthropy, but also secures a valuable increment to the population of the community and an ultimate increase of its wealth. The people of the more prosperous and less congested districts owe a debt of hospitality to the older communities from which many of them came" (196). The ideas of children as benefit and hospitality as debt suggest a translation of the values of orphan fiction and magazine rhetoric to the public sphere.

16. Wayne Carp contends that the Bureau, a modestly staffed and modestly funded division of the Department of the Interior, quickly "established itself as the nation's leading expert on children" and, moreover, on adoption, coordinating policy, conducting surveys, and vetting others' researches into child placement (22–23). As an outpost of professional women within an overwhelmingly male federal bureaucracy, it thus represents an interesting blend of the trained scientific expert and the private and feminine.

17. Such "before and after" photographs have been subject to manipulation. Gould reports the retouching of pictures of impoverished Kallikaks "to produce an appearance of evil or stupidity," while a picture of a Kallikak confined to a mental institution was left alone, presumably to show that she had been "saved from depravity" (172, 171). And in the 1870s, British child-saver Thomas Barnardo posed impoverished but marginally respectable children in rags and bare feet to make them look more like street waifs in fund-raising photographs (Mavor 185).

6. Adoption Up to Date

1. Another 51,035 were in unsubsidized foster care or "free homes," 22,243 were in paid foster care, and 4,933 were listed as unclassified, a category that included those "in almshouses and other institutions not primarily for dependent children" (Thurston 149).

2. Consider Karen Samples's newspaper story on Charles Collins, a Kentuckian placed in foster care in 1949 at age ten. Collins reports that, until he fled the placement in 1956, he "worked like an indentured servant" and endured neglect and abuse; his foster mother's cousin agrees that the fostering couple "just used him." His account is not unique.

3. This is not to suggest that unabashedly sentimental rhetoric no longer existed; it could still be found, although it was now often relegated to the provinces

and to the work of writers who lacked scientific or social-scientific credentials. One adjective-filled article in the Omaha *World-Herald* from 15 December 1921 reports the arrival of an orphan train containing a shipment from the New York Foundling Hospital: the "car load of joy," noted the reporter effusively, brought with it "thirty-five of the most wonderful babies imaginable," "ranging in age from twelve months to 5 years." The adoptive mothers manifested "an outpouring of such affection as only a mother can give," while the adoptive fathers, duly subordinate, "reflected a portion of the joy radiating from the faces of their wives." Needless to say, the children "all fill[ed,] to the most minute detail, the requirements of the new parents" ("Train" 11).

4. As in Willsie's article and indeed in almost all discussions of sentimental adoption by married couples from the 1850s onward, the wife is presented as the instigator of the adoption.

5. Some adoptive parents, such as the author of "An Adopted Mother Speaks" (*The Survey,* 1922), asserted that having passed a lengthy screening process in order to be granted a child, they possessed parenting credentials superior to those of adults "whose children are more often accidental than desired" (962).

6. From its inception in the 1910s, syndicate-produced series fiction relied heavily on orphans and half-orphans, perhaps because such young people were considered to be less trammeled by domesticity and hence more likely to have adventures. The well-known Stratemeyer Syndicate charted the careers of or-phaned or motherless adolescents engaged in an assortment of activities, from work in the film industry (the Motion Picture Chums, Moving Picture Girls, and Moving Picture Boys) to detection (Nancy Drew, the Hardy Boys, the Dana Girls, and others). Earlier in the decade, Lawrence had ghostwritten Stratemeyer's Betty Gordon series, another set of adventures describing the exploits of an orphan girl (Johnson 60).

7. This insistence that orphans may be better off in modest homes because these homes are more in touch with everyday reality and the domestic virtues is present as early as *The Wide, Wide World,* and appears also in Progressive Era nonfiction by adoption workers. Within post–Civil War fiction, however, the emphasis on the normal often lost out to rags-to-riches drama (as in *Tattered Tom, A Little Princess, Pollyanna,* and so on), which dominated until the 1920s.

8. Joy, a bewitching toddler with golden hair, is the ideal adoptable child of the period; the older children, undemonstrative David and recalcitrant red-headed Patty, would have posed greater challenges for a placement agency. That Linda and Miss Gilly extend a warm welcome to both attractive and unattractive orphans has a didactic function in that it suggests that "real" families are collections not of stereotypes or ideals but of whatever individuals fate happens to send, and that a child's need is more important than an adult's whims or prejudices.

9. As Chapin's *Heredity and Child Culture* makes clear, a number of scientific experts in the 1920s were arguing that environment trumps biological inheritance.

10. I use the term "selected" advisedly. Parker notes that when her Research Bureau was given scope to determine which case histories would become part of the study, it chose not only the "oldest adoption cases about which recent information was available, regardless of the favorable or unfavorable outcome," but also "a few of a surprisingly large number of unsuitable adoptions which have come to the attention of social organizations within recent years" (77). In other words, her sample is to some extent deliberately skewed toward the negative.

11. The interracial angle seems particularly disturbing to Parker, who devotes more space to this case history than to any other and who also passed the reference along to legal writer Joseph Newbold as an example of the potential evils of adoption. In Newbold's rendition, the husband was found to have abused two of his wife's adopted daughters (606).

12. Parker takes a dim view of adoptions by relatives, on the ground that unless the child is certifiably an orphan, such adoptions usually signal family dysfunction or immorality or both.

Works Cited

Addams, Jane. "Child Labor and Pauperism." In *Proceedings of the National Conference of Charities and Correction at the Thirtieth Annual Session Held in the City of Atlanta, May 6–12, 1903,* ed. Isabel C. Barrows. N.p.: Frederick J. Heer, n.d. 114–21.

"An Adopted Mother Speaks." *Survey* 47 (18 March 1922): 962–63.

Alcott, Louisa May. *Little Women* and *Good Wives.* 1868–69. New York: Bantam, 1983.

———. *Rose in Bloom: A Sequel to "Eight Cousins."* 1876. Boston: Little, Brown, 1927.

———. *Under the Lilacs.* 1878. Garden City: Nelson Doubleday, n.d.

Alden, Lyman P. "The Shady Side of the 'Placing-Out System.'" In *Proceedings of the National Conference of Charities and Correction, at the Twelfth Annual Session Held in Washington, D.C., June 4–10, 1885,* ed. Isabel C. Barrows. Boston: George H. Ellis, 1885. 201–10.

Alger, Horatio, Jr. *Julius or The Street Boy Out West.* 1874. Rpt. in *Strive and Succeed: Two Novels by Horatio Alger.* New York: Holt, Rinehart and Winston, 1967. 1–146.

———. *Tattered Tom; or, The Story of a Street Arab.* 1871. Philadelphia: Henry T. Coates, n.d.

Altschuler, Mark. "Motherless Child: Huck Finn and a Theory of Moral Development." *American Literary Realism* 22.1 (Fall 1989): 31–42.

"As Others See the Homeless Child: More Letters from Prominent People Who Are Interested in the Child-Rescue Campaign." *Delineator* 71.2 (February 1908): 251–53.

Ashby, LeRoy. *Endangered Children: Dependency, Neglect, and Abuse in American History.* New York: Twayne, 1997.

———. *Saving the Waifs: Reformers and Dependent Children, 1890–1917.* Philadelphia: Temple University Press, 1984.

Askeland, Lori. "Orphans and Orphanages." In *Girlhood in America: An Encyclopedia,* ed. Miriam Forman-Brunell. Vol. 2. Santa Barbara: ABC–Clio, 2001. 483–89.

Avery, Gillian. *Behold the Child: American Children and Their Books 1621–1922.* Baltimore: Johns Hopkins University Press, 1994.

Banta, Martha. *Taylored Lives: Narrative Productions in the Age of Taylor, Veblen, and Ford.* Chicago: University of Chicago Press, 1993.

Baym, Nina. *Woman's Fiction: A Guide to Novels by and about Women in America, 1820–1870.* Ithaca: Cornell University Press, 1978.

Berebitsky, Julie. *Like Our Very Own: Adoption and the Changing Culture of Motherhood, 1851–1950.* Lawrence: University Press of Kansas, 2000.

"Both Sides of Orphan Triangle." Rpt. from *El Paso Morning Times,* 10 October 1904. *Crossroads* 22 (December 1992): 7–9.

Brace, Charles Loring. "The Best Method of Founding Children's Charities in Towns and Villages." In *Proceedings of the Seventh Annual Conference of Charities and Correction, Held at Cleveland, June and July, 1880,* ed. F. B. Sanborn. Boston: A. Williams, 1880. 227–37.

———. *The Dangerous Classes of New York: And Twenty Years' Work among Them.* 1872. Washington, D.C.: National Association of Social Workers, 1973.

———. "The Little Laborers of New York City." *Harper's New Monthly Magazine* 47 (August 1873): 321–32.

———. "The Poor Boy's 'Astor House.'" *St. Nicholas* 3 (April 1876): 360–63.

———. "Wolf-Reared Children." *St. Nicholas* 9 (May 1882): 542–54.

Brodhead, Richard H. *Cultures of Letters: Scenes of Reading and Writing in Nineteenth-Century America.* Chicago: University of Chicago Press, 1993.

Burnett, Frances Hodgson. *A Little Princess.* 1905. New York: Dell, 1979.

———. "Little Saint Elizabeth." *St. Nicholas Magazine* 16.2 and 16.3 (December 1888 and January 1889): 133–36 and 204–208.

———. *Sara Crewe, or What Happened at Miss Minchin's.* 1888. New York: Putnam's, 1981.

Butler, Amos W. "Saving the Children." In *Proceedings of the National Conference of Charities and Correction at the Twenty-Eighth Annual Session Held in the City of Washington, D. C., May 9–15, 1901,* ed. Isabel C. Barrows. Boston: George H. Ellis, 1901. 204–19.

Butler, Edmond J. "The Essentials of Placement in Free Family Homes." *Foster-Home Care for Dependent Children.* Washington, D.C.: Government Printing Office, 1924. 33–50.

Canfield, Dorothy. "Out of the Wilderness." *Delineator* 76.3 (September 1910): 159, 224–26.

———. *Understood Betsy.* 1917. New York: Grosset and Dunlap, 1946.

Care of Dependent Children in the Late Nineteenth and Early Twentieth Centuries. Intro. Robert H. Bremner. New York: Arno, 1974.

Carp, E. Wayne. *Family Matters: Secrecy and Disclosure in the History of Adoption.* Cambridge: Harvard University Press, 1998.

Carpenter, Mary. "What Should Be Done for the Neglected and Criminal Children of the United States." *Proceedings of the Conference of Charities, Held in Connection with the General Meeting of the American Social Science Association, Detroit, May 1875.* Boston: Tolman and White, 1875. 66–76.

Carstens, C. C. "Dependent and Neglected Children." In *Social Work Year Book 1929,* ed. Fred S. Hall and Mabel B. Ellis. New York: Russell Sage Foundation, 1930. 128–37.

"The Case of the New York Foundlings in Arizona." *Charities* 13 (4 February 1905): 448–52.

Chapin, Henry Dwight. *Heredity and Child Culture.* New York: E. P. Dutton, 1922.

"Child Emigrants." Ravenna, Ohio *Republican-Democrat,* 14 April 1880. Rpt. *Crossroads* 14 (January 1991): 10.

"Children Given Away: Little Waifs from the New York Juvenile Asylum Find Homes." Burlington, Iowa *Gazette,* 3 October 1889. Rpt. *Crossroads* 15 (April 1991): 10.

Clement, Priscilla Ferguson. *Growing Pains: Children in the Industrial Age, 1850–1890.* New York: Twayne, 1997.

Cole, Elizabeth S., and Kathryn S. Donley. "History, Values, and Placement Policy Issues in Adoption." In *The Psychology of Adoption,* ed. David M. Brodzinsky and Marshall D. Schechter. New York: Oxford University Press, 1990. 273–94.

Commander, Lydia Kingsmill. "The Home without a Child." *Delineator* 70.5 (November 1907): 720–23 ff.

"Concerning the Magazine." *Delineator* 74.7 (July 1910): 3.

Conn, Peter. *The Divided Mind: Ideology and Imagination in America, 1898–1917.* Cambridge: Cambridge University Press, 1983.

Coppée, François. "Adoption." *Chautauquan* 53.2 (January 1909): 249–55.

"Cradles Instead of Divorces." *Literary Digest* 77.2 (14 April 1923): 35–36.

Crenson, Matthew A. *Building the Invisible Orphanage: A Prehistory of the American Welfare System.* Cambridge: Harvard University Press, 1998.

Crockett, Beverly. "Outlaws, Outcasts, and Orphans: The Historical Imagination and *Anne of Green Gables.*" In *Imagining Adoption: Essays on Literature and Culture,* ed. Marianne Novy. Ann Arbor: University of Michigan Press, 2001. 57–81.

Crumley, H. L. "The Orphan Children of Georgia." *Charities* 10.23 (6 June 1903): 566–68.

Dale, Florence D. "Foster-Children and the Shop: A Study of the Inter-Action of Placing-Out Standards and Child-Labor Laws in Different States." *Charities* 12.13 (2 April 1904): 343–46.

"Debate on the Papers." In *Proceedings of the Seventh Annual Conference of Charities and Correction, Held at Cleveland, June and July, 1880,* ed. F. B. Sanborn. Boston: A. Williams, 1880. 237–41.

"The Delineator Child-Rescue Campaign: For the Child That Needs a Home and the Home That Needs a Child." *Delineator* 70.5 (November 1907): 715–19. Dates of identically titled articles in subsequent issues of the magazine are noted in the text.

Devine, Edward T. "Care of Children." *Municipal Affairs* 6 (June 1902): 294–96.

"Discussion." In *Proceedings of the National Conference of Charities and Correction, at the Eleventh Annual Session, Held at St. Louis, October 13–17, 1884,* ed. Isabel C. Barrows. Boston: George H. Ellis, 1885. 354–62.

"Discussion." In *Proceedings of the National Conference of Charities and Correction, at the Twelfth Annual Session Held in Washington, D.C., June 4–10, 1885,* ed. Isabel C. Barrows. Boston: George H. Ellis, 1885. 459–62.

"Discussion." In *Proceedings of the National Conference of Charities and Correction at the Twenty-Ninth Annual Session Held in the City of Detroit, May 28–June 3, 1902,* ed. Isabel C. Barrows. Boston: George H. Ellis, 1902. 401–18.

"Discussion." In *Proceedings of the National Conference of Charities and Correction at the Thirtieth Annual Session Held in the City of Atlanta, May 6–12, 1903,* ed. Isabel C. Barrows. N.p.: Frederick J. Heer, n.d. 542–48.

"Discussion of Miss Carpenter's Paper." In *Proceedings of the Conference of Charities, Held in Connection with the General Meeting of the American Social Science Association, Detroit, May 1875.* Boston: Tolman and White, 1875. 78–84.

Dixie, Dolly. "The Colored Mammy and Her White Foster Child: A True Story." *Our Young Folks* 4.3 (March 1868): 137–40.

Dobson, Joanne. "The Hidden Hand: Subversion of Cultural Ideology in Three Mid-Nineteenth-Century American Women's Novels." *American Quarterly* 38.2 (Summer 1986): 223–42.

Dodge, Mary Mapes. *Donald and Dorothy.* 1883. New York: Century, 1900.

"Doesn't Anybody Want a Little Boy?" *Delineator* 71.3 (March 1908): 424.

Dosch, Arno. "Not Enough Babies to Go Around." *Cosmopolitan* 49.4 (September 1910): 431–39.

Douglass, John W. "The Board of Children's Guardians, District of Columbia." In *Proceedings of the National Conference of Charities and Correction at the Twenty-Eighth Annual Session Held in the City of Washington, D.C., May 9–15, 1901,* ed. Isabel C. Barrows. Boston: George H. Ellis, 1901. 239–44.

Downs, Susan Whitelaw, and Michael W. Sherraden. "The Orphan Asylum in the Nineteenth Century." *Social Service Review* 57 (June 1988): 272–90.

Dubbert, Joe L. "Progressivism and the Masculinity Crisis." In *The American Man,* ed. Elizabeth H. Pleck and Joseph H. Pleck. Englewood Cliffs: Prentice Hall, 1980. 303–20.

Dulberger, Judith A. *"Mother Donit fore the Best": Correspondence of a Nineteenth-Century Orphan Asylum.* Syracuse: Syracuse University Press, 1996.

Dunbar, Olivia Howard. "Miss Hildreth: 'Mother of Ten.'" *Harper's Bazar* 46 (September 1912): 443–44.

"Editorial." *Charities* 10.16 (18 April 1903): 377–79.

Evans, Mrs. J. H. "Child Placing by Volunteers." In *Proceedings of the National Conference of Charities and Correction at the Thirty-Seventh Annual Session Held in the City of St. Louis, Mo., May 19th to 26th 1910,* ed. Alexander Johnson. Fort Wayne: Archer, n.d. 131–34.

Faderman, Lillian. *Odd Girls and Twilight Lovers: A History of Lesbian Life in Twentieth-Century America.* New York: Columbia University Press, 1991.

Fearing, Alden. "A Home and a Chance in Life." *World's Work* 28.2 (June 1914): 192–97.

Ferris, John C. "Child Helping in Tennessee." In *Proceedings of the National Conference of Charities and Corrections,* 1883. 336–41. Rpt. *Care of Dependent Children in the Late Nineteenth and Early Twentieth Centuries,* intro. Robert H. Bremner. New York: Arno, 1974.

Fink, Rychard. "Horatio Alger as a Social Philosopher." In *Ragged Dick* and *Mark, the Match Boy.* By Horatio Alger. New York: Collier, 1962. 5–33.

Folks, Homer. "Institution vs. Family." *Charities Review* 8.12 (February 1899): 546.

———. "The Under-side of the Price Mark." *Charities* 12.13 (2 April 1904): 342.

Ford, I. N. "The Fresh-Air Fund." *St. Nicholas Magazine* 10 (June 1883): 616–26.

Foster, John N. "Ten Years of Child-Saving Work in Michigan." In *Proceedings of the National Conference of Charities and Correction, at the Eleventh Annual Session, Held at St. Louis, October 13–17, 1884,* ed. Isabel C. Barrows. Boston: George H. Ellis, 1885. 132–42.

"Fritz." "Paul Goldschmeid, the Boy Fiddler." *Merry's Museum and Parley's Magazine,* n.s. 10 (November and December 1860): 139–41, 164–66.

Frost, Leslie Elaine. "'The Revolt of the Beavers': Performing Childhood on the Federal Theater Project Stage." Paper presented at the meeting of the Modern Language Association, San Francisco, California, 28 December 1998.

Gannon, Susan R. "'But I Wanted It to Be the Other Way': Fictions of Rescue and Their Function in *St. Nicholas Magazine.*" *Nineteenth-Century Contexts* 21 (1999): 259–88.

Gay, Peter. *The Bourgeois Experience: Victoria to Freud.* Vol. 1: *Education of the Senses.* New York: Oxford University Press, 1984.

Gilmer, Elizabeth M. "The Dream Regained." *Good Housekeeping* 56 (June 1913): 829–31.

———. "When the Dream Fails." *Good Housekeeping* 56 (May 1913): 683–84.

"Good News from the Delineator Family: Homes That Have Found Children and Children That Have Found Homes Are Happy." *Delineator* 74.2 (August 1909): 134.

Gordon, Linda. *The Great Arizona Orphan Abduction.* Cambridge: Harvard University Press, 1999.

Gould, Stephen Jay. *The Mismeasure of Man.* New York: Norton, 1981.

Griswold, Jerry. *The Classic American Children's Story: Novels of the Golden Age.* 1992. New York: Penguin, 1996.

Grossberg, Michael. *Governing the Hearth: Law and the Family in Nineteenth-Century America.* Chapel Hill: University of North Carolina Press, 1985.

Haber, Samuel. *Efficiency and Uplift: Scientific Management in the Progressive Era, 1890–1920.* Chicago: University of Chicago Press, 1964.

Hacsi, Timothy A. *Second Home: Orphan Asylums and Poor Families in America.* Cambridge: Harvard University Press, 1997.

"Half a Century of Child Saving." *Charities* 9.23 (6 December 1902): 550–52.

Hall, Edward A. "Destitute and Neglected Children: The Relations between Their Care and Education in the Home and in the Institution." In *Proceedings of the National Conference of Charities and Correction at the Twenty-Sixth Annual Session Held in the City of Cincinnati, Ohio, May 17–23, 1899,* ed. Isabel C. Barrows. Boston: George H. Ellis, 1900. 177–88.

Hart, Hastings H. "Placing Out Children in the West." In *Proceedings of the National Conference of Charities and Correction, at the Eleventh Annual Session, Held at St. Louis, October 13–17, 1884,* ed. Isabel C. Barrows. Boston: George H. Ellis, 1885. 143–50.

Hartlie, A. "The Birthday Box: A Parlor Drama." *Our Young Folks* 2 (December 1866): 741–47.

Healy, William. "Types of Children as Predeterminable for Placement." *Institution Quarterly* 7.2 (30 June 1916): 173–75.

Hebberd, Robert W. "Placing Out Children: Dangers of Careless Methods." In *Proceedings of the National Conference of Charities and Correction at the Twenty-Sixth Annual Session Held in the City of Cincinnati, Ohio, May 17–23, 1899,* ed. Isabel C. Barrows. Boston: George H. Ellis, 1900. 171–77.

Henderson, Charles R. "Home-Finding: An Idea That Grew; The Story of the Great Movement That Has Put 27,000 Homeless Children into Happy Homes." *Delineator* 71.4 (April 1908): 609–11.

Hewins, Katharine P. "The Development of Placing-Out Work by Institutions." In *Foster-Home Care for Dependent Children.* Washington, D.C.: Government Printing Office, 1924. 97–111.

Hoffman, Frederick L. "The Social and Medical Aspects of Child Labor." In *Proceedings of the National Conference of Charities and Correction at the Thirtieth Annual Session Held in the City of Atlanta, May 6–12, 1903,* ed. Isabel C. Barrows. N.p.: Frederick J. Heer, n.d. 138–57.

Hofstadter, Richard. *The Age of Reform: From Bryan to F.D.R.* New York: Vintage, 1955.

———. *Social Darwinism in American Thought.* Revised ed. Boston: Beacon, 1955.

Holloran, Peter C. *Boston's Wayward Children: Social Services for Homeless Children, 1830–1930.* Rutherford, N.J.: Fairleigh Dickinson University Press, 1989.

Holt, Marilyn Irvin. *The Orphan Trains: Placing Out in America.* Lincoln: University of Nebraska Press, 1992.

Huffaker, Lucy. "Waifs Who Have Become Famous: Some Geniuses Who Have Honored Their Foster-Parents' Names." *Delineator* 71.6 (June 1908): 1005–1006 ff.

Hurley, Daniel I. *One Child at a Time: A History of the Children's Home of Cincinnati, 1864–1989.* Cincinnati: Children's Home of Cincinnati, 1990.

"The Jail at the Carter Republic." *Charities* 10.11 (14 March 1903): 250.

Jenks, Horace H. "Safeguarding the Dependent Child's Physical and Mental Health." In *Foster-Home Care for Dependent Children.* Washington, D.C.: Government Printing Office, 1924. 113–34.

Joachimsen, Philip J. "The Statute to Legalize the Adoption of Minor Children." *Albany Law Journal* 8 (6 December 1873): 353–57.

Johnson, Deidre A. "Community and Character: A Comparison of Josephine Lawrence's Linda Lane Series and Classic Orphan Fiction." In *Nancy Drew and Company: Culture, Gender, and Girls' Series,* ed. Sherrie A. Inness. Bowling Green: Bowling Green State University Popular Press, 1997. 59–73.

Johnston, Annie Fellows. *Big Brother.* 1893. Boston: L. C. Page, 1909.

Karcher, Carolyn. "Lydia Maria Child and the *Juvenile Miscellany.*" In *Research about Nineteenth-Century Children and Books,* ed. Selma K. Richardson. Urbana-Champaign: University of Illinois, 1980. 67–84.

Keiger, Dale. "The Rise and Demise of the American Orphanage." *Johns Hopkins Magazine* (April 1996). Online at <*http://www.jhu.edu/~jhumag/496web/orphange.html*>. 1–7. Accessed 12-20-02.

Kelsey, Carl. "The Importation of Dependent Children." *Annals of the American Academy of Political and Social Science* 18 (1901): 90–98.

Kelso, Robert W. "Passing of the Stone Age in Care and Custody." In *Proceedings of the National Conference of Social Work at the Fiftieth Anniversary Session Held in Washington, D.C. May 16–23, 1923.* Chicago: University of Chicago Press, 1923. 203–209.

Kerley, Charles Gilmore. "The Adoption of Children." *Outlook* 112 (12 January 1916): 104–107.

Kidd, Kenneth. "Farming for Boys: Boyology and the Professionalization of Boy Work." *Children's Literature Association Quarterly* 20.4 (Winter 1995–96): 148–54.

Kimmel, Michael S. "Men's Responses to Feminism at the Turn of the Century." *Gender and Society* 1.3 (September 1987): 261–83.

King, Frederick A. "Self-Government and 'The Bunch': An Experiment in Handling Unruly and Delinquent Boys." *Charities* 13.1 (1 October 1904): 36–41.

Kingsley, Sherman C. "Child-Saving and the Standards of the Naturalist." *Charities* 13.11 (10 December 1904): 276–78.

———. "The Substitution of Family Care for Institutional Care for Children." *Charities* 10.16 (18 April 1903): 387–92.

Kinkead, Thomas L. "The Institutional Care of Children." *Charities* 10.16 (18 April 1903): 392–96.

Knoper, Randall. "'Away from Home and amongst Strangers': Domestic Sphere, Public Arena, and *Huckleberry Finn.*" *Prospects* 14 (1989): 125–40.

Kunzel, Regina G. *Fallen Women, Problem Girls: Unmarried Mothers and the Professionalization of Social Work, 1890–1945.* New Haven: Yale University Press, 1993.

Lasch, Christopher. *Haven in a Heartless World: The Family Besieged.* New York: Basic Books, 1977.

"The Latest Applicants." *Delineator* 73.5 (May 1909): 695.

Lawrence, Josephine. *Linda Lane*. New York: Barse and Hopkins, 1925.

———. *Linda Lane Experiments*. New York: Barse and Co., 1927.

———. *Linda Lane Helps Out*. New York: Barse and Co., 1925.

———. *Linda Lane's Big Sister*. New York: Barse and Co., 1929.

———. *Linda Lane's Plan*. New York: Barse and Hopkins, 1926.

———. *Linda Lane's Problems*. New York: Barse and Co., 1928.

Lears, T. J. Jackson. *No Place of Grace: Antimodernism and the Transformation of American Culture, 1880–1920*. New York: Pantheon, 1981.

Lee, Eula. "The Crossing Sweeper." *Merry's Museum and Woodworth's Cabinet* n.s. 23 (1867): 172–75.

Letchworth, William Pryor. "Dependent Children and Family Homes." *Charities Review* 7 (September 1897): 577–86.

"Letters from Mr. Weller, Mr. Sehon, Mr. Sherrard and Mr. Hurley." *Delineator* 71.3 (March 1908): 428–29.

"Letters from the First Members of the National Child-Rescue League." *Delineator* 73.1 (January 1909): 103 ff.

Leverenz, David. *Manhood and the American Renaissance*. Ithaca: Cornell University Press, 1989.

Lewis, Judd Mortimer. "Dealing in Babies." *Good Housekeeping* 58 (February 1914): 194–98.

"Machine Charity as Found in the Orphan Asylum—The States That Have No Home-Placing Agencies." *Delineator* 72.5 (November 1908): 781–82.

MacLeod, Anne Scott. *American Childhood: Essays on Children's Literature of the Nineteenth and Twentieth Centuries*. Athens: University of Georgia Press, 1994.

———. "Howard Pyle's Robin Hood: The Middle Ages for Americans." *Children's Literature Association Quarterly* 25.1 (Spring 2000): 44–48.

"The Making of a Father." *Woman's Home Companion* 40.2 (February 1913): 5.

Marsh, Margaret, and Wanda Ronner. *The Empty Cradle: Infertility in America from Colonial Times to the Present*. Baltimore: Johns Hopkins University Press, 1996.

Marshall, Gregory. "Blood Ties as Structural Motif in *Huckleberry Finn*." *Mark Twain Journal* 21.3 (Spring 1983): 44–46.

Mathews, Byron C. "The Duty of the State to Dependent Children." In *Proceedings of the National Conference of Charities and Correction at the Twenty-Fifth Annual Session Held in the City of New York, May 18–25, 1898*, ed. Isabel C. Barrows. Boston: George H. Ellis, 1899. 367–74.

Mavor, Carol. "Dream-Rushes: Lewis Carroll's Photographs of the Little Girl." In *The Girl's Own: Cultural Histories of the Anglo-American Girl, 1830–1915*, ed. Claudia Nelson and Lynne Vallone. Athens: University of Georgia Press, 1995. 156–93.

May, Elaine Tyler. *Barren in the Promised Land: Childless Americans and the Pursuit of Happiness*. New York: Basic Books, 1995.

McCausland, Clare L. *Children of Circumstance: A History of the First 125 Years (1849–1974) of Chicago Care Society*. Chicago: Donnelly, 1976.

Michaels, Walter Benn. "An American Tragedy, or the Promise of American Life." *Representations* 25 (Winter 1989): 71–98.

Mills, Alice. "Pollyanna and the Not So Glad Game." *Children's Literature* 27 (1999): 87–104.

Modell, Judith S. *Kinship with Strangers: Adoption and Interpretations of Kinship in American Culture.* Berkeley: University of California Press, 1994.

Moon, Michael. "'The Gentle Boy from the Dangerous Classes': Pederasty, Domesticity, and Capitalism in Horatio Alger." *Representations* 19 (Summer 1987): 87–110.

Morey, Anne. "'Have *You* the Power?' The Palmer Photoplay Corporation and the Film Viewer/Author in the 1920s." *Film History* 9.3 (1997): 300–19.

[Morris, Edmund]. *Farming for Boys.* Serialized in *Our Young Folks* 1 and 2 (1865 and 1866).

Morse, Lucy G. "The Ash-Girl." *St. Nicholas* 3 (April 1876): 386–92.

———. "Cathern." *St. Nicholas* 4 (March 1877): 302–10.

"The National Child-Rescue League: Suggestions for Work for New Members." *Delineator* 73.2 (February 1909): 251.

Nelson, Claudia. "'In these days of scientific charity': Orphanages and Social Engineering in *Dear Enemy.*" In *Children's Literature and the Fin de Siècle,* ed. Roderick McGillis. Westport, Conn.: Greenwood, 2002.

———. "Nontraditional Adoption in Progressive-Era Orphan Narratives." *Mosaic* 34.2 (June 2001): 181–97.

"New York Foundlings in North Dakota." *Charities and The Commons* 15 (9 December 1905): 348–49.

Newbold, Joseph W. "Jurisdictional and Social Aspects of Adoption." *Minnesota Law Review* 11 (1927): 605–23.

Nodelman, Perry. "Progressive Utopia: Or, How to Grow Up without Growing Up." Rpt. in *Such a Simple Little Tale: Critical Responses to L. M. Montgomery's "Anne of Green Gables,"* ed. Mavis Reimer. Metuchen, N.J.: Scarecrow, 1992. 29–38.

O'Hagan, Anne. "The Biography of a Foundling: The Story of a New York Waif, Telling How He Got a Name and a Religion, and How He Passed through the Dangers That Are Fatal to Most Babies in the City Institutions." *Munsey's Magazine* 25.3 (June 1901): 308–16.

The Orphan Trains. Video. Prod. and dir. by Janet Graham and Edward Gray. Written by Edward Gray. 1995. Aired on *The American Experience,* PBS.

"The Orphans." Columbus, Kansas *Star-Courier,* 21 June 1894. Rpt. *Crossroads* 15 (April 1991): 11.

Otis [Kaler], James. "Jenny's Boarding-House." Serialized in *St. Nicholas* 14 (February–August 1887).

"Our Adopted Son: An Experience in Bringing Up Two Boys Who Are Not Blood Brothers." *Ladies' Home Journal* 41 (April 1924): 35 ff.

Parker, Ida R. *"Fit and Proper"? A Study of Legal Adoption in Massachusetts.* Boston: Church Home Society, 1927.

Patterson, Ada. "Giving Babies Away." *Cosmopolitan* 39.4 (August 1905): 405–12.

Porter, Eleanor H. *Just David.* New York: Grosset and Dunlap, 1916.

———. *Pollyanna.* 1913. New York: Puffin, 1987.

Presser, Stephen B. "The Historical Background of the American Law of Adoption." *Journal of Family Law* 11 (1971): 443–516.

Proceedings of the Conference on the Care of Dependent Children Held at Washington, D.C. January 25, 26, 1909. 1909. New York: Arno, 1971.

Putnam, Elizabeth C. "Auxiliary Visitors: Volunteer Visiting of State Wards in Connection with Official Work." In *Proceedings of the National Conference of Charities and Correction, at the Eleventh Annual Session, Held at St. Louis, October 13–17, 1884,* ed. Isabel C. Barrows. Boston: George H. Ellis, 1885. 123–31.

Redfield, Susan Curtis. "Jack's Cure." *St. Nicholas* 17 (March 1890): 382–95.

Reeder, R. R. "To Country and Cottage: The Effect on Institution Children of a Change from Congregate Housing in the City to Cottage Housing in the Country." Serialized in *Charities and The Commons* 14 and 15 (1904 and 1905).

Regier, C. C. *The Era of the Muckrakers.* 1932. Gloucester, Mass.: Peter Smith, 1957.

"Rescued from the Streets." New York *Tribune,* 21 January 1880. Rpt. *Crossroads* 43 (March 1998): 15–20.

Reynolds, W. S. "Essentials in Placing Children in Foster Homes." *Ohio Bulletin of Charities and Correction* 23.1 (February 1917): 13–17.

Richardson, Anne B. "The Massachusetts System of Placing and Visiting Children." In *Proceedings of the Seventh Annual Conference of Charities and Correction, Held at Cleveland, June and July, 1880,* ed. F. B. Sanborn. Boston: A. Williams, 1880. 186–200.

Riis, Jacob A. "God's Children: Give Them a Chance; A Comparison of the Influence of Heredity and Environment." *Delineator* 71.5 (May 1908): 809–10.

———. *How the Other Half Lives: Studies among the Tenements of New York.* 1890. New York: Dover, 1971.

Riley, James Whitcomb. "Little Orphant Annie." 1885. Rpt. in *The Oxford Book of Children's Verse,* ed. Iona and Peter Opie. New York: Oxford University Press, 1973.

Ross, Mary. "Children Who Had a Second Chance: The Story of How Nine Hundred and Ten Foster Children Turned Out." *Survey* 52 (1924): 382 ff.

Rotundo, E. Anthony. *American Manhood: Transformations in Masculinity from the Revolution to the Modern Era.* New York: Basic Books, 1993.

———. "Body and Soul: Changing Ideals of American Middle-Class Manhood, 1770–1920." *Journal of Social History* 16 (Summer 1983): 23–38.

Rutherford, L. M. "Frances Hodgson Burnett." In *British Children's Writers 1880–1914,* ed. Laura M. Zaidman. Dictionary of Literary Biography 141. Detroit: Gale, 1994. 59–78.

Samples, Karen. "Ex-Orphan Wants Apology: Says He Was Given to Man as a Servant." *Cincinnati Enquirer,* 23 January 2000: C2.

Schwartz, Joel. *Fighting Poverty with Virtue: Moral Reform and America's Urban Poor, 1825–2000.* Bloomington: Indiana University Press, 2000.

Sedgwick, Catharine Maria. *A New-England Tale; or, Sketches of New-England Character and Manners.* 1822. Ed. Victoria Clements. New York: Oxford University Press, 1995.

Segal, Harry G. "Life without Father: The Role of the Paternal in the Opening Chapters of *Huckleberry Finn.*" *Journal of American Studies* 27.1 (April 1993): 19–33.

Shulman, Robert. "Fathers, Brothers, and 'the Diseased': The Family, Individualism, and American Society in *Huck Finn.*" In *One Hundred Years of Huckleberry Finn: The Boy, His Book, and American Culture,* ed. Robert Sattelmeyer and J. Donald Crowley. Columbia: University of Missouri Press, 1985. 325–40.

Silverman, Arnold R., and William Feigelman. "Adjustment in Interracial Adoptees: An Overview." In *The Psychology of Adoption,* ed. David M. Brodzinsky and Marshall D. Schechter. New York: Oxford University Press, 1990. 187–200.

Simpson, Eileen. *Orphans: Real and Imaginary.* New York: Weidenfeld and Nicolson, 1987.

Slingerland, W. H. *Child-Placing in Families: A Manual for Students and Social Workers,* intro. Hastings H. Hart. New York: Russell Sage Foundation, 1919.

Smith, Bruce. *The History of Little Orphan Annie.* New York: Ballantine, 1982.

Smith, Daniel Scott. "Family Limitation, Sexual Control, and Domestic Feminism in Victorian America." In *A Heritage of Her Own: Toward a New Social History of American Women,* ed. Nancy F. Cott and Elizabeth H. Pleck. New York: Simon and Schuster, 1979. 222–45.

Smith, Virginia T. "The Work of the Temporary Homes and of Finding Homes for Children in Connecticut." In *Proceedings of the National Conference of Charities and Correction, at the Twelfth Annual Session Held in Washington, D.C., June 4–10, 1885,* ed. Isabel C. Barrows. Boston: George H. Ellis, 1885. 210–19.

Smith-Rosenberg, Carroll. *Disorderly Conduct: Visions of Gender in Victorian America.* New York: Knopf, 1985.

Snedeker, Caroline Dale. *Downright Dencey.* 1927. Garden City, N.Y.: Doubleday, n.d.

Southworth, E.D.E.N. *The Hidden Hand, or Capitola the Madcap.* 1859. New Brunswick: Rutgers University Press, 1988.

Stewart, Barbara. "For Children of the City, Memories of Country Days." *New York Times,* 3 May 1998: A29.

Stewart, Veronica. "Mothering a Female Saint: Susan Warner's Dialogic Role in *The Wide, Wide World.*" *Essays in Literature* 22.1 (Spring 1995): 59–74.

Stoneman, A. H. "Social Problems Related to Illegitimacy: Safeguarding Adoptions, Legally and Socially." In *Proceedings of the National Conference of Social Work at the Fifty-First Annual Session Held in Toronto, Ontario June 25–July 2, 1924.* Chicago: University of Chicago Press, 1924. 144–50.

Stratton-Porter, Gene. *Freckles.* 1904. Bloomington: Indiana University Press, 1986.

Susman, Warren I. *Culture as History: The Transformation of American Society in the Twentieth Century.* New York: Pantheon, 1984.

Theis, Sophie Van Senden. "How Foster Children Turn Out." In *Proceedings of the National Conference of Social Work at the Fifty-First Annual Session Held in Toronto, Ontario June 25–July 2, 1924.* Chicago: University of Chicago Press, 1924. 121–24.

———. *How Foster Children Turn Out: A Study and Critical Analysis of 910 Children Who Were Placed in Foster Homes by the State Charities Aid Association and Who Are Now Eighteen Years of Age or Over.* 1924. New York: Arno, 1974.

———. "Minimum Qualifications of a Good Child-Placing Agency." In *Proceedings of the National Conference of Social Work at the Forty-Ninth Annual Session Held in Providence, Rhode Island June 22–29, 1922.* Chicago: University of Chicago Press, 1922. 121–24.

Thorne, Olive [Harriet Mann Miller]. "Little Housemaids." *St. Nicholas* 6 (April 1879): 403–10.

Thurston, Henry W. "How Much Child Dependency Is There in the United States?" In *Proceedings of the National Conference of Social Work at the Fifty-Third Annual Session Held in Cleveland, Ohio May 26–June 2, 1926.* Chicago: University of Chicago Press, 1926. 148–51.

Tichi, Cecelia. *Shifting Gears: Technology, Literature, Culture in Modernist America.* Chapel Hill: University of North Carolina Press, 1987.

"Town Meeting Day at Freeville: A Hint as to the Psychology of Boy Politics at the George Junior Republic." *Charities* 10.23 (6 June 1903).

"Train Brings 18 Babies to Nebraska: Trainload of Thirty-Five Arrive in Omaha for Distribution in Three States; Four Mothers Wait." Omaha *World-Herald,* 15 December 1921. Rpt. *Crossroads* 14 (January 1991): 11.

Twain, Mark [Samuel Langhorne Clemens]. *The Adventures of Huckleberry Finn.* 1884. Garden City: Nelson Doubleday, 1954.

"Uncle Hiram's Pilgrimage." *Merry's Museum and Parley's Magazine* 9 (1860): 36–37.

Warner, Susan. *The Wide, Wide World.* 1850. Afterword by Jane Tompkins. New York: Feminist Press, 1987.

Wells, Carolyn. *The Story of Betty.* Serialized in *St. Nicholas* 26 (January-October 1899).

"What Others Think of Our Campaign for the Child: The Comment of Many Prominent People as Expressed in Their Letters to the Editor." *Delineator* 71.1 (January 1908): 100–103.

"'Where 100,000 Children Wait'—The Answer: *The Delineator* Article Has Aroused a Wave of Sympathy for Unfortunate Children." *Delineator* 73.1 (January 1909): 120–21.

Whitmore, William H. *The Law of Adoption in the United States, and Especially in Massachusetts.* Albany: Joel Munsell, 1876.

Wiggin, Kate Douglas. *Rebecca of Sunnybrook Farm.* 1903. Mahwah, N.J.: Watermill, 1981.

———. *Timothy's Quest: A Story for Anybody, Young or Old, Who Cares to Read It.* 1890. Boston: Houghton, Mifflin, 1893.

Williams, C. V. "Child-Placing Conditions in Ohio." *Ohio Bulletin of Charities and Correction* 23.1 (February 1917): 18–23.

Williams, Henry Smith. "What Shall Be Done with Dependent Children?" *North American Review* 164 (1897): 404–14.

Williams, Susan S. "Widening the World: Susan Warner, Her Readers, and the Assumption of Authorship." *American Quarterly* 42.4 (December 1990): 565–86.

Willsie [Morrow], Honoré. "The Adopted Mother." *Century Magazine* 104.5 (September 1922): 654–68.

Wirth-Nesher, Hana. "The Literary Orphan as National Hero: Huck and Pip." *Dickens Studies Annual* 15 (1986): 259–73.

Wishy, Bernard. *The Child and the Republic: The Dawn of Modern American Child Nurture.* Philadelphia: University of Pennsylvania Press, 1968.

Wright, Henrietta Christian. "State Care of Dependent Children." *North American Review* 171 (1900): 112–23.

Youcha, Geraldine. *Minding the Children: Child Care in America from Colonial Times to the Present.* New York: Scribner, 1995.

Yundt, Thomas M. *A History of Bethany Orphans' Home of the Reformed Church of the United States, Located at Womelsdorf, Pa.* Reading, Penn.: Daniel Miller, 1888.

Zelizer, Viviana A. *Pricing the Priceless Child: The Changing Social Value of Children.* New York: Basic Books, 1985.

Ziff, Larzer. *The American 1890s: Life and Times of a Lost Generation.* 1966. New York: Viking, 1968.

Index

CLAUDIA NELSON is Associate Professor of English at Southwest Texas State University. She is the author of *Invisible Men: Fatherhood in Victorian Periodicals, 1850–1910* (1995) and *Boys Will Be Girls: The Feminine Ethic and British Children's Fiction, 1857–1917* (1991). Other publications include two edited books, as well as numerous articles and chapters in edited collections. She became an adoptive mother in 1998.